RECOLLECTIONS
OF
A MILITARY LIFE

RECOLLECTIONS

OF

A MILITARY LIFE

BY

GENERAL SIR JOHN ADYE, G.C.B., R.A.

GYAN

Published by

GYAN

Gyan Publishing House
5, Ansari Road
Daryaganj, New Delhi-110002
Phone: 011-47034999, 9811692060
E-mail: books@gyanbooks.com

Distribution Network
gyanbooks.com
India, USA, Canada, UK, Australia, France

ISBN: 978-81-212-7099-1 (PB)
First Published, 1895

2nd Impression 2024

Printed at: Gyan Press, Delhi.

RECOLLECTIONS OF A MILITARY LIFE
Author: JOHN ADYE

RECOLLECTIONS

OF

A MILITARY LIFE

HEAD QUARTERS, CRIMEA. WINTER OF 1854

Farm House, in which Lord Raglan died

RECOLLECTIONS

OF

A MILITARY LIFE

BY

GENERAL SIR JOHN ADYE, G.C.B., R.A.

New York
MACMILLAN AND CO.
1895

INTRODUCTION

Having served for many years in the Royal Artillery, and taken part in some of the campaigns in which the British army has been engaged during my period of service, I am in hopes that my recollections may be of some interest, and my views on military subjects worthy of record; and I therefore publish them, dedicating my book to the Officers and Men of the Regiment amongst whom I have passed my career.

1895.

CONTENTS

LIST OF ILLUSTRATIONS

FULL-PAGE ILLUSTRATIONS

ILLUSTRATIONS IN TEXT

MAPS

RECOLLECTIONS

OF

A MILITARY LIFE

CHAPTER I

DAYS OF PEACE

'Wakening the echoes of joys long fled.'

IN recording personal recollections of the varied scenes and events in which, during a long military service, it has been my lot to take part, it is scarcely necessary to enter into family details, and I will therefore merely state that my grandfather, Stephen Payne Adye, entered the Royal Artillery in 1762, and served in the war in Germany and in America; and since that date various members of the family have served in uninterrupted succession in the regiment down to the present day.

Of his four sons, three became officers of artillery. The eldest, Ralph Willett Adye, was the author of the 'Pocket Gunner,' which was a standard book of reference for many years. He died at Gibraltar in 1804, and his monument still exists there, in the so-called Trafalgar Cemetery.

The second son, Stephen Gallwey Adye, saw much active service. He was with Sir Ralph Abercromby in Egypt in 1801, and was slightly wounded in action near Alexandria. He was also at Walcheren in 1809, at Cadiz in 1813, and at Quatre Bras and Waterloo. He died a Major General and Superintendent of the Laboratory, Woolwich Arsenal, in 1838.

The third son, John Miller Adye, was an officer in the Royal Navy. He served as a Lieutenant in Lord Nelson's flagship, the 'Vanguard,' at the battle of the Nile, and was wounded. In 1815 he was in command of the 'Partridge' corvette cruising off the Island of Elba, and conveyed Sir Neil Campbell (who was British Commissioner there) to Leghorn in February. Sir Neil, having received information that Napoleon intended to escape, returned hastily to Elba, but owing to light winds was delayed, and only arrived on the morning of February 28th to find that Napoleon had left on the night of the 26th. The 'Partridge' went in pursuit towards the Antibes, but, it being uncertain to what part of the coast he had sailed, failed to overtake him.[1]

[1] *Napoleon at Elba*, Sir Neil Campbell.

The fourth son, James Pattison Adye (my father), was also in the Artillery, and was present at Copenhagen in 1806, and served for several years in the Mediterranean.

In 1834 I received a nomination to a cadetship at the Royal Military Academy Woolwich from the Master General of the Ordnance, Sir James Kempt, and went up for examination in February, at the age of fourteen. There was no competition fortunately in those days, and the whole affair, including medical examination, only lasted an hour and a half, and I was reported as having passed very satisfactorily. My career at the Academy was a happy one. I was treated with much kindness, and experienced none of the bullying or ill-usage which was supposed to exist. An amusing incident occurred soon after I joined. Each room contained four cadets, the head of my room being the late General William Gardner, R.A. He was at that time about twenty-one years of age, and having quarrelled with another cadet, who was a good fighter with his fists, a meeting was arranged in the Racket Court. Gardner, however, said that a pugilistic encounter was very well for boys, but as a man he claimed to fight with pistols.

This gave a more serious turn to the matter, and I, as junior of the room, was ordered to prepare the bullets for the duel, and well remember remaining up late at night, melting lead in the fire shovel, and pouring it into bullet moulds. These serious preparations led to some arrangement, and the affair never came off.

Colonel Parker was at that time Captain of the Cadets, and Wilford one of the subalterns. Parker, a fine old soldier, had lost his leg at Waterloo and wore a wooden one. He was nicknamed Peg Parker.

One Sunday afternoon the cadets were being marched to church across the 'barrack field' at Woolwich, Parker as usual riding in front on a small white pony. All at once Wilford ran up to him and said, 'Beg your pardon, sir, but you have lost your leg!' and sure enough, on looking down, Parker saw that his wooden one was missing. It had tumbled off. Wilford, however, who had picked it up, screwed it on again, and the march was resumed.

In December 1836, after nearly three years' residence, I received my commission as a second lieutenant. I was head of the Academy, and just seventeen. The late Sir Frederic Campbell was second, and we both selected the Royal Artillery.

In the spring of 1837 I attended a levee of William IV., and, to my surprise, on hearing my name he kindly spoke to me and asked what relation I was to General Adye. The current story was that the king asked me what relation I was to my uncle, and that in my confusion I replied grandson; but this is apocryphal.

Speaking of William IV. reminds me of a story about him which I believe is well founded. Soon after becoming king he one day visited Woolwich, and after inspecting the Artillery, &c., inquired who was Commanding Officer of the Marines, and was told it was Sir John McCleverty. The king said that Sir John was an old friend and comrade of his, and went off at once to call on him at the Barracks. He expressed great pleasure at seeing his old companion, and asked if he could do anything for him, adding, 'You know I am a king now, and can do what I like.' Old Sir John McCleverty replied: 'Yes, your Majesty, you can do something for me. My son not long ago was a lieutenant on board a man-of-war, and in the Channel one night in a thick fog, when he was on watch, they came into collision with another ship, and the Admiralty have in consequence tried him by Court Martial, cancelled his commission, and have nearly broken my heart, for he is an excellent officer.' The king promised that he should be restored, was as good as his word, and the son rose afterwards to some distinction, commanding the 'Terrible' in the Black Sea during the Crimean war.

As the earlier years of my service were passed

during a period of peace, they call for little remark. Towards the end of 1840 I embarked at Woolwich with my company for Malta in an old sailing transport, the 'Numa Pompilius,' and, owing chiefly to bad weather in the bay, the voyage occupied no less than two months. We sailed into Malta on the same morning that the British fleet under Sir Robert Stopford arrived from the capture of Acre.

In 1843, having returned home, I was appointed Adjutant of the Artillery in Dublin, and was present when Daniel O'Connell was put into prison in Richmond Bridewell, and made a sketch of the building, which was published in the 'Illustrated London News.' I also witnessed the great procession through the streets of Dublin when O'Connell and the other prisoners were released.

In 1845 I was appointed to C Troop, Royal Horse Artillery, at Woolwich. There were three troops there, each consisting of two guns, a waggon, and forty horses. They were all commanded by officers who had been present at Waterloo thirty years before—Fox Strangways, Frank Warde, and Ingilby; but only one of them (Strangways) was even a Brevet Major, and they were all between fifty and sixty years of age. Those were days of slow promotion.

On one occasion Major Chalmers, R.A., had an interview with William IV., who incidentally asked him how long he had been a Captain of Artillery. 'Twenty-three years, your Majesty,' replied Chalmers. The king hastily said, 'I didn't ask you how long it was since you were born, but how long you had been a captain.' 'Well, your Majesty,' says Chalmers, 'I am very sorry, but I have been twenty-three years in that rank.' The king, who apparently could hardly believe it, laughed and said, 'And a very fine position, too.' 'Oh yes,' said Chalmers, 'undoubtedly so.'

In the spring of 1848 I was in command of an artillery detachment in the Tower of London. There was at that time much anxiety about the Chartists, and as to the result of a meeting under Fergus O'Connor which took place on Kennington Common on April 10. The walls of the Tower and the top of the Bank and the Mansion House were to some extent prepared for defence, and sandbags were placed to form loopholes for musketry, an attack by the mob being apprehended. The Lord Mayor applied for some hand-grenades to be thrown from the Mansion House in case of need, and I sent him a boxful in a cab, at the same time giving a hint that in using them he should not hold them too long in his hand, as they might explode prematurely. This caused a little uneasiness, and subsequently a bombardier was ordered to give him instructions as to throwing them.

The clerks in the Ordnance Department at the Tower were sworn in as special constables, and were served out with batons cut out of old mop-sticks. On the morning of April 10 Sir George Cathcart, then Lieutenant of the Tower, sent for me. He had three large canvas frames in his drawing-room, and on them was painted in great letters: 'The Tower guns are loaded to the muzzle. If you attempt to enter, they will be fired!' He said his intention was, when the expected mob came, to hang them (the frames, not the mob) over the walls, with a bit of string. I ventured to point out that, if loaded as stated, the guns, which were old cast-iron carronades, would infallibly burst, but he replied that it was only to frighten the people, who would probably run away. We waited all day, but no crowd ever came near the Tower, and the whole affair collapsed.

It is often said that extravagance prevails amongst the officers in some regiments of the army, and there is probably a good deal of truth in the remark. But at all events in the earlier days of my service real economy prevailed in the Artillery, as is proved by the following facsimile copy of my mess-bill in Dublin in May 1850, now in my possession.

May 1850

	£	s.	d.
Share of Mess Guest			2½
To Ale			4
2 Cigars			10
Luncheon		2	0
Share of H.R.H. Prince George's Luncheon			6½
3 Breakfasts		3	9
1 Cigar			5
2 Cigars			10
Luncheon and Soda Water		1	11
19 Dinners	1	18	0
	2	8	10

Entertaining royalty for 6½*d.* can hardly be considered extravagant.

CHAPTER II

COMMENCEMENT OF CRIMEAN WAR—INTERVIEW WITH NAPOLEON III

It is time now to pass on from the early reminiscences of a period of peace to the more interesting and important events of active service, in which for some years it was my good fortune to share.

In the spring of 1854, after a peace which in Europe had lasted nearly forty years, the British navy and army were again called upon to take part in a great war; and the whole nation soon became deeply absorbed in the stirring events of the Crimean campaign. Lord Raglan at that time was Master General of the Ordnance and was also appointed to command the expedition, and I had the good fortune to be selected as Brigade Major to the artillery under General Cator.

There is perhaps no operation of war more difficult than that which this country has to undertake in the embarkation of its army for a continental campaign. It is not merely as regards its *personnel*; but large reserves of ammunition and stores, and the armaments and equipments of the artillery, engineers, medical, commissariat, clothing, and other departments have to be embarked, and all so arranged as to be prepared for rapid landing after a long voyage, and possibly in the face of an enemy. In proceeding to the Crimea eight batteries of horse and field artillery, several siege train companies, and large reserves of munitions for the army were embarked in Woolwich dockyard during March and April. The combined naval and military arrangements were efficiently carried out; and although the field artillery were conveyed in sailing vessels, and were several weeks at sea before arrival at Constantinople, the loss of horses was only 4 per cent. out of about 1,600 embarked.

Towards the end of April Colonels Strangways and Lake, Captains Patton, Gordon, and myself (all artillery officers) were directed to proceed *viâ* France to Marseilles for Malta. On arrival at Paris, Colonel Strangways, who was personally known to the Emperor Napoleon, received a message that his Majesty wished to receive him and his brother officers at the Tuileries. Strangways informed our ambassador, Lord Cowley, who, however, said it was not according to etiquette, and that we ought to attend a levee in the usual way, and declined to go with us; so we put on our uniforms and drove to the Tuileries in a *fiacre* without him. The servant at the entrance seemed rather surprised when we said we had come to see the Emperor; but after conference with a staff officer, we were conducted through the 'Salle des Maréchaux' to an inner room, and were received very kindly by Napoleon, who was in the uniform of a general. He made inquiries about the amount of artillery we had embarked for the East; spoke about the difficulty of conveying horses for a long voyage; and expressed a hope that the French and English armies combined would be able to act decisively—and then, wishing us prosperity, he invited us to come and see him again on our return. Alas! we were not destined to do so. Strangways was killed at Inkerman; Lake, who had a horse shot under him at Alma, and another at Inkerman, was invalided and died soon after; Captain Patton died of cholera at Balaclava; and many years elapsed before I had another interview with Napoleon, under very altered conditions, shortly before his death at Chiselhurst.

We arrived at Malta about the middle of May. The streets were full of French soldiers on their way to the East; and there was a great deal of cheering and enthusiasm. On the 15th we embarked in the 'Medway' for Constantinople with the 55th regiment. As we approached the Dardanelles we passed a sailing transport, with part of a cavalry regiment on board, and as they had been some weeks at sea, and were making no progress owing to calm weather, we induced our captain to take her in tow. The officers in the transport made signs of their wish to communicate, so we lowered a bottle tied to a long string, which they picked up as it floated past, and we then pulled it back. We expected their inquiries might be as to the position of the Russians and the progress of the war, but their message was: 'Can you tell us who won the Two Thousand Guineas? We have several bets, and are very anxious!' As we entered the Dardanelles we were boarded by two French officers from a small transport, who begged assistance, as they were short of provisions, having only biscuits, and no water. We provided them with what was requisite, and also took them in tow. They belonged to the Chasseurs d'Afrique, and had been forty days on passage from Algiers. Passing Gallipoli, where there were several men-of-war at anchor and considerable French and English encampments on shore, we arrived at Constantinople on May 20.

Our troops of the various arms were now arriving daily, and were accommodated either in the great barrack at Scutari, or encamped on the plain outside, in close proximity to large Turkish cemeteries. All was bustle and animation. The scene, however, soon changed, and at the end of May the Light Division under Sir George Brown re-embarked, entered the Black Sea, and landed at Varna, followed shortly after by the whole of the allied armies.

Until my arrival at Constantinople, I had never seen Lord Raglan. Owing, however, to the failure of General Cator's health almost immediately on his landing, and to the numerous artillery matters which required discussion and decision, it so happened that I had from that time almost daily interviews with the Commander-in-chief. In fact, during the succeeding twelve months, and until his death in June 1855, it was my good fortune to be closely associated with Lord Raglan in the great events which rapidly succeeded each other. General Cator's advice to me was, never to trouble Lord Raglan more than absolutely necessary with details, to listen carefully to his remarks, to try and anticipate his wishes, and at all times to make as light as possible of difficulties. These excellent suggestions I did my best to carry out.

The original intention in massing the allied armies at Varna was with a view of an advance to the Danube, although, in regard to land transport, the English force was but little prepared for rapid movement. However, the raising of the siege of Silistria towards the end of June and the retreat of the Russians led to an entire change of plan, and the expedition to the Crimea was decided on. The Duke of Newcastle was then Minister for War, and in his despatch to Lord Raglan, of June 29,[1] he gave instructions that no

[1] Committee of the House of Commons on the state of the army before Sebastopol.

campaign in the Principalities should be undertaken, but that measures should at once be concerted for the siege of Sebastopol.' Lord Raglan's reply on July 19 said, that 'the descent on the Crimea is decided upon, more in deference to the views of the British Government than to any information in the possession of the naval and military authorities as to the extent of the enemy's forces or to their state of preparation.'

Owing to the continued and severe illness of General Cator he was invalided home in August, and had to be carried on board ship in a hammock, being succeeded in command of the artillery by General Strangways. Lord de Ros, Quartermaster General, went home ill at the same time. During the month of August incessant preparations were made for the embarkation of the great expedition. The fleets of the allied powers arrived, and the bay of Varna was crowded with hundreds of transports, steam-tugs, flat-bottomed boats, and rafts; and the beach was strewn with thousands of gabions, fascines, and baggage of all kinds. Towards the end of the month the troops commenced embarking. One morning early, whilst superintending the departure of some batteries from the shore, Lord Raglan came up and spoke to me. He remarked that the artillery staff was insufficient, and that I had too much to do; and added, 'If you were a field officer I would appoint you Assistant

Adjutant General, and give you help.' Having heard a rumour that an officer of high rank was coming from England as chief of the artillery staff, I ventured to say that I hoped Lord Raglan would not supersede me. He replied at once: 'Certainly not. I will take good care that you are not superseded.' The next day he sent for me, and said, 'I have got the Duke of Newcastle in a corner.' This rather puzzled me for the moment, but he continued: 'I have requested him at once to give you either brevet or local rank as a Major, and then the difficulty will be met.' The result of this was that within a month I was gazetted as a Major.'

After the expedition had been decided on, and even after it had embarked, great difference of opinion existed amongst the generals and admirals of both nations as to its expediency. The late season of the year, the want of accurate information as to the actual force of the Russians and of the condition of the defences of Sebastopol, all were matters of grave concern. The prevalence of cholera and fever—which had greatly weakened the allied armies and fleets, and which continued after leaving Varna—also added to the difficulties. These considerations, however, were not allowed to prevail, and on August 25 Marshal Saint-Arnaud issued a proclamation to the French army, in which he said that Providence had called them to the Crimea, a country healthy as France, and that ere long the three united flags should float over the ramparts of Sebastopol. Lord Raglan also issued his instructions, which were as follows: 'The invasion of the Crimea having been determined on, the troops will embark in such ships as shall be provided for their conveyance.'

Notwithstanding his proclamation, Saint-Arnaud, even when approaching the shore of the Crimea, remained in a somewhat vacillating condition of mind. During the voyage across, he made a signal requesting Lord Raglan and Admiral Dundas to come and see him on board the 'Ville de Paris.' They proceeded alongside in the 'Caradoc,' but Lord Raglan, having only one arm, was unable to go on board.[1] Admiral Dundas, however, visited Saint-Arnaud, who at the time was very ill and in great pain, and unable to converse. He handed the Admiral a paper without signature, in which it was urged that it would be too hazardous to land in face of a powerful enemy having a numerous cavalry; that the season was too late for a siege of Sebastopol, which, moreover, was known to be stronger than anticipated; and that consequently it was necessary to reconsider the situation and the measures to be adopted.

Admiral Dundas, accompanied by some French

[1] This account is taken from a pamphlet written by the late General Sir W. Brereton, R.A., who was on board Admiral Dundas's flagship at the time.

generals, then returned to the 'Caradoc,' and a long debate took place with Lord Raglan, who at length ended the discussion by declaring that he would not now consent to alter a decision which had been come to after careful consideration at the last council at Varna. Without doubt the enterprise was a bold and dangerous one, undertaken at a late period of the year, with troops that were physically weak from cholera and fever. The orders of the French and English Governments were, however, peremptory, and therefore the allied generals had in reality no option in the matter.

On the morning of September 14 the allied fleets and transports arrived off the coast of the Crimea, and the troops at once commenced landing on the shore about twenty-five miles from Sebastopol. The French were very quick in their movements, and, on our part, the Light Division under Sir George Brown lost no time; by the end of the day almost the whole of the British infantry, and twenty field guns horsed and equipped, were on shore. Just as the disembarkation commenced in the early morning a Russian officer with a Cossack orderly, rode up on some high ground between the French and English landing places, dismounted, and leisurely surveyed the scene; and then as our men on landing approached, he re-mounted and quietly trotted away. With that solitary exception, no enemy came near us during the five days occupied in disembarkation.

The first night on shore it rained heavily, our troops were without tents or shelter, and the operations on several subsequent days were considerably retarded by rough weather and a heavy surf, rendering our position somewhat precarious. It has always appeared inexplicable why Prince Menschikoff should have allowed so critical an operation on the part of the allies to be completed, without any attempt on his part to oppose or delay it; for nothing can be more helpless than an army with men, horses, and material of all kinds huddled together in boats, and landing on an open beach. The probabilities are that he was occupied in concentrating his troops at the strong position on the Alma, and felt himself unable to disturb our operations. One morning after landing, I rode with General Strangways inland for a mile or two to get water for our horses, and found a battalion of the Rifle Brigade in possession of a large farm. The officers complained that some of the French soldiers were pillaging the neighbourhood, and driving off the cattle, &c. Sir George Brown had sent a remonstrance to the French on the subject. As we left the farm we saw a French staff officer, evidently very angry and in pursuit of some of his men, and General Strangways recognised

Prince Jerome Napoleon, who was in command of the division close by.

At length, on September 19, all being ready, the allied armies commenced their celebrated march on Sebastopol. The French were close to the shore, and the order of march is shown on the following plan.

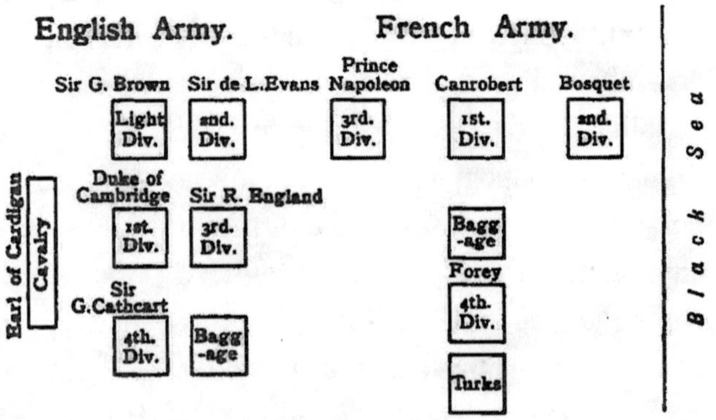

DIAGRAM OF FRENCH AND ENGLISH ARMIES

The strength of the British Army was approximately as follows:

		Officers and men
Cavalry		1,200
Artillery	60 guns	2,000
Infantry		25,000
	Total	28,200

The French were rather stronger in infantry, but had no cavalry. The division of Turks was about 6,000 strong.

The troops were in excellent spirits at the prospect of immediate action. The country was open and undulating; the distant smoke of burning villages, and the occasional appearance of a few Cossacks hovering about on the flank, were the only evidences that we were in an enemy's country. The arrival in the afternoon at the small fresh stream of the Bulganac was most welcome to the men and horses of the allies, who for days had suffered from a scanty supply of indifferent water. Late in the afternoon the enemy's cavalry showed in considerable force, at a distance almost out of range, beyond the stream, and Lord Raglan with his staff moved to the front, accompanied by the Light Cavalry under Lord Cardigan. Suddenly a Russian battery opened fire and a round shot passed through the Light Cavalry, taking off a man's leg, and bounding like a cricket ball over the heads of the staff. That was the first shot of the campaign in the Crimea. Two batteries of Horse Artillery were at once sent forward, and on their coming into action the enemy fell back out of range, covered by a cloud of skirmishers. Our loss was four troopers severely wounded. It was almost dusk, and Lord Raglan, being anxious to inform Prince Napoleon of what had occurred, as he was with his division about a mile distant, directed Colonel Count Lagondie, the French military attaché, to ride over and give him the necessary information. The French colonel was riding a fat Flemish mare which he called 'Medore,' and as he cantered leisurely off the remark was made, 'If Lagondie does not move a little faster it will be a long time before he comes back.' He never did come back, as will be explained presently.

Shortly after dusk all staff officers were directed to attend at head quarters, which were established in a small hut close to the Bulganac. General Airey, the Quartermaster General received us, and desired that all general officers should be informed that the enemy in considerable numbers being in the vicinity, a good look-out must be kept during the night, and that there should be no sounds of drums or trumpets. He then went on to say that the Russian army, computed at 45,000 men with a powerful artillery, occupied a strong entrenched position on heights beyond the Alma, a few miles distant, and that a general action was imminent on the morrow. The night passed quietly.

CHAPTER III

BATTLE OF ALMA

'Though till now ungraced in story,
Scant although thy waters be,
Alma, roll those waters proudly;
Roll them proudly to the sea.'

September 20.—In the early morning the allied armies formed up in position as on the previous day's march, in readiness for the battle. It was then discovered that Colonel Lagondie was absent from head quarters, and inquiries were made without result. As it was supposed he might have remained during the night with his French comrades, a message was sent to Prince Napoleon. The prince, however, said that Lagondie had arrived the previous evening with Lord Raglan's message, and then left. The mystery of his absence remained for the time inexplicable. Soon after the battle of the Alma, however, Menschikoff's carriage, containing a number of his papers and letters, was captured, and amongst them a note from a lady in Sebastopol saying how much pleased they were with the charming French colonel he had sent in to them, and hoping he would soon send some more. This at once cleared up the mystery of our friend Lagondie; and it subsequently transpired that on leaving Napoleon at dusk, being short-sighted, he had missed his way, and had ridden straight into the Russian cavalry and was made prisoner.

Considerable delay occurred on the morning of September 20, before our troops were prepared to advance, owing to numerous cases of cholera and fever amongst the men during the previous night, and the necessity of conveying them to the shore, for embarkation in the transports. The French, being close to the sea, had a considerable advantage in this respect. During the morning Marshal Saint-Arnaud, with a large staff and an officer carrying a silk tricolor standard, rode along the front of the British Army to confer with Lord Raglan, and was loudly cheered by our men. Whether the French marshal was a great general or not, I had no means of judging; but when we consider that he was then suffering from a mortal disease—of which, indeed, he died a few days later on board a French man-of-war—I think that he evinced a brave and heroic spirit under such circumstances in leading and commanding a French army in a great and successful battle.

At about eleven o'clock the allied armies advanced, the whole front covered by a cloud of skir-

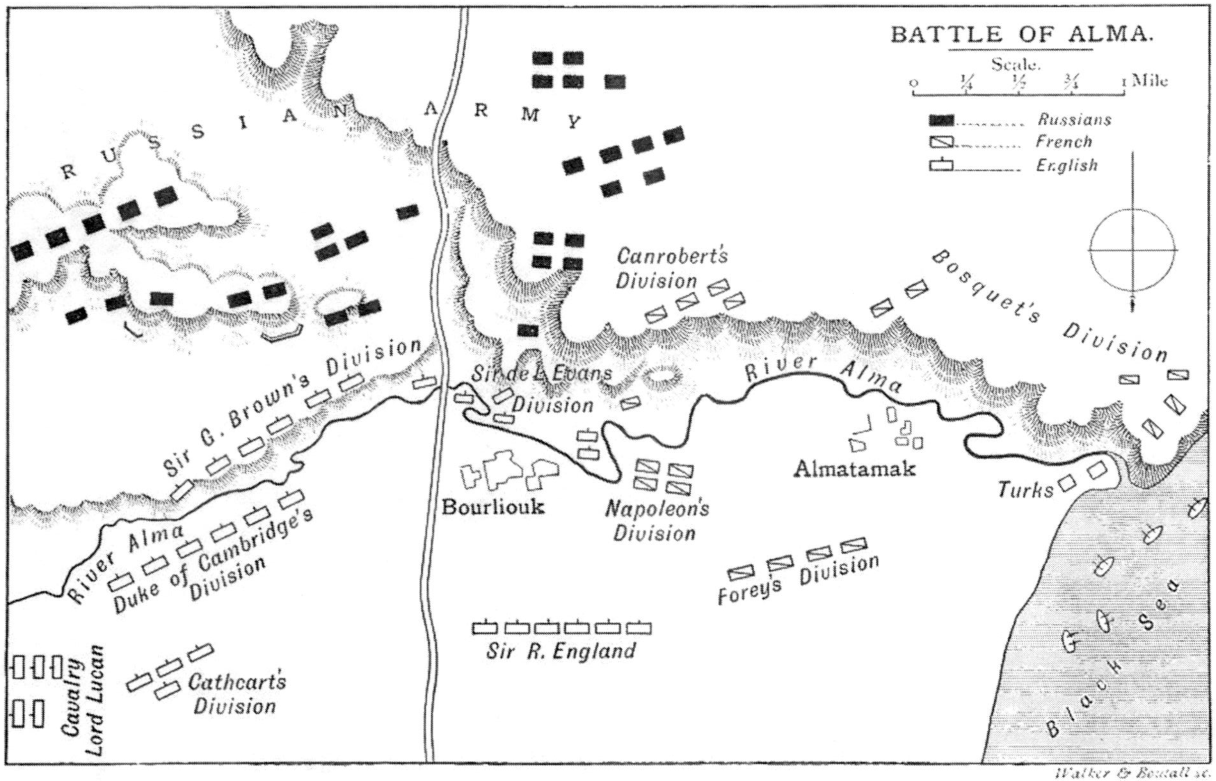
BATTLE OF ALMA.
Scale.
0 ¼ ½ ¾ 1 Mile
Russians
French
English
RUSSIAN ARMY
Canrobert's Division
Bosquet's Division
Sir G. Brown's Division
Sir de L. Evans Division
River Alma
Almatamak
Turks
Bourliouk
Napoleon's Division
River Alma
Duke of Cambridge's Division
Forey's Division
Black Sea
Sir R. England
Cavalry Lord Lucan
Cathcart's Division
Walker & Boutall sc.

mishers. The order of battle was an *échelon* from the right. General Bosquet's division led off, marching along the sea shore, with the Turkish force in rear. Then came the divisions of Canrobert and Prince Napoleon, with that of General Forey in rear in reserve. The English then took up the *échelon*; the second division under De Lacy Evans being next to that of Napoleon, then the Light Division under Sir George Brown, followed in a second line by the troops of Sir Richard England and the Guards and Highlanders under the Duke of Cambridge, the batteries of artillery in the intervals of brigades—the fourth division under Sir George Cathcart and the cavalry under Lord Lucan being held in reserve on the outward flank, which was three or four miles from the shore.

As the armies thus advanced to the attack we were able to take a more complete survey of the Russian position, and whilst the ground in front of the French was seen to be precipitous and difficult, it was evident that the main body of the Russians was in position, and partly entrenched, on slopes which the English forces were about to storm.

It has sometimes been argued that the English ought to have attempted a movement turning the Russian right; but when it is considered that our base was the sea, it is, I think, evident that the only prudent course in attacking a strong, partially entrenched position on the other side of a river, was the *échelon* movement as described. It was about noon when the first gun was fired; Bosquet's brigades crossed the river near its mouth, and commenced climbing the precipitous slopes, their advance being assisted by the fire of some vessels of the fleet. The enemy, however, were not in great force at this point, and the French gained the crest with comparatively few casualties. The divisions of Canrobert and Prince Napoleon as they reached the river crossed in succession, and were vigorously opposed as they swarmed up the heights. Great difficulties also were encountered in bringing up their artillery; but a flank movement of Bosquet's troops along the crest finally enabled the French Army to make good the ascent, although with considerable loss, and the Russians were compelled to yield the ground.[1]

So far the battle had satisfactorily progressed, but a sterner and far more terrible struggle had commenced on the left. The two leading English divisions as they approached the river and came within long range of the enemy's guns were deployed into line, and, whilst waiting for the completion of the French attack, were ordered to lie down. The English batteries came into action; but the enemy's guns were both powerful and numerous, and on command-

[1] General Canrobert was slightly wounded during the attack.

ing ground, so that at the beginning we were rather at a disadvantage.

Urgent messages having been received from the French, it was apparent that the moment of action had at length arrived, and Lord Raglan then gave the order for the advance of the whole army. The village of Burliuk on our side of the river, in front of Sir De Lacy Evans' division, was set on fire by the enemy, and led to the temporary separation of his two brigades, one passing it on either side. Lord Raglan, having given the order, passed with his staff through the burning village to the right, and by a narrow lane came suddenly down to a ford of the river. In riding through the village we passed the body of Lieutenant Cockerell, a young officer of artillery, who with his horse had just been killed by a round shot from the heights. A sharp skirmish was going on between the Russian outposts and the Zouaves of Napoleon's division as we reached and crossed the ford. At that moment Lieutenant Leslie, of the Life Guards, orderly officer to Lord Raglan, fell from his horse, shot through the shoulder, and was laid under the bank on the opposite side. The horse of Captain Fortescue, R.A, was killed at the same time by a bullet in the head.[1] Lord Raglan pressed on, and passing some French skirmishers in

[1] Nearly two years afterwards, when peace was signed, I re-visited the scene of the battle, and found the skeleton of the horse lying in the lane, with its skull pierced by a bullet.

the vineyards, soon reached high ground, from which he had an excellent view of the Russian position. Perceiving the important advantage he should gain by artillery fire from this spot, he consulted General Strangways and then sent me back for some guns. Fortunately Captain Turner's battery was just crossing the ford, and two guns were quickly brought up, followed shortly by the others. Their fire, directed against the Russian columns and batteries, who were now heavily engaged with the advance of the Light and Second Divisions, had a powerful effect, not only materially but morally, as showing the Russians that whilst their front was being stormed their flank was already turned. Lieutenant Walsham, R.A., was killed whilst with these guns.

In the meantime the two leading divisions, covered by skirmishers, moved steadily across the plain. Their ranks became somewhat disarranged by the gardens and vineyards as they approached the river, and still more so as they waded across the stream, which was fordable at many places. They, however, found a momentary shelter behind the broken ground on the opposite bank, and then the great crisis began. It was a moment of intense anxiety as the men of the Light and part of the Second Divisions jumped from their cover, and with a rattling fire commenced the charge. The ground over which they had to pass was of the nature of a smooth, steep

BATTLE OF ALMA, 20TH SEPTEMCER, 1854

glacis, and was swept by infantry and artillery fire. Three of our batteries, however, had converged towards the bridge over the Alma, and gave material support to the advancing troops. Up to this time every advantage had been on the side of the enemy. The scale, however, now began to turn. As the English line approached the Russian columns, its formation, straggling and irregular as it was, enabled it to open a continuous line of fire. The enemy's forces could be seen opening out and endeavouring to deploy; but it was too late—our regiments were close upon them. Then the Russian masses began to shake; then men from the rear were seen to run; then whole columns would turn and retire, halting and facing about at short intervals, but, with artillery smashing on their flank, and with Codrington's and Pennefather's brigades still streaming upwards, the enemy's troops could no longer hold their ground, but fled disordered up the hill. The converging fire of their batteries, however, still made a fearful havoc in the English ranks, and a wide street of dead and wounded, the whole way from the river upwards, showed the terrific nature of the fight. Breathless, decimated and much broken, but with victory crowning their efforts, the centre regiments at length dashed over the main entrenchment and captured two guns. But the battle was even then by no means over. The Russian reserves moved down, and

Codrington's brigade, whose force was almost expended, was obliged to give way, and victory for a moment seemed doubtful. Succour, however, was at hand. The three regiments of Guards, with the Highlanders on the left, the whole under the Duke of Cambridge, were now advancing up the hill in grand array. Some slight delay occurred until Codrington's brigade had fallen back and cleared the front, during which time the casualties were numerous, but then the chance of the Russians was over and their whole army retreated in some confusion. Lord Raglan in the meantime had left his position on the hill and joined his victorious troops, and by his orders five batteries of artillery were concentrated and fired on the broken columns of the enemy until they were out of range. It was a great victory, not only in its immediate result, but in its general effect on the Russian army.

Our losses in killed, wounded, and missing were very severe—amounting to 2,006 officers and men. About half of the entire number occurred in the Light Division alone.

The following diagram gives the position of the infantry regiments chiefly engaged, and of the casualties in each:

19th	23rd	33rd	7th Fus	95th	55th
226	210	239	222	193	115

Coldstream Guards	Scots Guards	Grenadier Guards
80	181	122

The joy and excitement of the English troops were intense as Lord Raglan rode along the line formed on the heights they had just won. On coming to the Highland Brigade rather an amusing incident occurred. Sir Colin Campbell addressed the Commander-in-Chief, and begged him to do him a favour. Lord Raglan, in reply, said it would give him pleasure to serve him in any way. Sir Colin then said: 'My lord, you have in years gone by shown me kindness when I was a young officer, and now I am an old one. My request is that, so long as I am at the head of the Highland Brigade, I may be allowed to wear the Highland bonnet.' This delighted the Scotchmen, and great cheering followed.

In addition to the two guns captured, two Russian generals were taken prisoners and about 900 of their wounded men were left on the field. The total loss of the Russians in the battle is stated to have been upwards of 5,000. The battle ended about four o'clock in the afternoon, the head quarters camp being pitched near the river, and Lord Raglan then went in search of his orderly officer, Lieutenant Tom Leslie, and with the help of some guardsmen, with a stretcher, brought him to his tent. Lord Raglan asked me if I knew Tom's mother, and on my replying in the negative, he said: 'A charming woman. I must write to her. How proud she will be to hear that he has a bullet in his shoulder!'

Several years after the battle, when in India, I met an old artillery man at Delhi, who claimed my acquaintance, and reminded me of the incident of bringing up Turner's guns from the ford. He said he was one of the drivers of the battery at the time, and that I rode up to him in the river and said: '"Johnson," says you, "you'll not spare whip nor spur till you get to the top of that hill, for Lord Raglan wants you."' I cannot vouch for the absolute correctness of his personal reminiscences, but the main fact is correct enough.

The two days following the victory were passed in collecting our wounded (upwards of 1,400), and carrying them in hammocks and stretchers to the beach for embarkation. Amongst others I remember saying a few words to Baring of the Coldstream Guards, as he was carried away from the field. He had lost an arm. Reserves of ammunition were also landed from the transports to meet the expenditure, which, however, was not large, the infantry having fired about six rounds a man and the artillery fifteen rounds a gun. The Russians' muskets, lying about the field in thousands (many of them with the old flint lock) were broken, and the accoutrements, knapsacks, &c., collected in heaps and burned.

The Russian Commander-in-Chief having omitted to send in a flag of truce, or to make any inquiry as to his wounded left on the ground, they were collected in a field and as far as possible attended to. An English medical officer, having volunteered, was left in charge of them as we marched away; a message being sent to Prince Menschikoff informing him of the arrangement.

CHAPTER IV

THE FLANK MARCH

On the morning of September 23 the allied armies left their position on the Alma, and after a march of about seven miles arrived at the Katcha, meeting with no opposition, and on the following day reached the Belbec, a small stream within a short distance of Sebastopol. From our pickets on the heights we could see the harbour and their line-of-battle ships at anchor.

Hitherto the intention of the allies had been to attack the forts on the north side, but the plans were suddenly altered, chiefly in consequence of the recommendation of Sir John Burgoyne. In a very able memorandum, written the day after the Alma, he pointed out in the first place, that the city of Sebastopol, with its docks, wharves, reserve armaments and stores—in fact, its chief resources—were on the south side of the harbour, and that the land defences there were imperfect and incomplete. In the second place, that the harbours of Kameisch and Balaclava would give the allied forces a safe base of operations, and free communication with the fleet, whereas on the north they had only the sea shore to rely on. Under these circumstances he recommended the abandonment of the north altogether, and establishing ourselves to the south of the city. The strategical advantages of this course were apparent, and the plan was adopted, and on September 25 the flank march began, the English army leading off, and proceeding for some miles in a south easterly direction through the woods. I remember when the Duke of Cambridge received the order to march south-east through the forest, he remarked that he had received many orders in his day, but that was the first time he had ever marched by compass.

It so happened that on the same morning Prince Menschikoff, ignorant of our sudden change of plan, was moving a considerable force inland from Sebastopol, in order to take the allies in flank, and as we emerged from the woods on the open ground at Mackenzie's farm, our advanced troops suddenly ran into the rear guard of the Russians. In fact, both the opposing armies were making a flank march at the same time, and the head of one came into collision with the tail of the other. Both sides were taken unawares, but some of our cavalry and Maude's troop of Horse Artillery at once pursued and captured a few prisoners and a considerable number of waggons, with ammunition, supplies, and baggage. This unexpected encounter must have rather mystified the

D 2

enemy; but Lord Raglan, knowing that his forces were scattered for some miles on a long thin line, pushed on, and towards sunset the Light and First Divisions reached the bridge over the Chernaya on the road leading to Balaclava, and bivouacked for the night.[1]

The following morning the march was resumed across the plain for two or three miles to Balaclava, that small fishing village, with its land-locked harbour scarcely larger than a dock, which was destined to be the British base throughout the war. As the staff and leading troops approached the village, a deputation of the inhabitants came out bearing bread and salt as a token of submission. Almost at the same time a gun was suddenly fired from the ruins of the old castle on the heights, and a shell splashed into the marshes close by, followed by another. Lord Raglan, through an interpreter, asked the deputation the reason of this unexpected demonstration, as bread and salt and bursting shells seemed inconsistent with each other; but the only explanation they could give was that the small garrison had not been formally summoned to surrender. The troops of the Light Division at once swarmed up the heights, and half of C troop of Horse Artillery, under Brandling, came into action; the other half I took, by Lord Raglan's orders, up the steep hill overlooking the

[1] Lord Raglan's Despatch, September 28, 1854.

castle. Just as we got into action, the 'Agamemnon,' with Admiral Sir Edmund Lyons, arrived off the harbour, and the small garrison, finding themselves under a converging fire from three sides, hoisted a white handkerchief on a pole in token of surrender. Their armament consisted of four antiquated brass mortars. The commandant, an old Greek colonel, had been wounded in the foot, and was carried down to Balaclava, where he met the staff who had just ridden in. The commandant's wife, on seeing her husband's condition, rushed out of her house in a flood of tears, fell on his neck, and kissed him repeatedly. Lord Raglan, however, spoke kindly and reassured her. In the meantime some Russian ladies who had left Sebastopol and taken refuge in Balaclava, terrified by our sudden arrival, crossed the harbour in a small boat in the vain hope of escape. Accompanied by another officer I followed them across, and we tried to reassure them. Knowing nothing of their language this was a difficulty. We tried 'Buono, Russ buono,' but it was not sufficient. Fortunately, at length we found one who spoke a little French, and then they became comforted and returned with us to the village, and were taken care of. Such was the capture of Balaclava.

Many years after, in 1872, on re-visiting the Crimea with the late Colonel Charles Gordon of Khartoum, we found that the old commandant

(Colonel Mammoo) was still alive, being over eighty, and we called on him. He was much pleased to see us and to talk over old days, and said that he should never forget the kindness he had received from the English when a prisoner of war. The officers and men of the navy in the man-of-war which took him to Constantinople treated him, he said, like a prince.

In the meantime the condition of Marshal Saint-Arnaud had become critical, and on September 25 he resigned the command of the French army, and was succeeded by General Canrobert, who was then forty-five years of age. Saint-Arnaud embarked at Balaclava on board the 'Berthollet,' and was visited by Lord Raglan and Sir Edmund Lyons. He was then almost at the point of death, and his last words to Lord Raglan were: 'Je vous suivrai toujours par la pensée.'[1] He died on board on September 29.

At the end of September the allied armies took up their position on the plateau in front of Sebastopol, the French on the left with their base at Kameisch; Lord Raglan establishing his head quarters at a farm house.

The land defences of the city at the time were incomplete and not continuous. On the east stood a round tower with four guns (the Malakoff), and on the west a crenelated wall, with another tower over-

[1] Bazancourt, ii. 276.

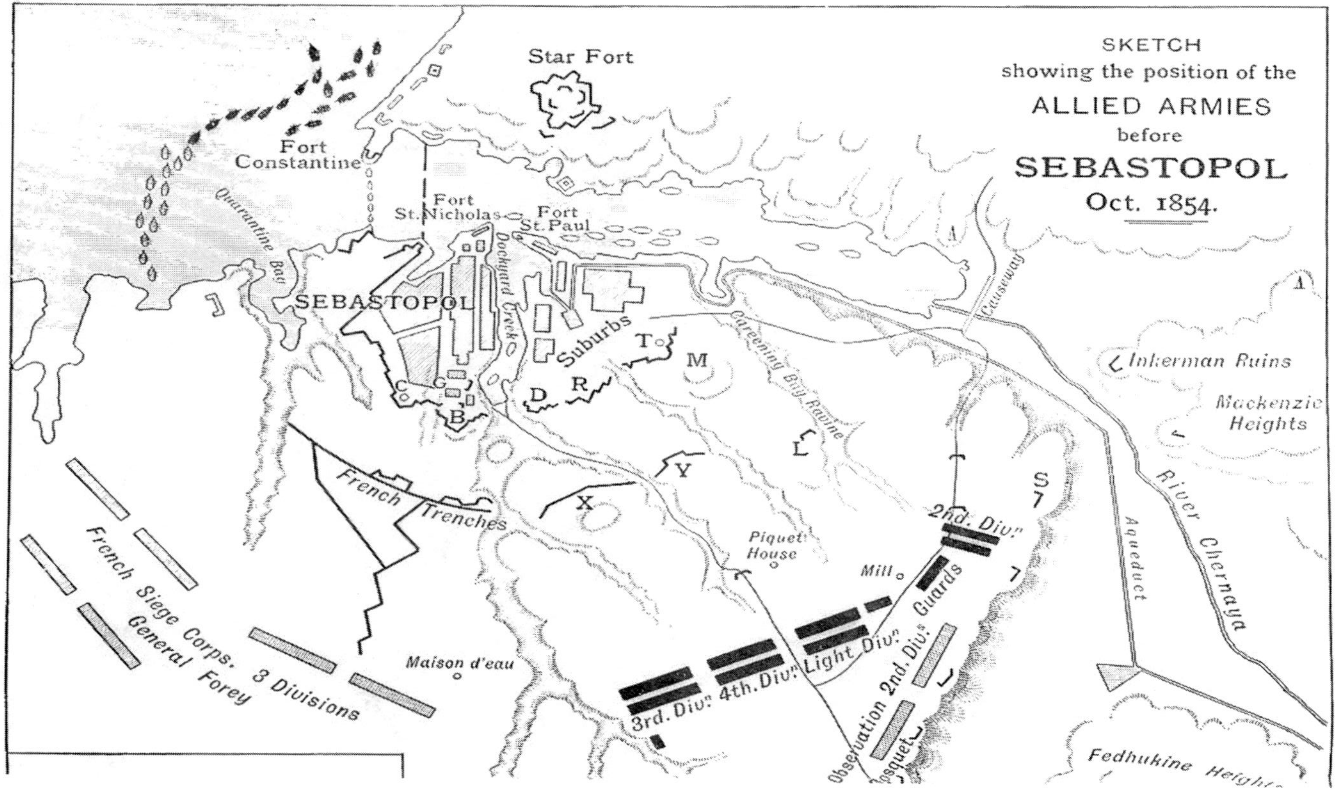
SKETCH
showing the position of the
ALLIED ARMIES
before
SEBASTOPOL
Oct. 1854.
Star Fort
Fort Constantine
Fort St. Nicholas
Fort St. Paul
Quarantine Bay
SEBASTOPOL
Dockyard Creek
Suburbs
Careening Bay Ravine
Causeway
Inkerman Ruins
Mackenzie Heights
River Chernaya
Aqueduct
Fedhukine Heights
French Trenches
French Siege Corps. 3 Divisions
General Forey
Maison d'eau
Piquet House
Mill
2nd. Divn
Guards
Light Divn
4th. Divn
3rd. Divn
Observation 2nd. Divn
Pisquet

REFERENCES.

Russian Names.

T. *Malakoff Tower* — *Korniloff Bas.*
M. *Mamelon. Gordon's Hill*
R. *Great Redan* — *Bastion No. 3*
D. *Barrack Batteries*
G. *Garden Batteries*
B. *Bastion dù mât* — *Bastion No. 4*
C. *Bastion Centrale* — *Bastion No. 5*
L. *Lancaster Battery*
X. *Left Attack. Chapman's Batteries*
Y. *Right Attack. Gordon's Batteries*
S. *Sand bag Battery at Inkerman.*

English
French.

References to Balaclava.

A. B. C. D. E. F. { *English Batteries.*

1. 2. 3. 4. 5. 6. { *Redoubts manned by Turks.*

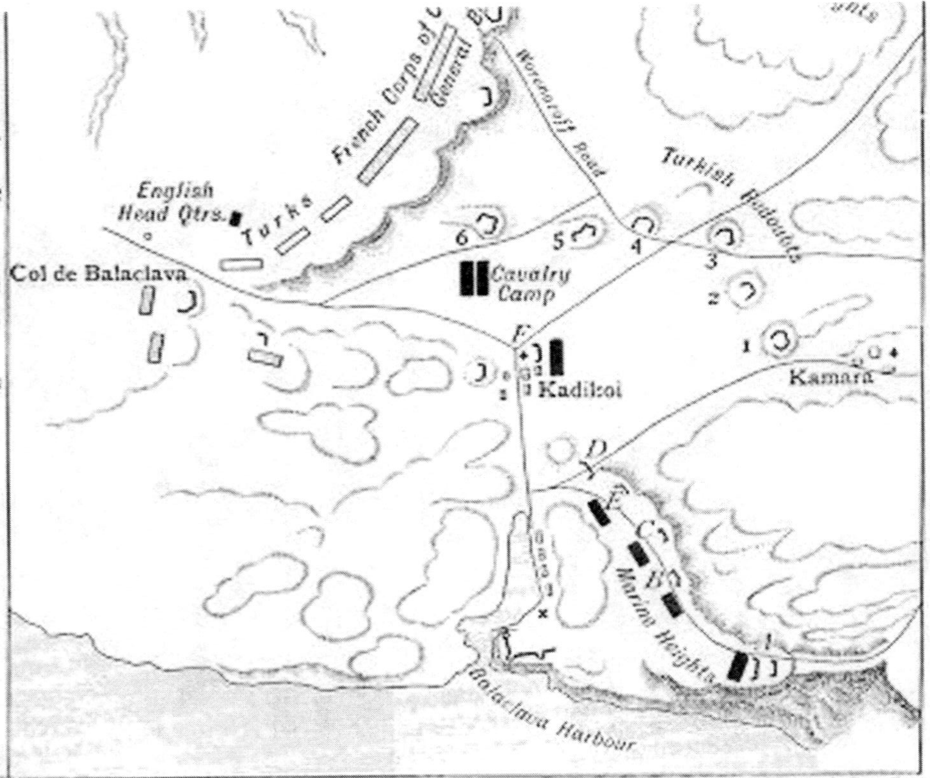

Walker & Boutall sc.

looking Quarantine bay, and between these were some earthworks (called afterwards the Redan, Bastion du Mât, &c.), unfinished and unarmed. These defences were not formidable, and the idea of an immediate assault suggested itself and was advocated by some officers of high rank. On the other hand, the garrison was almost equal in number to the allies; the approaches were commanded by guns, although few, of heavy calibre; and the enemy had so placed their line-of-battle ships in the harbour as to sweep the ravines leading down to the city. On the whole it was considered more prudent to land the French and English siege trains, with a view to a bombardment, to be followed by a general assault.

As to the general plan of attack, Sir John Burgoyne, having, with Lord Raglan, surveyed the position, drew up a memorandum in which he indicated the Malakoff as the chief point for consideration. He said: 'On the right, the great tower appears to be the key of the whole position, and the only work to prevent an assault at any time; a good site, or sites for not less than eight guns . . . must be sought for to demolish that tower.' The French, however, demurred to this view, and it was finally decided that the main attack should be made by them on the Bastion du Mât, an earthwork in their immediate front on the left. When we remember that at the end of the siege, which lasted nearly a twelve-month, the city fell chiefly by an assault on the very position originally indicated by Sir John Burgoyne, we have a striking proof of the clear insight and great ability of that distinguished soldier.

During the first fortnight of October the allied armies were incessantly occupied in landing and moving up heavy guns and ammunition from Kameisch and Balaclava, and in constructing batteries and trenches in front of Sebastopol, and it was arranged that the bombardment should open on the 17th, to be followed by a general assault, the combined fleets simultaneously attacking the forts at the mouth of the harbour. Lord Raglan's order was as follows: 'The fire upon Sebastopol to commence at 6.30 A.M. from the French and English batteries, in co-operation with the allied fleets—the signal to be the discharge of three mortars by the French. The troops off duty to be ready to fall in at a moment's notice. Horses of the field batteries to be harnessed.' A thousand seamen with heavy guns were landed from the British fleet, and formed a naval brigade to act in co-operation with the Royal Artillery in the trenches.

The enemy, however, were equally energetic in developing and completing their earthworks, and, having an almost unlimited supply of heavy ordnance and munitions close at hand, they were in reality, as the event proved, able to strengthen their defensive position faster than the allies could concentrate their powers of attack.

The bombardment commenced at daylight on October 17, the infantry and field artillery being held in readiness for a general assault during the day. Our hopes and expectations were, however, destined to a great and speedy disappointment. The French siege batteries in front of the Bastion du Mât were soon seen to be in difficulties, being overmatched by those of the enemy; and early in the morning one of their magazines exploded, followed by a second, resulting in great loss of life, and practically putting an end for the time to their fire. The Russians, having thus gained a considerable advantage in one direction, turned their attention more immediately towards the English position, and a vigorous bombardment was maintained on both sides. Lord Raglan, in his despatch of October 18, alluding to the British batteries, speaks in high terms of the conduct of the sailors and of the Royal Artillery. He says that they kept up their fire with unremitting energy throughout the day, to his own and the general satisfaction, and to the admiration of the French army.

About three o'clock in the afternoon, a magazine blew up in the Redan, and for a time the Russian guns were silent. Lord Raglan said that, under other circumstances, this explosion would have been the proper moment for assault. The combined fleets during the day also engaged the sea forts and suffered considerably, but from our inability to take advantage of their action no decisive results were achieved. In short, the great bombardment of October 17 was a *coup manqué*, and although the conflict was still vigorously maintained, and although the French in a few days partially re-opened fire, it began to be apparent that the allies were growing weaker by the wearing out of their guns and carriages and the exhaustion of their ammunition, whilst the Russian defences were becoming consolidated and their armaments augmented.

General Canrobert did not at first take so gloomy a view of the position. Writing a few days after, he stated that his means of attack were concentrated on the Bastion du Mât, and that, assisted by the English, he hoped soon to gain possession of it. Lord Raglan, however, writing on the 23rd, said that the fire of the enemy was not seriously diminished; that, with plenty of men and unlimited resources, they were able to repair their works, remount guns, and re-open fire from batteries which had been silenced, and that consequently, he was unable to say when ulterior measures could be undertaken. The situation was growing serious.

In the meantime the enemy were also beginning to appear in strength on the Chernaya, in the direction of Balaclava. Since our arrival, at the end of September, considerable attention had been given to the defence of this important base of our operations. Defensive entrenchments were constructed on the heights immediately surrounding and overlooking the harbour, armed with guns of position, and held by a force of marines; whilst the 93rd Highlanders and a battery of artillery were in front of Kadikoi, the whole under the command of Sir Colin Campbell. In the plain beyond, and about a mile in advance, a girdle of small detached hills extended in a curve across the valley, and upon these, several battalions of Turks were distributed and began to entrench themselves. As they had no ordnance suitable, some cast-iron howitzers were by Lord Raglan's direction lent to them for the purpose. Such were the main outlines of the precautions taken for the defence of Balaclava. They were by no means too strong; but what with the incessant duties before Sebastopol and the great extent of ground to be covered, our troops were overworked, and no more were available for the defence of this flank of the position, covering, indeed, the sole base of our supplies of food and munitions.

CHAPTER V

BATTLE OF BALACLAVA

'Not once or twice in our rough island story,
The path of duty was the way to glory.'

Early on the morning of October 25, the Russian army having received large reinforcements, General Liprandi advanced in force and attacked the unfinished redoubts held by the Turks; and although the latter were supported in the plain by the British cavalry and Maude's troop of Horse Artillery, they were not able to hold their ground, and, after a short defence, fell back disordered to Balaclava, leaving their guns behind, many of the Turks calling out 'Ship—Johnnie—Russ no bono' as they ran past our troops. It was during this early part of the action that Captain Maude[1] was seriously wounded and had his horse killed under him.

Soon after the commencement of the battle, Lord Raglan, General Canrobert, and their staffs, arrived, and took up a position on the edge of the Sebastopol plateau overlooking the plain, and thus gained a

[1] The late Sir George Maude, Crown Equerry.

complete panoramic view of the scene below. Lord Raglan, on perceiving the defeat of the Turks in the outlying forts, at once ordered the First Division under the Duke of Cambridge, and the Fourth under Sir George Cathcart, to proceed from the front to strengthen the force at Balaclava. The enemy, having somewhat easily gained an important advantage by the capture of the Turkish position, after a short delay made a further movement towards the inner line of defence, and a large mass of Russian cavalry advanced rapidly and with great boldness across the plain. One portion approached the 93rd, who were in line in front of Kadikoi, but, being received with perfect steadiness by the Highlanders, they did not follow up the attack. The main body bore down towards the English Heavy Cavalry under General Scarlett, who, however, wheeled into line as the Russians approached, and charged straight into them. Having been sent with an order to Brandling's C Battery of Horse Artillery, it so happened that I was at the moment only a few hundred yards distant, and witnessed the whole affair. For a few minutes it seemed as if our cavalry, owing to the great superiority of the enemy's numbers (estimated at three to one), were almost surrounded. Then small bodies of red-coats could be seen vigorously fighting and in close personal combat with the Russians. At length the latter gave way, their retreat being hastened by the fire of two batteries of Horse Artillery. Lord Raglan in his despatch said that the charge was one of the most successful he had ever witnessed. It was made at an opportune moment, and completely checked the enemy's movements, their infantry remaining at a distance, partially concealed behind the captured Turkish forts. A pause now ensued.

Whilst the events just related were taking place, the First and Fourth Divisions were marching down, and arrived in the plain. In the meantime, the Light Cavalry under Lord Cardigan had moved to the outer valley, just beyond the Turkish forts. A small force of French Chasseurs d'Afrique was on their left. Lord Raglan, being anxious to recover the position lost by the Turks, sent the following order in writing to the Earl of Lucan, who was in chief command of the cavalry: 'The cavalry to advance and take advantage of every opportunity to recover the heights. They will be supported by infantry, which has been ordered to advance on two fronts.' Instructions of a similar purport were sent to the infantry divisions. As some delay occurred and the object was not accomplished, and, further, as Lord Raglan from his position on the heights observed that the enemy were removing the captured guns, he sent a second order, *also in writing*, to Lord Lucan, by Captain Nolan, as follows: 'Lord Raglan wishes

BALACLAVA. SCENE OF LIGHT CAVALRY CHARGE, 25TH OCTOBER, 1854

the cavalry to advance rapidly to the front, follow the enemy, and try to prevent them carrying away the guns. Troop of Horse Artillery may accompany, French cavalry on your left. Immediate.'

The fair construction of the above orders would appear to be that the cavalry were to follow the retreating enemy, and that they were to be supported by artillery and two divisions of infantry. What followed is thus related by Lord Lucan himself. 'After carefully reading this order, I hesitated, and urged the uselessness of such an attack and the dangers attending it. The aide-de-camp, in a most authoritative tone, stated that they were Lord Raglan's orders that the cavalry should attack immediately. I asked, where and what to do, neither enemy nor guns being in sight? He replied in a most disrespectful but significant manner, pointing to the further end of the valley: "There, my Lord, is your enemy; there are your guns." So distinct, in my opinion, was your written instruction, and so positive and urgent were the orders delivered by the aide-de-camp, that I felt it was imperative on me to obey, and I informed Lord Cardigan that he was to advance, and to the objections he made, and in which I entirely agreed, I replied that the order was from your Lordship.'

Such are the main outlines of the circumstances which led to the celebrated Light Cavalry charge.

Formed as shown in the diagram, they moved rapidly and steadily down the plain. They did not attack the enemy behind the Turkish entrenchments, nor did they attempt to intercept the captured howitzers which were being withdrawn, but rode straight into the main body of the Russian army, far away at the other end of the valley. Artillery opened upon them on either flank and in front, but still they rode on, and at length passed right through

Formation of Light Brigade under the Earl of Cardigan.

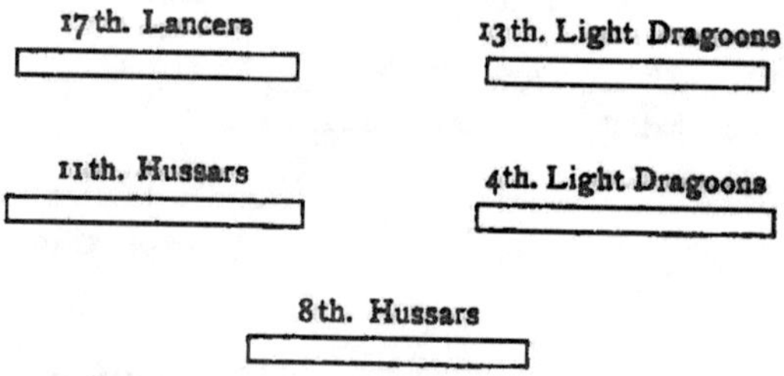

the enemy's guns; but assailed by artillery, infantry, and cavalry they were at length almost broken up, and only scattered fragments of each regiment ever came back. The Chasseurs d'Afrique, who were on the flank of the Light Brigade, gallantly charged the enemy on the Fedhukine heights, and thus made an important diversion, in which they suffered severely. The loss of the cavalry during the day amounted to 40 officers and 353 men killed, wounded, and missing; and 381 horses killed.

Having been sent a second time to Balaclava with orders and my horse becoming lame, I was returning leisurely just as the charge took place, but, owing to the ridge of intervening hills intercepting the view, was not aware of it. Meeting H.R.H. the Duke of Cambridge a few minutes afterwards at the head of the Guards, he spoke of the sad loss the army had just sustained; and, seeing that I was ignorant of the circumstances, went forward a little and pointed down the outer valley, where small groups could be seen in the distance of men and horses of the Light Cavalry lying about, and in some cases being attended to by the Russians. The Duke added: 'The officer who brought the order lies dead in that ditch.' There, a few yards off, was the body of Captain Nolan, with a large wound in his chest. In the course of the afternoon part of Sir George Cathcart's division advanced a short distance, and re-took one of the outlying forts, in which were found two of the lost howitzers upset in the half-formed entrenchment.

Lord Raglan, in his despatch of the Battle of Balaclava, alluding to the circumstances which led to the Light Cavalry charge, limited his remarks to the statement that 'from some misconception of the instruction to advance, the Lieutenant-General considered that he was bound to attack at all hazards.' The Earl of Lucan, however, took exception to this description of his action in the matter, and, persisting in his objections, was ultimately recalled.

The consequences immediately resulting from the battle of the 25th were not of a decisive character. The enemy had no doubt achieved a partial success in getting possession of the outer line of defence, but had not obtained their main object—the capture of Balaclava. The position however, was precarious, and two regiments of Highlanders were added to Sir Colin's force, and a brigade of French infantry were encamped on the heights in rear. Still Lord Raglan was anxious, and in his despatch of November 3 says that he should be more satisfied if he could have occupied the position in considerably greater strength. Greater anxieties were, however, awaiting him.

On the afternoon following the battle of Balaclava the Russians came out in considerable strength from Sebastopol (about 6,000 men and 16 guns) and attacked the right of our position on the heights of Inkerman, but were vigorously met by the artillery and infantry of the Guards and Second Division, and were driven back into the city with a loss of about 600 men. This attempt of the enemy proved to be the shadow of a coming event.

During the next few days no incident of special importance occurred, but the crisis was approaching, and the Russians, having received large reinforcements, on November 5 made another determined attack in great force on the right of the English position, which, had it succeeded, would not only have raised the siege, but would probably have entailed the abandonment of the Crimea by the allies. Indeed, although unsuccessful in its main purpose, still the results of the great battle on that day were by no means insignificant. The allies were compelled to postpone any idea of assault, and they thus afforded the enemy time to complete their defences, which enabled the city to hold out for ten months longer. In connection with this subject there is another point which deserves consideration. Although probably fortuitous, still it is a fact that both on landing in the Crimea, and on taking up ground in front of Sebastopol, the English army occupied on each occasion the exposed flank, so that at the three successive battles the brunt of the actions, and consequently the chief losses, fell upon them. Not only that, but whilst their numbers—owing to deaths, wounds, and sickness—were constantly and rapidly diminishing, they had, in addition to their work in the trenches, to guard a very extended position. General Canrobert, perhaps unduly cautious, did not feel able at that time to give us any more assistance in the defence of Balaclava.[1] Lord Raglan himself so informed me at the time.

[1] See Lord Raglan to the Duke of Newcastle, November 8, Kinglake's *Inkerman*, p. 45.

As regards the ground at Inkerman on which the great conflict took place, it did not in itself offer any very inviting facilities to an enemy's attack. It formed the right-hand corner, as it were, of our position on the elevated plateau south of the city; and the ascent to it from Sebastopol and the Chernaya was precipitous, its area being restricted by the Careening Bay ravine on one side, and by steep slopes on the other—so that the enemy's columns as they arrived were rather huddled together, and got in each other's way.

Todleben wrote: 'Although the nature of the ground rendered this position a strong one in itself, it was to be considered that the number of English troops which occupied it was very weak.'[1]

The general plan was as follows:[2]

Two corps of the Russian army under General Dannenberg, computed at 40,000 infantry and 135 guns, were detailed for the attack. One under Dannenberg and Pauloff was to cross the marsh at the mouth of the Chernaya, climb the heights, and force the English right; whilst the other, under Soimonoff, was to leave Sebastopol, near the Malakoff, and advance up the *left side* of the Careening Bay ravine. These arrangements would appear to be simple enough, but as it turned out they were in a great measure frustrated by a singular mistake. It appears that

[1] Kinglake's *Inkerman*, p. 56.

[2] See Kinglake's *Inkerman*, pp. 110 and 498; Dannenberg's orders to Soimonoff.

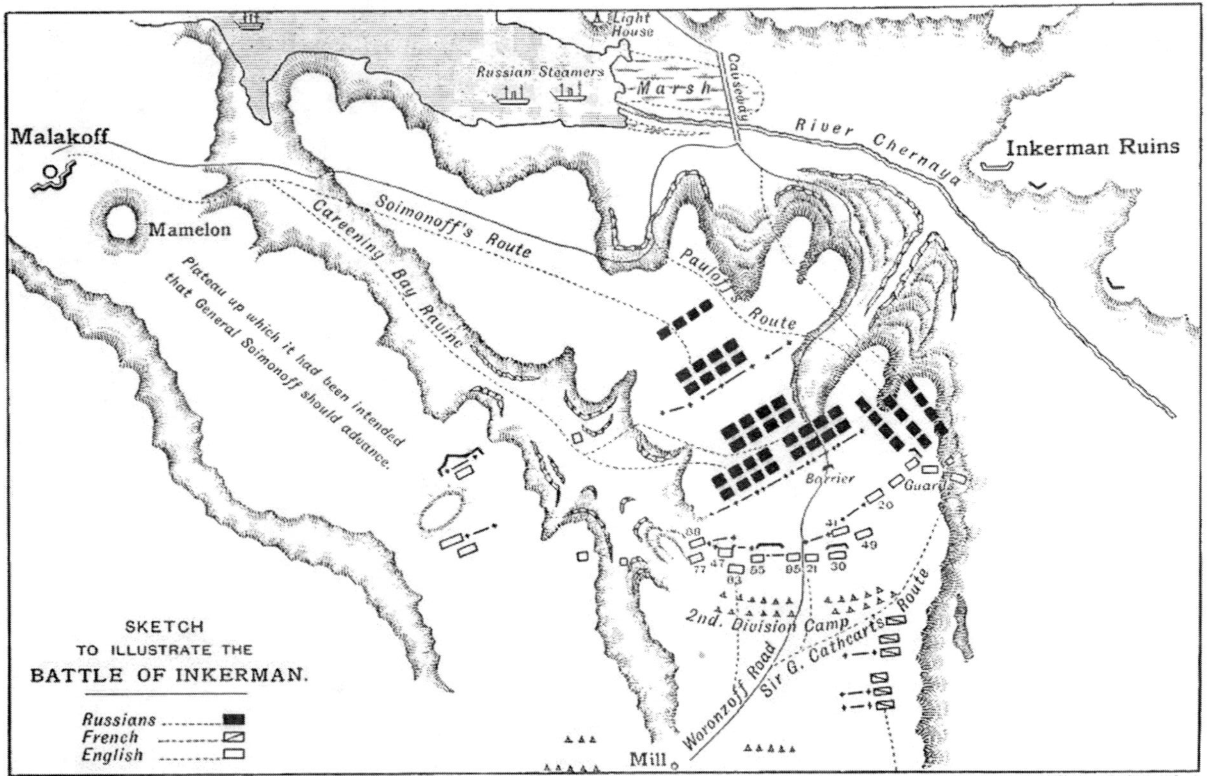

Walker & Boutall sc.

General Soimonoff, looking from Sebastopol, imagined that he was to advance up the *left side* of the ravine as he saw it from that point of view, whereas the intention was precisely the reverse. The intention of General Dannenberg seems clear from the following short extract from his instructions to Soimonoff, issued the day before. He says: 'Votre flanc gauche sera parfaitement couvert par le ravin du Carénage, et la coopération des troupes qui traversent la Chernaya.' Again he says: 'Un ravin profond et très long, connu sous le nom de ravin du Carénage, nous sépare, le général Soimonoff et moi, au commencement de l'attaque.'

As it was, however, before daybreak on the 5th Soimonoff led his corps across the ravine, and marched up on the other side, so that when Pauloff arrived immediately after he found the heights already occupied and the battle begun. This initial blunder (although we were of course ignorant of it at the time) hampered the Russians throughout the day; and the death of Soimonoff early in the action probably rather added to their confusion. A Russian account quite confirms this view. It says: 'The disadvantage of this false direction was that from the confined nature of the ground Soimonoff's troops were very much in the way of Pauloff's columns, and neither the one nor the other could find space to deploy.' . . . . 'While the Russians were moving about in columns, the English were drawn up in a line two deep, and their long-ranging guns enabled them to inflict mortal wounds on the Russians at a time when the latter were unable to reach them at all with their firearms.'

As regards the arrangements of the English previous to the battle, 500 men of the Second Division and three guns were detailed daily to watch the ground at Inkerman, and one or two slight earthworks were thrown up; a picket of the Light Division being also posted in the Careening Bay ravine, which, however, was captured on the morning of the 5th.

CHAPTER VI

BATTLE OF INKERMAN

Before giving a slight sketch of the events of this momentous day, it is necessary to bear in mind that the original numbers of the English army had become much reduced since their landing, by the casualties of war and by sickness; that they had also to guard the trenches day and night, and to be ready to defend the extended position in front of Balaclava. In short, their numbers were not by any means adequate to the various and widely detached duties they were called upon to perform. The consequence was that on the day of Inkerman they had only 8,000 infantry and 36 guns available for the defence of the position.

It was dark and wet and a thick fog lay on the ground as day dawned on Sunday, November 5. My servant came into my tent and woke me about daylight, saying that heavy firing had just commenced not far away. In a few minutes I was off, but found that Lord Raglan and General Strangways had already left. On approaching the scene, and riding through the camp of the Second Division, it was apparent that the enemy were close at hand. Round shot were bounding along, tents were being knocked over, horses killed at their pickets, whilst blankets and great coats were lying about among the brushwood, thrown down, apparently, as our men had hastily fallen in and hurried to the front. The centre of our position on the ridge was held by the Second Division under Pennefather, with the Guards in advance on the right under the Duke of Cambridge and Bentinck, and one brigade of the Light Division under Buller on the left—six batteries of artillery being in action in the intervals. On joining Lord Raglan about 7 A.M. it was evident from the very heavy fire both of infantry and artillery that the Russian columns were close upon us, and were indeed forcing our position at various points. In fact, owing to the rain and thick mist, the troops of both the opposing forces were in immediate proximity several times during the day almost before they were aware of it.

On the extreme right, and in advance, a small sandbag work had been established and armed with two 18-pounders many days previously, not with a view to local defence, but to silence some Russian guns on the other side of the Chernaya which annoyed our camp, and having achieved the object our guns had been withdrawn. It was in the neighbourhood of this earthwork that very severe fighting took place, and it was captured and re-taken several times, the Guards especially sustaining the brunt of the conflict and suffering great losses. The Russian account says: 'The battle raged forward, backward, beneath, above, among bushes and underwood; above all, the sand-bag battery on the wing had been the object of many an attack, until at length General Bentinck led up his Guards, the *élite* of the English army. These chosen troops pressed irresistibly forward to the redoubt, and tore it from the Russians. . . .'

In the meantime Sir George Cathcart, with part of the Fourth Division, arrived to the support of our hardly pressed troops. Conceiving the extreme right to be the point most open to danger, he was marching in that direction when he received urgent messages requesting assistance in the centre and on the left. He accordingly detached the greater part of his brigade and a battery towards these points, but proceeded himself, with a small number of men, to reinforce the Guards. The enemy, in fact, were forcing our line at several places at once. Hardly had the battery just named got into action and fired a few rounds of case than it was run into and three of its guns momentarily captured, the officer commanding (Major Townsend) being killed. Three guns of Turner's battery were also taken and some of the gunners bayonetted at their posts; but in both instances the guns were re-taken immediately afterwards by the 77th and 88th Regiments.[1]

[1] Lord Raglan's despatch, November 8, 1854.

Sir George Cathcart, under the impression that he could assist the Guards by a flank movement, moved for some distance down the slopes, near the sandbag battery, but suddenly found himself surrounded by a superior force, and fell, shot through the heart; General Torrens, who was with him, being also severely wounded.[1]

At about 8 o'clock A.M., Lord Raglan with his staff was moving along the ridge, and halted about the centre of the line. Perceiving the advantage he should gain by the fire of heavy guns from such commanding ground, he sent an order for the two 18-pounders, which were near at hand at the mill, to be brought up. It so happened that the officers in charge of them, anticipating his wishes, had already packed the necessary ammunition in waggons, and were, therefore, ready when his message came. Colonel Gambier, R.A., in command, was wounded, and had to retire as they moved up; but under Colonel Collingwood Dickson[2] and Captain D'Aguilar these guns were speedily brought into action on the ridge, and rendered excellent service throughout the day. Prince Menschikoff, in his despatch after the battle, makes special allusion to the fire of the British heavy guns. There were no less than seventeen casualties with these two guns, and they fired about 84 rounds a gun.

[1] Lord Raglan's despatch, November 8, 1854.

[2] Now Generals Sir C. Dickson and Sir C. D'Aguilar.

Just before the arrival of the 18-pounders, Lord Raglan, accompanied by his staff, was on the ridge surveying the position, having General Strangways on his right. At that moment a shell, supposed to have been fired at long range from a Russian vessel in the harbour, passed between them and burst amongst the staff, killing the horses of Colonels Gordon and Paulet Somerset. These two officers, however, were unhurt.[1] A few seconds afterwards General Strangways turned round to me, saying, quite calmly, 'Help me off my horse,' and he was then seen to be falling. General Estcourt and myself jumped off and caught him as he fell; and we then found that his left leg had been taken off below the knee by the shell as it passed between him and Lord Raglan. We laid him on the ground and I tied my handkerchief round his shattered limb. The staff moved on a short distance, and I was left with him alone. The enemy at the time were close upon us. After looking about in vain for a doctor, or a stretcher to carry him away, I at length saw two men bearing a wounded comrade, and, when they had deposited

[1] It is interesting to note that nearly forty years before this day Lord Raglan and Strangways, then both young men of twenty-six years of age, had been present at Waterloo, when both were severely wounded, Lord Raglan losing his right arm.

The staff present were as follows: Sir John Burgoyne, Generals Estcourt, Strangways, and Airey; Colonels Steele, Paulet Somerset and the Hon. A. Gordon; Captains N. Kingscote, Lord Burghersh, Hon. L. Curzon, Hon. E. Gage, Wetherall, Stopford, Hon. S. Calthorpe, E. Gordon, and myself.

him in a tent, induced them to return with me. A medical officer also arrived. We gave the General some wine and water from a flask, which temporarily revived him. He did not seem to suffer pain, gave me many messages to his wife and daughter, and begged me to take him to the siege train camp, which was done. Almost his last words were, 'Take me to the gunners, let me die amongst the gunners.' As we were carrying him off we passed the body of another officer on a stretcher, and it proved to be that of Sir George Cathcart. On arrival at the hospital tent, General Strangways became faint and insensible; it was evident that no operation could be performed, and soon afterwards he passed away, with wounded gunners lying round him, Lord Raglan coming to see him just before he died. He was much beloved and respected by all his officers and men, and his death at such a critical time was a great misfortune. When General Strangways fell on the ridge, his horse got away in the confusion, but was afterwards recovered, and singularly enough, was untouched, not even the stirrup leather being cut.

On going up to rejoin Lord Raglan, after the death of Strangways, I met Sir Edmund Lyons, Captain Drummond, and other naval officers on ponies, and conducted them, at their request, to the front. Subsequent to the events just sketched out, from which it will be apparent that our position was very critical, the battle still continued with unabated energy for several hours. The arrival of some French battalions and batteries under Generals Bosquet and Bourbaki, however, gave valuable support to our sorely pressed troops, and Lord Raglan, in his despatch of November 8, drew special attention 'to the brilliant conduct of the allied troops.' 'French and English,' he said, 'vied with each other in displaying their gallantry and manifesting their zealous devotion to duty, notwithstanding that they had to contend against an infinitely superior force, and were exposed for many hours to a very galling fire. . . .' General Canrobert also joined Lord Raglan on the field, and was again slightly wounded. I remember his inquiring of me how many guns we had in action, and I replied: 'thirty-six, in addition to the two 18-pounders.'

The Russian account, though not altogether correct, is worth perusal. It says: 'The battle had now attained its climax. Most of the English generals were *hors de combat*. The Britons, sadly reduced in numbers and exhausted by the struggle, defended themselves but faintly. More and more the fortunes of the day inclined to the Russians. It was about 11 o'clock when, on a sudden, the shrill tones of horns were heard above the rolling and rattling of the fire. The third act, the turning point of the battle, commenced. The French arrived. In the same proportion as the assurance of their timely aid revived the sinking spirits of the English, it discouraged the Russians, who felt themselves at once on the point of being deprived of the fruit of five hours' hard fighting.'

About noon I was directed by Lord Raglan to go to General Codrington, whose brigade was on the other side of the Careening Bay ravine, to inquire how he was getting on, and whether he required assistance. Codrington's brigade, be it observed, was on the very ground up which it had been intended that Soimonoff should advance. I found his troops lying down, and temporarily out of action. General Codrington informed me that he had been occasionally attacked by Russian troops coming suddenly out of the ravine, but that he had driven them back, and that they were not in great force. As the fog was lifting he invited me to go with him some distance to the front, to try and gain a better general view of the Russian position. We did so, and looking across the ravine to Inkerman were able, for the first time, to see the great masses of the enemy. Whilst carefully observing their movements, the Russian batteries were seen to be retreating in *échelon.* Codrington looked at his watch—it was ten minutes to one. He then desired me to return forthwith to Lord Raglan and let him know what we had seen. On delivering the message to the Commander-in-Chief, and saying that the battle seemed coming to an end, his reply was: 'Yes, I believe so,' showing that he had already become aware of the commencement of the retreat.

Lord Raglan's despatch, speaking of the latter part of the battle, said: 'Subsequently to this, the battle continued with unabated vigour and with no positive result, the enemy bringing upon our line, not only the fire of all their field batteries, but those in front of the works of the place, and the ship guns, till the afternoon, when the symptoms of giving way first became apparent; and shortly after, although the fire did not cease, the retreat became general, and heavy masses were observed retiring over the bridge of the Chernaya, and ascending the opposite heights, abandoning on the field of battle 5,000 or 6,000 dead and wounded, multitudes of the latter having already been carried off by them.'

The Russian account says: 'Thus ended the battle, one of the most sanguinary on record, at 2 o'clock P.M., after lasting eight hours.' It attributed their defeat partly to the bravery and steadiness of the English and French troops, partly to the superiority of their arms, and finally to the wrong direction of Soimonoff. When it is considered that the English had only 8,000 infantry and 38 guns available for the defence of the position, and with this small force had to bear the brunt in all the earlier hours of the battle, it is not necessary to dwell on the courage and discipline of the officers and men ; the facts speak for themselves. And the quotation I have given from Lord Raglan's despatch is sufficient proof of the timely support and great gallantry of our brave allies.

The English losses were very serious : no less than eight generals and 2,614 officers and men were killed, wounded, or missing.[1]

The names of the generals are as follows :

Killed	Sir George Cathcart Fox Strangways Goldie
Wounded . . .	Sir George Brown Adams, died of his wounds Torrens, died of his wounds Bentinck Buller

The losses of the Russians are computed to have been between 11,000 and 12,000. We also captured one gun-carriage and five ammunition carts, left on the heights. Our allies, the French, lost about 930 officers and men, killed and wounded. Late at night on the 5th I was sent for by Lord Raglan, who wished for information as to the supply of ammunition at Inkerman, in the event of a second attack. H.R.H. the Duke of Cambridge was with him. I was able to give a satisfactory statement, and to inform him that Captain Gage, R.A., who had been sent during the

[1] Eighty artillery horses were killed.

battle down to Balaclava to bring up a large supply, both for infantry and artillery, had just returned, reporting that the mill, which was our magazine at the front, was amply stocked.

It appears that Prince Menschikoff and two Russian Grand Dukes were present on the field of Inkerman during the day; and that reminds me of a curious incident which occurred in relation to one of them long years afterwards. A gunner of the Royal Artillery served throughout the war, and was wounded, receiving the Victoria Cross for his gallant conduct. Subsequently he served during the Indian mutiny, and was again wounded. After he was pensioned I was partially instrumental in obtaining for him an appointment in the Yeomen of the Guard. Being on one occasion on duty in one of the corridors of Buckingham Palace (at a State Ball, if I remember rightly), a foreign officer, who proved to be a Russian Grand Duke, came up, spoke to him, and examined his decorations. He asked him about his Victoria Cross, and then, seeing he had the Crimean medal and clasp for Inkerman, said: 'Were you at that battle?' 'Yes, sir,' was the reply. 'So was I,' said the Grand Duke. The old Yeoman, in telling me the story, said he thought he might be so bold, so he replied to the Grand Duke, 'Well, sir, if you was at Inkerman, I hope we may never meet again on so unpleasant an occasion.'

CHAPTER VII

THE WINTER OF 1854

WHATEVER hopes or expectations might have been previously entertained as to the speedy fall of Sebastopol, the battle of Inkerman, at all events, utterly and rudely dispelled them. The facts were now plain enough—nearly 100,000 Russians were on the spot, with an almost unlimited supply of guns and ammunition to defend their city, whilst the allies had not much more than half the number of men; and their siege material was nearly worn out and its ammunition expended. The fortresses in the Mediterranean might in some degree help us to replenish our batteries, but there was no hope of efficient operations being renewed until the allied armies had been largely reinforced, both with men and material. Months must thus elapse, during which time the enemy would have leisure to strengthen their armaments and complete their defences. Thus the first attempt on Sebastopol had failed. But even these were by no means the worst features of the case. The allies had open trenches to maintain, and at the same moment a widely extended frontier to guard from attack.

It is as well to pause for a moment and to consider the circumstances of the English army at the time. In the first place the force sent to the East had been raised with difficulty, was quite inadequate to the occasion, and was insufficiently provided with commissariat and transport. Mr. Sidney Herbert, Minister for War, said: 'The army in the East has been created by discounting the future. Every regiment at home or within reach, and not forming part of the army, has been robbed to complete it.' Again, it was entirely devoid of reserves. The House of Commons Committee of 1855 reported 'that the men sent to reinforce the army were recruits who had not yet become fit for foreign service. When the Duke of Newcastle acquainted Lord Raglan that he had 2,000 recruits to send him, he replied that those last sent were so young and unformed that they fell victims to disease, and were swept away like flies—he preferred to wait . . .'

We must, however, go further. It will be remembered that the expedition proceeded to the Crimea at a late season, and after much sickness at Varna, in obedience to the orders of the Home Government—who apparently did not foresee the probability of a winter campaign with open trenches before a half-beleaguered city, and the inevitable hardships and losses which must ensue. For some time during the winter of 1854 the English army was diminishing from invaliding and casualties at the rate of 100 men a day. In short the winter was upon them, and standing on the bare plateau, with greatly diminished numbers, several miles from their base, and without proper food, shelter, or clothing, they must now be prepared to maintain their dangerous position. A consideration of these circumstances will enable us to form some idea of the difficult position of Lord Raglan at that time. He had, moreover, other anxieties pressing upon him—anxieties of divided councils, and of indecision in his French colleague—who, however brave as a soldier, allowed himself to be swayed and overborne by incessant and rash proposals from Paris, and even by subordinates on the spot. These latter facts were not generally known at the time, and the people of England were misled; but in proof of them I will shortly enter into some details, quoting official documents published afterwards. There is almost always an element of weakness in allied operations, but during the earlier part of the Crimean War they became more than usually apparent and mischievous.

On the death of General Strangways, Colonel Dacres[1] succeeded to the command of the artillery, and one morning soon after, he waited on Lord

[1] The late Field-Marshal Sir Richard Dacres, G.C.B.

Raglan, who, in his usual good-natured way, asked him how he was getting on. 'My Lord,' said Dacres, 'when a man has been twenty-one years a subaltern, he never can get on.' However, his turn came at last. At the beginning of 1855 he was only a Lieutenant-Colonel, but before the year was at an end he had been promoted to Colonel, Brigadier-General, Major-General, and Lieutenant-General, and had received the Order of the Bath, the Legion of Honour, the Medjidi, and an Italian order.

The English army had hardly begun to realise the difficulties and sufferings it was destined to endure throughout the winter when an additional misfortune was caused by a terrific gale on November 14, during which no less than fifteen transports containing clothing, food, ammunition, forage, and other stores were sunk in the Black Sea. A large number of tents on the plateau were also blown down, and great misery ensued. Notwithstanding all our troubles, there were occasional incidents of an odd and amusing kind, which now and then helped to enliven us. Among others was one relating to a dead man, who came to life and appeared at Woolwich. Soon after our arrival before Sebastopol it was found that many men of the different regiments were unaccounted for, some having died on the march, others been carried on board ship sick, and some taken prisoners. Courts of Inquiry were held, and as regards the artillery the results sent home. Some time afterwards a letter was received from the Horse Guards that a Gunner Brown, who was reported as dead, had arrived at Woolwich, and an explanation was requested. The officer commanding the battery, in reply to the query, stated to the effect 'that Brown was an old comrade of his, that he had visited him when he was dying, and attended his funeral; therefore,' he said, 'I know he is dead, and am surprised to hear of his return to Woolwich, but am not responsible for his subsequent movements.'

On December 26 I had the gratification of receiving a note from Lord Raglan of which the following is a copy: 'December 26, 1854. My dear Adye,—I have great satisfaction in announcing your promotion to the rank of Lieutenant Colonel, and that of Captains Fortescue, Gordon, and Gage to the rank of Major. Captains Paynter,[1] Wodehouse, Maude, Swinton, D'Aguilar, Brandling, Turner, Anderson, Morris, Hamley, Hoste, Yates, and Pennycuick have also got a step. A pretty Christmas box for you all. Pray accept my congratulations, and offer them to Captains Fortescue, Gordon, and Gage. Yours faithfully, Raglan.'

The rations served out by the Commissariat during the winter of 1854 were not very varied or

[1] These were all artillery officers.

specially inviting, and consisted chiefly of lumps of salt beef or pork (with occasional fresh meat), ship's biscuits and rum, but no bread or milk. Luxuries of any kind were difficult to obtain at Balaclava, and were expensive. A ham cost two guineas, beer three shillings a bottle, and so on. Our chief difficulty, however, was fuel. There were several English travellers, called T.G.'s (travelling gentlemen), who paid the Crimea a visit during the winter. On one occasion I was asked if I would entertain one of these travellers at dinner, as the Headquarters' Farm was full and the accommodation limited, and of course consented. My friend turned out to be an old gentleman of position and large fortune, but of delicate health, and was accompanied by a valet. What induced him to come out at such a time is inexplicable. As my tent was rather larger than the others, the three or four officers of the Artillery Staff usually dined together in it. The table was a plank, and the seats chiefly empty boxes on end. As soon as our friend arrived, dinner was served, cooked, of course, in a hole in the open air, and consisted of a lump of salt pork, more or less boiled. It was soon apparent that the old gentleman was making a wretched effort, and I tried to encourage him with a glass of rum and some biscuit; but he said he had a poor appetite, which was evident. Presently he turned round to me and said, 'You won't be offended, will you?' I replied, 'Not in the least. What is it?' 'Well,' he said, 'I don't mind for myself, but I know my valet can't eat salt pork; if I were to give him a sovereign, do you think he could go to some place of refreshment near, and buy some food?' I assured him that there was nothing better to be had nearer than Constantinople, which was several hundred miles away. After that he collapsed, and left for England the next morning.

The history of the siege for the next few months is a record of hardships and privations nobly borne. The officers and men of the naval brigade, the artillery and infantry, who had to take their turn of duty in the trenches for twenty-four hours at a time, were the chief sufferers; having to lie in muddy ditches and batteries, without shelter, with scanty clothing, and very indifferent food. There were officers and men, however, in all branches of the service who, in spite of hardships, went through the whole siege and never missed a tour of duty. In January 1855 the English sick list amounted to 13,000 men. The country was often deep in snow, and the road to Balaclava became almost impassable. Four fifths of the artillery horses died.

Pending the arrival of wooden huts from England several officers dug holes in the ground, and by means of planks and tarpaulins obtained rather better shelter than was afforded by a tent. Among others, Colonel Wood, R.A.,[1] constructed a rough hut of the kind. He had brought out a French cook, whom he accommodated in the hut, living himself in a covered cart. On being asked his object in this arrangement, his reply was that if he could save the life of the cook, the latter in return would do the same for him by giving him good food, otherwise both would probably perish. His precaution proved successful. Warm clothing, in large quantities, was sent out from England, and as the weather began to hold up in February the condition of the troops gradually improved. In addition to Government supplies, many persons in England, deeply affected by the sufferings of the army, sent out bales of mitts, comforters, flannels, under-garments, and even plum puddings. Occasionally the distribution was somewhat embarrassing. For instance, on one occasion, in opening some parcels for the artillery, we found a warm pair of drawers ticketed, 'For the brave Jones in the trenches.' Who was the brave Jones? We also sometimes received curious letters and inquiries about artillerymen, of which the following is an example:—'To the Right Honourable Colonel, Commanding the 12th Battalion Royal Artillery, field of Battle, Crimea. Your Honour—Your Petitioner is extremely anxious to know it

[1] The late General Sir David Wood, G.C.B., R.H.A.

James Winch under your command is still alive, if otherwise, by sword or epidemic.'

Subsequently to the great battle of November 5 it became evident that the English army, which was so rapidly diminishing in numbers, could not adequately guard the positions at Balaclava and on the heights, in addition to the hard work in the trenches. Consequently, the ridges and slopes of Inkerman were gradually occupied by a portion of the French army. The Russians, ever on the alert, came out in February, and established outworks near the harbour, beyond the Careening Bay ravine—known subsequently as the 'ouvrages blancs'—and it became necessary to dislodge them. The duty was undertaken by the French, and on the night of February 23, after a severe fight, in which they suffered considerable loss, the position was captured, but was not held, so that a few days afterwards it was again occupied and strengthened by the Russians; and it is important to bear in mind that no further attempt was made to dislodge them until after General Canrobert had resigned his command at the end of May. In fact, the Russians, who had received large reinforcements, became more bold and aggressive daily, and during March commenced and armed a formidable outwork on the Mamelon, considerably in advance of the Malakoff. Their night sorties against the trenches of the allies were both vigorous and frequent, with severe losses on all sides. It is computed that the Russian army in April amounted to nearly 150,000 men.

The English batteries during the long severe winter only maintained a desultory fire on the city, waiting for fresh armaments; and as ammunition ran short we had frequently to obtain supplies from the navy for current use. I was sent on many occasions to Admiral Sir Edmund Lyons in connection with these details. On one occasion, on being shown into his cabin on board the flagship, he said: 'Colonel Adye, whenever I see your face it always reminds me of a 68-pounder shot.' I thought at first he meant that it was too round, or was wanting in expression, and began to explain that I was not altogether responsible; but he said it was not that, but whenever I came to see him I always wanted a fresh supply of 68-pounder shot. My reply was that he had exactly foreseen my request, and promised if he would meet our wishes they should be safely delivered the next day into Sebastopol. The argument convinced him, and he complied at once.

Flag of Truce.—The following extract from my journal refers to rather an interesting event. '23rd of March. Accompanied Lord Burghersh, A.D.C., with a flag of truce, by order of Lord Raglan. We first went to the advanced French trenches on the left, near the sea, hoisted a white flag, and sounded a bugle. In a few minutes firing ceased on both sides. We stepped over the parapet, advanced about 100 yards, and were met by the enemy's riflemen out of their pits. A Russian officer on horseback, with two orderlies, galloped out to meet us, dismounted, and the conversation was then carried on in French. We handed him some letters, clothes, and money for French and English officers who had been taken prisoners, also a letter for Madame Osten-Sacken from Lord Raglan. His letter enclosed one from the mother of the midshipman (Giffard) who was killed in the fight at Odessa. It appears that Madame Osten-Sacken had cut off a lock of the poor boy's hair, and had sent it to his mother, who sent a letter of thanks. We offered the Russian officer a cigar, which he declined, and we also asked him a few questions, but his manner was stiff, and he shortly remounted and rode off. We returned to the trenches; the white flag was pulled down, and firing re-commenced. The French soldiers were always cheerful and good-natured in their monotonous duties. Lord Burghersh, as we passed along through their trenches, heard two of them chatting. One, looking over the parapet, said to his comrade: "Alphonse, êtes-vous prêt?" "Oui, mon ami, toujours prêt." "Eh bien! Allons faire la guerre;" and then they both jumped up and fired away through the loop-holes at the Russians.'

During the month of March strenuous efforts were made by the allies to prepare for a second bombardment, and, fresh armaments having arrived, it was decided to re-open with nearly 500 guns on April 9. It was, however, at this period that considerable hesitation and conflicting opinions became more or less evident at French Head Quarters. It was understood that the Emperor of the French would shortly arrive and take the command, and De Bazancourt, in his history of the campaign, states that General Canrobert received secret instructions which tied his hands. Their general scope was that the siege should be turned into a blockade, and a campaign undertaken in the interior of the Crimea.[1] The French army had about this time received large reinforcements, and was divided into two corps, one under Bosquet on the extreme right, the other under General Pélissier (who arrived in March) on the left; the English holding the centre of the position. The French strength was estimated at about 80,000 men. Omar Pasha also arrived in April with 20,000 Turkish troops. Great events were therefore anticipated.

[1] The history of the Crimean campaign by the Baron de Bazancourt is often incorrect, and sometimes unjust as regards the British army, and is therefore not altogether to be relied on. But in his account of the French views and proposals he has more complete knowledge, and, in fact, usually quotes official documents, and I have therefore made some quotations from his work, especially as to this critical juncture.

CHAPTER VIII

BOMBARDMENT OF APRIL

On April 9 the second bombardment, for which such incessant preparations had been made during the winter, at length commenced, and was vigorously maintained for the following ten days; and although the Russians carried out numerous sorties, and were also unceasing each night in repairing their shattered batteries, still it became evident that the allies had achieved a virtual mastery and had laid open paths for a general assault. It was a momentous crisis. As regards the condition of Sebastopol at that time, Todleben, writing of the Bastion du Mât, said[1] 'that after having undergone a constant and violent bombardment, the work was in a desperate plight. Its artillery had been dismounted, its embrasures and its merlons almost entirely demolished, and a part of its salient had fallen in,' . . 'that they were constantly expecting to see the enemy take advantage of the critical state to which the bastion was reduced, and advance to the assault of the work.' He adds,

[1] Kinglake, vii. 192.

that the French might have advanced to the assault of the bastion with an absolute certainty of success . . . and that would have carried with it the fall of Sebastopol.' . . .

The allied armies were indeed in full expectation of being at length led to the assault, and the result was almost a foregone conclusion, but no order was issued and no decisive action taken. The real history of the case was not known at the time, but the accounts published by De Bazancourt in 1856, and confirmed long afterwards by Kinglake's account, have cleared up the mystery. De Bazancourt [1] said: 'La pensée d'une opération à l'extérieur planait toujours, on le voit, sur les décisions, et empêchait de tenter contre la place une action décisive. Les instructions secrètes du général Canrobert lui liaient les mains, à moins de force majeure.' Again, he quotes a despatch of Canrobert of April 24 as follows: 'Les officiers généraux des armes spéciales des deux armées, les chefs de nos deux corps d'armée, ont été unanimes pour céder dans cette circonstance aux cris de nos soldats français et anglais, demandant l'assaut. Lord Raglan partage fermement leur avis. J'ai pensé que mon devoir était de m'y joindre. . . .' It seems remarkable, considering the unanimity which prevailed amongst the allied generals, and that the French Commander-in-Chief himself said he felt

[1] Bazancourt, ii. 239-242.

it his duty to join them, that no assault took place. Kinglake,[1] however, by means of French official documents brought to light after the fall of the Empire, proves that General Canrobert was in reality held back by instructions from Paris and by the influence of General Niel, and, in view of the expected arrival of the Emperor, would not join in a general assault.

Lord Raglan had apparently been informed of the expected arrival of the Emperor Napoleon, which he considered ill-advised, but both he and the English Government were kept for some time in the dark as to the special instructions which fettered the action of General Canrobert. Various interviews took place towards the end of April between the two Commanders-in-Chief, and in my journal I find a remark as follows: 'Met Lord Raglan out riding; he invited me to dinner, but added: "Canrobert is coming to a Council of War at half-past six, so we shall be late." The Council did not break up till ten P.M.'

Days thus passed away, and the allies were gradually losing the opportunity for which they had so long waited. In fact, the second bombardment of Sebastopol failed, from causes, however, very different from those which prevailed in the first. In October, 1854, our failure was due to want of power; in April, 1855, it was from want of

[1] Kinglake, vii. 121.

will. Events, however, were hurrying on, and the crisis soon came.

Towards the end of April the Emperor Napoleon [1] relinquished his intention of coming to the Crimea, but sent out his proposed plan of an external campaign, to which, however, Lord Raglan strongly objected.[2] Whilst matters thus drifted, and whilst the batteries of the allies were again becoming weak and their ammunition exhausted, a new actor appeared on the scene in the person of General Pélissier, who was commanding the French *corps d'armée* on the left. Amongst other matters, he pointed out to Canrobert in clear and forcible language [3] that the Russians were establishing counter approaches in his front, and that he, and those under him, were fully convinced that the enemy's new position must be taken by a *coup de main.* He concluded: 'S'il m'était donner de décider, je n'hésiterais pas.' General Canrobert wavered, but at length accepted the responsibility, and the order for the attack was given for May 1. In my journal is a record as follows: 'Returned from Balaclava about 10 o'clock P.M. on the 1st of May and had an interview with Lord Raglan. Lord Stratford was there, when a message came that a severe battle was going on in front of the French trenches

[1] Kinglake, vii. 245, and De Bazancourt, ii. 266.

[2] De Bazancourt, ii. 266–274.

[3] *Ibid.* ii. 252.

near the sea. We went off to a post of observation. The scene was striking. The sky was lit up with constant flashes—shells whizzing through the air; and amidst the incessant rattle of musketry could be heard the cheers of the troops as they stormed the works. It lasted four hours. Canrobert was with us, walking up and down, flourishing his stick and greatly excited. The result was that the French captured an outwork, and took eight mortars, and also five officers prisoners.'

In addition to the many difficulties of Lord Raglan's position at this time, he was also much worried by receiving a notification that Lord Panmure was about to abolish the Master-General and Board of Ordnance, and to absorb their duties in the newly constructed War Department. Speaking to me one day, he deplored the change, and said that the Ordnance was one of the most efficient and economical departments of the State, and that a much greater man than himself, the late Duke of Wellington, was of the same opinion.[1]

In the meantime, Lord Raglan, backed by the opinions of Admirals Bruat and Sir Edmund Lyons, strongly advocated a naval and military force being sent to Kertch at the entrance to the Sea of Azov, with a view of cutting the Russian communications and stopping their supplies; and the expedition,

[1] See also Clode's *Military Forces of the Crown*, ii. 287.

consisting of about 12,000 troops (one-fourth being English) started at the beginning of May. Hardly had it got out to sea than General Canrobert received an order by telegraph from Paris to concentrate all his troops for an external attack, and in consequence recalled the Kertch expedition, to the dismay, not only of Lord Raglan, but of the admirals and generals, and indeed of the officers and men of the allied fleets and armies.[1] Matters were evidently coming to a deadlock.

On May 14 Lord Raglan, Canrobert, and Omar Pasha had a long and final consultation as to the proposal of the Emperor Napoleon, which was in effect to separate the allied forces into three armies acting independently—one to blockade Sebastopol, the second to storm the Mackenzie Heights, and the third to march to the centre of the Crimea. The scheme was rejected on the broad ground that it would render each separate force liable to attack and defeat in detail.[2] This decision brought affairs to a crisis, and on May 16 General Canrobert telegraphed to the Emperor resigning his command, partly on the plea of ill health, but chiefly because his recall of the Kertch expedition and the rejection of the Emperor's scheme had placed him in a false position.[3] General Canrobert's resignation was accepted,

[1] Kinglake, vii. 260–278.
[2] Kinglake, vii. 287; also De Bazancourt, ii. 273–276.
[3] *Ibid.* 278.

and by his own wish he resumed command of his old division.

On May 19 General Pélissier was appointed Commander-in-Chief of the French army, and the situation was at once completely altered. Writing to Marshal Vaillant, Minister for War at Paris, he said: 'I have already seen Lord Raglan, and we are in complete accord; please ask the Emperor to give me liberty of action indispensable under the actual conditions of the war, and especially in view of the preservation of the intimate alliance of the two countries.' Efforts, however, were still made from Paris to regulate the strategy of the campaign, but they were virtually disregarded, and General Pélissier, acting with Lord Raglan, in the course of a few days carried out a series of important movements which put an end not only to the delays and disappointments that had so long trammelled the actions of the allies, but entirely altered the conditions of the campaign. The strength of the allies towards the end of May was approximately as follows:

French	**100,000**
English	**25,000**
Sardinians	**15,000**
Turks	**45,000**

May 18.—Accompanied Lord Raglan and La Marmora round the English trenches.

The first movement by Pélissier was a renewed attack on the Russian counter approaches in front of the French left, on the night of May 23; and as, owing to the desperate nature of the fighting, the object was not fully accomplished he refused an armistice to bury the dead, and followed it up the following evening with complete success, and his troops then entrenched themselves in the captured cemetery. I accompanied Lord Raglan and Omar Pasha on the second night to the French post of observation. The losses on both sides were very severe, being computed at 2,303 on the part of the French, and at 3,081 of the Russians.[1]

On May 25 General Canrobert was ordered to take up the line of the Chernaya, which he accomplished with ease and almost without loss. In this operation he was assisted by the Sardinians under La Marmora, who had arrived some days previously. I remember riding in the morning down to the Chernaya with Lord Raglan and his staff on the occasion. General Canrobert galloped up to meet him, in the highest spirits, and speaking in French said: 'My Lord, when I was a great man and Commander-in-Chief you used to come and visit me, and now when I am only commanding a division you again come to see me.' Lord Raglan, in reply, expressed his pleasure that Canrobert had gained so extended a position, and with such trifling loss. He afterwards joined General La Marmora, and made

[1] Kinglake, viii. 25.

a reconnoissance towards Baidar, being altogether ten hours in the saddle. This movement in advance was of the greatest benefit to the allies, who, instead of being cooped up in a corner, had now ample space in a fertile valley, with plenty of grass, fuel, and fresh water at their disposal.

On May 24 the expedition to Kertch re-embarked, and sailed the following day. It consisted of 7,000 French, 3,000 English, and 5,000 Turks, with 5 batteries of artillery, and was attended with complete success. Kertch and Yenikale were captured without loss, the Russians retreating, after destroying large depots of supplies, &c. A considerable number of guns were taken, the Sea of Azov was opened to our fleets, and the enemy's communications interrupted. Sir Edmund Lyons reported that in four days the squadron had destroyed 241 vessels employed in transporting provisions to the Crimea, besides four war steamers and six million rations of flour and corn.[1]

[1] Lord Raglan's despatch, June 2, 1855.

CHAPTER IX

CAPTURE OF THE MAMELON AND QUARRIES—INTERVIEW WITH GENERAL PÉLISSIER

The next combined action of the allied forces took place against the Mamelon, the *ouvrages blancs*, and the quarries in front of the Redan. As the capture of these important outworks involved not only a partial re-armament of the siege batteries and a renewal of their munitions, but also a careful consideration of engineer arrangements, some short delay necessarily followed before decisive action could be taken. Towards the end of May a meeting was arranged to take place at the French head quarters between the senior artillery and engineer officers of the two armies, with a view to discuss the various details. As General Dacres was temporarily absent, owing to illness, and had gone for a few days to Constantinople, Lord Raglan directed me to accompany General Harry Jones, the Commanding Engineer. The meeting took place in a hut, at 6 A.M. To my surprise General Pélissier came in and presided; and, instead of the conference being limited to officers of the special arms, the following were present: French Generals Martimprey, Niel, Bosquet, Trochu, Frossard, Beuret, and Thiry, and one or two more; General Jones and myself being the only English officers at the meeting. Major Claremont and Prince Polignac were also in the room, to act as interpreters if required.

General Pélissier, in opening the proceedings, said it was decided that in a few days the French were to attack the Mamelon and other adjacent positions, whilst the English would seize the quarries in front of the Redan; and he invited those present to offer any remarks on details. A plan of Sebastopol was lying on the table for reference. General Niel began the discussion, stating that on an important occasion like the present it was necessary to take a general survey of the allied position and of the trenches, and he would begin with the left attack. Pélissier stopped him at once, and declined to enter into any such general considerations, saying that all he wanted was assistance as to details. He then took a ruler, laid it across the left attack, and said: 'L'attaque gauche n'existe plus.' General Niel under these circumstances abstained from taking any further part in the discussion.

General Bosquet having made a few remarks as to the troops to be detailed for the assault of the Mamelon, in which the Zouaves were to occupy a conspicuous place, Pélissier objected to the arrangement, contending that the Zouaves were not the best troops—'Pourquoi toujours les Zouaves?' he added. He went on to say that these, however, were small questions of detail to be settled afterwards. He was evidently determined to assert his position as Commander-in-Chief, and told us that there were persons in France of the highest position (evidently alluding to the Emperor) who read history and studied campaigns, and then sent him out their ideas as to what should be done. He told us that he had written respectfully to the Minister for War that, so long as he commanded the French army in the field, he declined to carry out any plans except such as were arranged and concerted between Lord Raglan and himself. A few other officers offered some observations, and then Pélissier turned to General Harry Jones. Apparently he had some difficulty in pronouncing his name, and approximately addressed him as General Hairy-Joze.[1] The General—who, I found afterwards, was considerably ruffled by Pélissier's arbitrary language—speaking in somewhat moderate French, said that when the French were ready to take the Mamelon the British troops were prepared to storm and capture the quarries in front of the Redan, and then sat down. Pélissier at once expressed his

[1] Soon afterwards, when he was knighted, he called him 'Sairey-Joze'! (Sir Harry Jones).

pleasure at hearing the statement of General Hairy-Joze. The English, he added, were evidently waiting for their allies, and with that 'solidité' which so distinguished them would no doubt succeed in what they undertook. The day and hour of the attack were known only to Lord Raglan and himself, but they should not have long to wait. Pélissier ended by stating that the discussion had been very interesting (no one having practically spoken except himself), and then he wished us all good morning.

Lord Raglan was much interested and amused when he heard of the interview, saying that had he known General Pélissier would be present he would have gone himself to listen to his lecture. It was known at the time that considerable differences existed between Pélissier and Niel. Years afterwards, in Kinglake's 'History of the Crimea,'[1] he quotes extracts of letters written at this time by General Niel to the Emperor Napoleon, and which evidently refer to the conference I have just described. In one General Niel says: 'At a meeting which took place yesterday he, General Pélissier, ordered me to be silent with a harshness not to be characterised. . . . We were in the presence of English officers.' Again, he writes to the Minister for War: 'Knowing nothing of what is going on, I abstain from all reflections. I

[1] 'Extracts from French Official Documents,' Kinglake, viii. 82 and 83.

asked leave to offer some observations on the state of the siege, and was told that it was not the time. . . .'

It must be borne in mind that the active measures which had been carried out by the allied generals during the latter part of May were by no means approved of in Paris, so much so that on June 5 Napoleon telegraphed to Pélissier as follows:[1] 'Je vous donne l'ordre positif, de ne point vous acharner au siège, avant d'avoir investi la place.' General Pélissier, however, entirely ignoring the veto, simply replied that he was in perfect accord with Lord Raglan, and was making final dispositions for the assault of the white redoubts, the Mamelon, and the quarries; and adds, that he should commence on the 7th and push on with the utmost vigour. And so he did.

A few days later, in writing to Paris, he speaks of himself as being at the paralysing extremity of an electric wire.[2] Lord Panmure, the Minister for War, however, about this time informed Lord Raglan that the English and French Governments had arranged that no orders should be sent out as to operations, without mutual consent,[3] and it seems curious that so obvious and common-sense a plan had not been in force throughout.

On the afternoon of June 6 the third great bombardment of Sebastopol commenced. My brother,

[1] Kinglake, viii. 89-90. [2] *Ibid.* viii. 129. [3] *Ibid.* 286.

Captain Mortimer Adye, R.A., was in command of an advanced battery in the trenches, and, the weather being hot, was fighting his guns in his shirt sleeves, when a shell from the enemy burst in the battery, exploding some loose gunpowder which was lying there, and burned him and two sergeants seriously; in fact, nearly blew them away. His face, neck, and arms were scorched, blackened, and blistered, and his flannel shirt smouldering. Some infantry soldiers, seeing his condition, threw some water over him, and he was then conveyed to camp; but some weeks elapsed before he was able to resume his duties.

The fire of the allied batteries soon obtained a mastery, and the Mamelon especially was in ruins. Todleben, speaking of the bombardment, said that more terrific than all else was the fire of the English.[1] It was arranged that the assault of the Russian advanced works should take place shortly before sunset, and during the afternoon of the 7th the French columns, in the highest spirits, marched under cover and unobserved down the ravines in readiness. The signal was given about half-past six, and the French first attacked and occupied the *ouvrages blancs*, near the Careening Bay ravine, taking several hundred prisoners. They then assaulted the Mamelon, took it with great rapidity and comparative ease, and hoisted their flag on the work; but, led away by success, they

[1] Kinglake, viii. 94.

impetuously, and contrary to the intention, followed the enemy even up to the glacis of the Malakoff. The Russians, however, came out in great force, and not only drove back the French columns, but followed them into the Mamelon and recaptured it, the French retreating down the slopes in disorder and with great loss. It was a critical moment, but Pélissier was equal to the occasion. Having large reserves in the adjoining ravine, he at once sent them forward and for a second time occupied the great outwork; and, darkness coming on, its entrenchments were turned during the night and the position firmly held. At the same time, whilst these serious battles were taking place, the English troops, consisting of part of the Light and Second Divisions, stormed the quarries in front of the Redan in the most brilliant manner; and although they were furiously attacked several times during the night by sorties from the Russian adjacent works, and suffered great loss, they resisted all efforts to dislodge them, and the next morning found them firmly established in comparatively close proximity to the Redan.

The great energy and activity of the allies during the fortnight since Pélissier had been in command of the French army and in full accord with Lord Raglan had thus been attended with important results, not only on the Chernaya and at Kertch, but also in depriving the enemy of the outworks in front of the city which they had established during the previous winter. Within a day or two of the successful actions of June 7, another meeting took place of the senior artillery and engineer officers of the two armies, at which I was present with General Dacres. The subject considered had reference to the arrangements in the trenches necessary for the further prosecution of the siege. Opinions rather differed, some considering that in view of the recent success, and its moral effect on the Russians, a general assault should speedily follow. Colonel Frossard, a distinguished engineer of the French army, however, urged that as we were still at a distance of some hundred yards from the Malakoff and Redan we should continue to advance cautiously by means of sap and trench as heretofore. He pointed out that an assault from our present position would involve the carrying of scaling ladders and woolbags to fill the ditches, for a considerable distance in the open under heavy fire, and that under all the circumstances we might be liable to defeat in assaulting prematurely. General Dacres entirely concurred in the views of Colonel Frossard, and the event proved that their misgivings were justified.

Some days passed away, during which time the batteries in the trenches were augmented and again prepared for a fresh effort, and it was finally decided that a general assault should be made on the Malakoff and Redan on June 18, to be preceded by a vigorous bombardment at daylight for two or three hours, so as to smash and silence the enemy's batteries and open a road for the attacking columns. It is important, however, to bear in mind that General Pélissier declined to make a simultaneous movement against the Bastion du Mât. A heavy fire was opened at daylight on June 17 from the English and French trenches, and continued throughout the day. In the evening Lord Raglan sent for me, and directed orders to be issued at once to all the batteries, that the renewed bombardment at daylight the next morning was not to be carried out. I ventured to remark that every preparation had been made, and that it would not only be a great disappointment to the navy and artillery, but it seemed to me that a concentrated fire for two or three hours on the points to be assaulted would produce a great effect. Lord Raglan replied that he entirely agreed with me, but, he added, it was useless to argue the question, as he had just received a message from General Pélissier altering previous arrangements, and saying that the French columns would attack at daylight.[1] The necessary orders were, of course, given.

[1] See Lord Raglan's despatch, June 19, 1855. Also Kinglake, viii. 310.

CHAPTER X

BATTLE OF JUNE 18 AND DEATH OF LORD RAGLAN

The night of the 17th was passed in concentrating the allied forces destined for the great assault. Lord Raglan and his staff arrived in the English trenches shortly before daylight. Two important circumstances occurred at the very outset, both of bad omen for the allies. One, that the Russians by some means had become aware of, and were consequently prepared for, the attack; the other, that one of the French generals, under a mistaken idea that the signal had been given, led his troops to the assault prematurely, and before all was ready. It was, in fact, still dark, when the ground in front of the Malakoff became suddenly the scene of a terrific conflict, of which for some time it was not possible to form a judgment, or to forecast the result.

As the day dawned it soon became apparent that the French were in difficulties, and were not within the Malakoff. Lord Raglan had always reserved to himself freedom of action as to the proper moment for ordering the advance of the

English. As he wrote to Lord Panmure afterwards, he felt that there ought to be some hope of the French success before committing his troops.[1] However, when he observed the serious condition of affairs, and that his allies were in dire conflict and suffering great losses, but were still persisting in their attack on the dominating position of the Malakoff, he felt that it was impossible for the English troops to remain inactive, and therefore gave the requisite signal. Our troops, composed of parts of the Light, Second and Fourth Divisions, accompanied by a storming party of seamen carrying scaling ladders and of gunners with means for spiking guns, jumped from their cover and made straight for the Redan; but the whole ground was torn and swept with grape and musketry from the enemy's works, both in front and on the flanks, and our men, gallantly as they were led and bravely as they advanced, were quite unable to enter the work. Lord Raglan, when the advance commenced, desired his staff to sit down in the trench; but he and General Jones, R.E., stood up together, anxiously watching the event. In the midst of the carnage, General Jones was struck on the forehead with a glancing grape-shot, and for a moment as he fell back it was feared the wound was mortal. He was

[1] See Lord Raglan's despatch, June 19, 1855. Also Kinglake, viii. 161.

taken away for medical aid, but in a minute or two suddenly returned with the blood streaming down his face, being anxious to speak to the Commander-in-Chief on some point which he deemed important; and it was with difficulty that he could be induced to have his wound attended to. It was about this time that Captain William Peel, R.N., who had led the seamen with the scaling ladders, passed us on his return, wounded, together with a great many other officers and men. The battle continued for some time, but at length ended in the failure of the allies at every point, and Lord Raglan then directed the batteries to re-open fire, in order to cover the retreat and to hold in check the Russian forces.

Soon after the termination of the various attacks, General Hugh Rose,[1] the British Commissioner at French head quarters, came to Lord Raglan with a message from General Pélissier, to ascertain his views on the situation. Lord Raglan said that in his opinion Pélissier had made two great mistakes—one, in attacking prematurely before a bombardment, and the other that he had not simultaneously assaulted the Bastion du Mât. 'However,' he added, 'I will go myself and see him,' and he then left the trenches with General Harry Jones, who in the meantime had returned, having tied a handkerchief over his forehead, making light of his wound. The

[1] Afterwards Field Marshal Lord Strathnairn.

losses during the day were serious. Of the English—General Sir John Campbell was killed, with many other officers of rank, and our total casualties were 1,443. The French suffered far more, their losses amounting to no less than 3,500. In fact, during the month that General Pélissier had been in command of the French army it is estimated that their casualties in killed, wounded, and missing amounted to upwards of 12,000 officers and men.

The failure of the great assault on Sebastopol on June 18 was undoubtedly the severest blow which the allies had received since their landing in the Crimea; and indeed it became difficult to forecast the future, as the activity, courage, and great resources of the Russians in men and material apparently rendered the capture of the city a somewhat remote and uncertain speculation. The British army were, however, destined in a few days to suffer another great misfortune, by the death of their beloved Commander-in-Chief on June 28. There is no doubt that the failure of the attack on Sebastopol, and the great losses on that eventful morning, had a serious effect upon Lord Raglan, following, as they did, on the accumulated anxieties of the previous months; so that his strong constitution at length gave way. Within a few hours of his death he happened to send for me on some matter of business, and then complained of illness and of great thirst; but he made light of it, and I had no idea that his condition was serious, or that it was destined to be my last interview with one with whom I had been so closely associated.

It will be well to consider briefly some of the great events which had occurred during the period of his command, as illustrative of his conduct and character during the campaign. In the first place, it must always be remembered that we entered into a war against a great Power after a peace in Europe of nearly forty years, when we had with difficulty collected about 30,000 men for the purpose; and when even these were inadequately provided with commissariat and transport, and there were no reserves existent to replace casualties as they arose. Again, the order to proceed to the Crimea came from home, without any specific knowledge of the resources and preparations of the Russians; it was given at a late season, and when the troops were physically weak; and as the Government did not anticipate a winter campaign, no provision had been made to meet it. In view of these circumstances Marshal Saint-Arnaud, as I have shown, hesitated at the last moment. It is true that he was then very ill—in fact, a dying man—but this must have added greatly to Lord Raglan's responsibilities at a critical time.

When the siege of Sebastopol commenced, the

failure of the first bombardment was due in a measure to the weakness of the French siege train, and to the the unfortunate explosion of some of their magazines. In the three great battles of Alma, Balaclava, and Inkerman, the English lost about 5,000 men, and as the winter came on, and found the allies with open trenches, it was evident not only that great sickness and suffering must ensue, but that our numbers and means were quite inadequate. In short, the English and French Governments entered into the war apparently under the impression that with a force of 60,000 men they could crush an empire, and that Sebastopol would fall by a *coup-de-main*. As regards the events which followed, I have quoted official documents which prove that General Canrobert, brave and good soldier as he was, still allowed himself to be constantly controlled and over-influenced by secret orders from Paris, which practically set at naught the plans of the allied generals and at last brought matters to a dead lock; and it is important to bear in mind also that, steadfast as Lord Raglan was in his opinions, yet so loyal was he to his colleague, and so magnanimous, that no word in his public despatches gave a hint of the enormous difficulties caused by the circumstance I have described. He submitted to great personal injustice, rather than say or do anything to weaken the *entente cordiale* between the two Powers, or to attach blame to others.

Again, when the allies landed in the Crimea their numbers were approximately equal, but, as the English had no reserves to replenish their rapidly diminishing ranks, the equality soon disappeared, and early in 1855 the French forces were at least three times greater than ours; and this disparity, whilst it gave increased authority to their views, must have tended to complicate Lord Raglan's position in council.

There is another point to be noticed—namely, that all the commanders of the allied armies and fleets, French, Sardinian, and Turkish, entertained the highest opinion of the ability, high courage, and character of Lord Raglan. I had good means of knowing, and believe there was no difference of opinion on the subject. General Canrobert always expressed these views, and indeed was anxious that Lord Raglan should be appointed to command all the allied forces. Pélissier, from the day he assumed command of the French army, was in complete accord with him, and so stated over and over again. Lord Lyons, I remember well, after the war told me that it was the proudest boast of his life that he should have been closely associated with Lord Raglan, during all the exceptional difficulties and dangers of his position.

I have recapitulated these points because they were by no means known to the people of England at the time; in fact, it was not until years afterwards, on the fall of the Empire, and by the publication of the French despatches, that many of the circumstances were brought to light. Finally, Lord Raglan, during all these months of incessant and harassing anxiety, had to bear a trial even greater than those I have attempted to describe. The English Press at home, and their correspondents in the Crimea, day after day continued to criticise his conduct, and to misrepresent his character in violent and unmeasured terms; describing him as indifferent, incompetent, and unfit for command; and attributing to his supposed incapacity and want of foresight the sufferings of the troops and the delays of the campaign, whilst during the whole time the facts were all the other way. Having been closely associated with Lord Raglan, and knowing a good deal of the circumstances, I feel it a matter of common justice to defend the memory of a great and distinguished man, the close of whose life was embittered by the feeling that the Government at home would not defend him, and that the people, grossly misled as they were, had withdrawn from him their confidence. One day, not long before his death, in conversation with him I expressed a hope that he would soon return to England, and have the opportunity of defending himself against the unjust attacks of which he was the object, when he replied—

smiling, perhaps, rather bitterly—'Return home? I shall never return home. Why, I should be stoned to death before I could get to Stanhope Street.'

But there is a still more important aspect of the case than the personal one. It is a great injury to the public service that a Commander-in-Chief in the field, surrounded, as he must be, by constant difficulties and anxieties, should be thus misjudged by violent and erroneous statements, and be attacked behind his back at a time when from absence, want of leisure, and from the nature of his position he is unable to reply. I must add that in almost every campaign in which I have borne a part, the same tendency to hasty criticism has been more or less observable, and always at moments when the people at home, being naturally anxious, are all the more susceptible and easily misled.

The death of Lord Raglan tended, no doubt, to diminish the influence of England in the councils of the war at a critical period of the campaign, and the *entente cordiale* between the generals of the allied armies which his influence and high character had done so much to maintain, gradually weakened. It was in every sense a calamity. The appointment, however, of General Simpson as his successor at all events prevented any divergence of opinion as regarded the immediate operations against Sebastopol. General Pélissier and himself were in entire accord that the Malakoff was the dominant feature of the situation; and although other parts of the enceinte, such as the Great and Little Redans and the Bastion du Mât, could not be left out of account, still in the final assault the attacks on these points would not necessarily lead to the fall of the place, and would, therefore, be subsidiary diversions, as it were, to the capture of the central position. In one of his first despatches General Simpson said that 'we were repairing and improving our works, to be in readiness to co-operate with the French, when their approaches towards the Malakoff shall be completed.' The opinion given at the beginning of the siege by Sir John Burgoyne, that 'the great tower was the key of the whole position,' had at length become the axiom of all.[1]

[1] General Pélissier, in his despatch of September 11 on the fall of Sebastopol, specially says that the Malakoff was the key of the defences, and that the other attacks were subordinate.

CHAPTER XI.

BATTLE OF CHERNAYA AND THE FALL OF SEBASTOPOL.

DURING the month of July and the early part of August the allies were occupied in pushing on their trenches, in obtaining fresh armaments and munitions, and adding to their batteries. About this time I was present at several interesting councils connected with these preparations, and partly with the consideration of suggestions from home. In my journal is a record as follows:—

First Conference, August 3, 1855. Present: Generals Pélissier, Simpson, Niel, Thiry, Barnard, Airey, Sir H. Jones;[1] Colonels Dupuis, Steele, and Adye. Subject: 'Whether, in case the town should not fall before the winter, it may not be necessary to raise the siege?' General Pélissier refused to entertain the idea, and the meeting broke up unsatisfactorily. The conference took place at the English head quarters, and during the discussion one of the French generals having made some remarks as to the great losses daily in the trenches, General

[1] General Dacres was at Constantinople sick.

Pélissier turned to him and said, 'Did you ever hear of a war without losses? We are not here to make war *à la* Monsieur Cobden!' After the meeting, in passing through General Simpson's room, Pélissier took up a book, and asked me what was the inscription on its cover. It was a Bible, and I told him the words were 'Society for the Promotion of Christian Knowledge.' He laughed, and said it was a good society, but whether he was a subscriber I do not know.

Second Conference, August 5. Present: Artillery and engineer officers of both armies only. Subject considered: 'A telegraphic despatch from England, Can the town be destroyed? Can it be taken? What will you do next?'

Answer: No amount of fire, both vertical and horizontal, would destroy the town—that is to say, the forts, docks, basins, and all that give importance to Sebastopol.

Answer to second question: This question is one for the Commanders-in-Chief to decide. The meeting stated the general condition of the trenches for their information. The third question was also for the Generals-in-Chief.

Third Conference, August 7. 'Two hundred mortars being expected from France and England, can the town be destroyed by this means and an assault obviated?'

Answer: No.

Fourth Conference, August 14. The French state that their batteries on the Mamelon and Careening Bay are ready to open. Proposed, therefore, that we open on the 17th all round, and then push forward our approaches.

In the meantime, and before the final preparations for the assault of Sebastopol were quite complete, the Russians determined to make one more effort to raise the siege by an attack on the position of the allies on the Chernaya. It was a desperate movement on their part. In the first place, the Fedhukine heights were held by 18,000 French troops with 48 guns, and the Sardinians on the hills to their right near Tchergoum were 9,000 strong with 36 guns, and in rear were 10,000 Turks in reserve. The heights themselves, which were well adapted for defence, had been strengthened by entrenchments, and the river Chernaya, as well as a narrow canal, acted as wet ditches along the front, and rendered an assault very difficult. It so happened also that a few days before the battle the allied generals had received information through spies of the intentions of the enemy, and were therefore fully prepared.

On August 12 I was sent to Balaclava to call upon General La Marmora, who wished that some English guns should be placed at his disposal, and by his invitation rode with him to the heights occupied by the Sardinian army, and received his directions as to the position to be taken up by the battery in the event of an assault. At daylight on August 16 the Russians advanced with great courage to the attack. General Pélissier, in his General Order to the French army on the following day, estimated the forces of the Russians as being 60,000 strong, with a numerous artillery and considerable masses of cavalry. Notwithstanding all the obstacles, the enemy succeeded in temporarily capturing the *tête-du-pont*, and in advancing for a considerable distance up the heights; but, after five hours' fighting, were ultimately driven back and defeated all along the line, losing more than 6,000 men, some of whom were drowned, and leaving 2,200 wounded and prisoners behind. General Pélissier specially alluded to the good service rendered by the English heavy battery, which took part in the action in co-operation with the Sardinians. C troop Horse Artillery was also present towards the close of the battle.

On the following day the allies commenced another bombardment, and in three days alone threw 10,000 shells from mortars into the doomed city, independently of the fire from the heavy guns. The batteries of the Malakoff and Redan were reduced to ruins and were almost silent. The end was approaching. The English artillery at this time, having been largely re-inforced, were about 7,000 strong, and, in addition to 200 pieces of ordnance in the trenches, they had 92 guns horsed and ready for the field. Under cover of this great bombardment, work in the trenches was actively carried on, and the French approached close to the counter scarps of the Malakoff. Their losses, however, were reckoned at 100 daily. In view of the crisis which was at hand, the Russians, towards the end of August, constructed a bridge of rafts across the harbour; an evident symptom of a possible withdrawal of the garrison and surrender of the city.

At the beginning of September a final meeting of the French and English officers of artillery and engineers took place, and a careful memorandum was then drawn up for the consideration of the Commanders-in-Chief. After recapitulating the general condition of the trenches, and pointing out that the French were within twenty-five yards of the place, they recommended that the whole of the batteries should re-open at once and maintain a vigorous fire for three days, and that the assault should then be given without delay; the Malakoff to be first attacked and captured, and then the Great and Little Redans, and the works near the Bastion du Mât, so as to divide the Russian forces as much as possible.[1]

[1] General Simpson's despatch of September 9, 1855, specially alludes to this report, which, he says, was agreed to and acted on.

The end had come at last. On September 5 the bombardment re-commenced, and the Russians were speedily driven to seek refuge in their numerous underground shelters, in the midst of crumbling ruins and dismantled batteries. On the morning of the 8th the troops of the allies marched quietly down to their allotted positions; and at noon, all being ready, General Mac Mahon led his division straight to the Malakoff, and in a few minutes entered it and hoisted the tricolor. This was the preconcerted signal, and then the other columns also rushed to the assault. On the extreme right, the French in great force attacked the Little Redan and works near the harbour, but, after a prolonged struggle and heavy losses, failed to maintain their ground. The English troops, composed of parts of the Light and Second Divisions and accompanied by a ladder and spiking party, advanced on the salient of the Great Redan, entered the work, and held it for some time. The interior of the work, however, was swept by the fire of artillery and infantry in rear, and they were ultimately forced back with great loss. At the same time, far away on the left, the Bastions Centrale and Du Mât were stormed by French columns, but also without success—in fact, the three subordinate assaults on the city all failed.

Mac Mahon, however, having once gained possession of the redoubt surrounding the old Malakoff tower, held it in spite of the furious efforts of the Russians for hours to drive him out. As one cause of the failure of the subsidiary attacks, it is as well to point out that they were all open works, swept by batteries and interior entrenchments; whilst, on the other hand, the ground round the Malakoff had been converted by the Russians into a closed redoubt which, whilst it may, at the outset, have added to the difficulties of its capture, still, when once taken, gave the French under Mac Mahon the advantage of comparative shelter.

The losses on all sides were very severe, and were as follows:

French	7,567
English	2,271
Russians	12,913
	22,751

Thus ended, after a siege of eleven months, the series of battles in front of Sebastopol. The Russians, aware that their position on the south side was no longer tenable, during the night set fire to the city, exploded their magazines, sunk their fleet, and, having withdrawn the garrison by means of the floating bridge across the harbour, then destroyed it, leaving their arsenal, docks, and large remaining supplies of guns and stores in the hands of the allies. As Pélissier said in his order of the day, 'Le boulevard de la Puissance Russe dans la Mer Noir n'existe plus.'

In the afternoon of the 9th Fort Paul blew up with a great explosion, and then all was still. What a comfort it was, after months of incessant anxiety, that the uproar had for a time ceased, and that there was nothing to do!

During the next few days we buried the dead, wandered about the desolate city, took stock of the armaments and reserves, and were occasionally shelled by the enemy at long range from the north side of the harbour. One large hospital which I visited presented a dreadful spectacle. There were hundreds of dead bodies of Russians lying in the beds; of men who had been wounded before the retreat, and then left at the last to die unheeded and alone. In a few of the beds were found wounded men still living!

With the fall of Sebastopol the Crimean war had virtually reached its termination, although several months elapsed before this was recognised. The Emperor of the French still hankered after a campaign in the interior; but the season was late, and the corner occupied by the allied armies formed a bad base for operations in the field. Marshal Pélissier, obstinate and determined as ever, would have none of it, and wrote to Paris: 'Thank God! it is not difficulties which frighten me. . . . But here the situation is not the same. I see the obstacles, but I do not perceive the success, nor even the hope of it.

I should be perplexed to form a plan of campaign, still more to carry it out.' In short, the fall of Sebastopol had destroyed the power of Russia in the Black Sea; and therefore the occupation of the Crimea, whilst it would entail great losses and considerable risk, would be of no special value.

The two allied Commanders-in-Chief, Simpson and Pélissier, were men of very different character and also of general appearance. The one was a tall, thin Scotchman; the other a short, stout, thick-set Norman. The first time they met after the capture of the city, Pélissier rushed up to the English general and embraced him with great fervour, having almost to climb up to reach his cheek. The English staff were amused at this demonstration, and said to Simpson, 'Why General, Pélissier kissed you!' And his reply, with a strong national dialect, was: 'Well, it was a great occasion, and I could na' resist him.'

As there was nothing specially to be done—at all events, until the English and French Governments had made up what they were pleased to call their minds as to future operations—I was fortunate enough in November to obtain a few weeks' leave, and went off to Malta for a holiday. On arriving at Constantinople I embarked in a small store steamer, in which there was only one passenger besides myself—a private soldier on his way to England. So, we talked of the war, and on my asking who had ordered him home, he replied: 'The Minister for War, sir.' On my asking why, he said, 'I'm in charge of his brother, sir.' This seemed rather incomprehensible, so I added, 'Where is his brother?' 'Sure, he's in the hold, sir.' This bewildered me still more; but it appeared that the soldier had been present at the funeral of Colonel the Honourable Lauderdale Maule, who died of cholera at Varna just before we left in the autumn of 1854, and had been sent to exhume the body and bring it to England at the request of his brother, Lord Panmure.

When I returned to the Crimea at the end of the year, although active operations were necessarily suspended for the winter, we were busily occupied in blowing up the docks, forts, and barracks, and in carrying off the Russian guns out of the arsenal (about 2,000 in number) and thus completing the destruction of Sebastopol. Preparations were also being made for a renewal of hostilities in the spring in some other part of the Russian Empire. But in reality a change was coming over the scene, and, instead of action, reaction had set in. In the first place, France was tired of the war. Her finances were exhausted and her troops anxious to return home. On the other hand, Russia also was crippled, both as to men and means. England, so tardy at the outset and so unprepared, was indeed the only Power which apparently had the will or vigour left to continue the contest. Our troops during the second winter were well clothed, housed, and fed, and as healthy as at home; and their numbers were daily increasing. At the beginning of 1856 we had upwards of 50,000 men and 96 field guns in the Crimea, with considerable reserves both at Malta and in England. The administrative departments, also, were becoming models of efficiency; and the transport branch, which hardly existed at the outset, had no less than 28,000 animals collected and ready for the field.

In the meantime the Turkish contingent had occupied Kertch and Enikale, at the entrance to the Sea of Azov; and in January 1856 I was sent by Sir William Codrington (who had succeeded Sir James Simpson as Commander-in-Chief) on a mission to General Vivian in command of the troops there. A French officer accompanied me, and we were conveyed in H.M.S. 'Stromboli,' our instructions being, in the first place, to make a rapid survey along the coast of the Crimea in order to ascertain if the Bay of Kaffa, or its neighbourhood, were fortified and held in strength by the Russians; and, if not, whether it offered facilities for landing. On arrival at Kertch, we were directed to confer with General Vivian as to the defences and to inquire whether he desired reinforcements or assistance of any kind, naval or military, and then to return forthwith to Sebastopol.

The fact was, that information had been received that Kertch was shortly to be attacked by the Russians in force, and the Commander-in-Chief was desirous of ascertaining General Vivian's views on the position. I remember when handing him the letter from Sir William Codrington, he confirmed the rumour of the expected attack, and as to holding out said, 'I can tell you at once; I shall be able to hold out for about five-and-twenty minutes.' He did not, of course, intend his words to be taken literally, but explained that in his opinion the place was not tenable against a powerful assault. Extensive earthworks had been constructed and armed on some of the heights; but they were commanded by others, and there was an entire deficiency of water in the outlying forts. However, after remaining a few days at Kertch, information was received of the probabilities of peace, and in February the representatives of the allied powers having met at Paris, towards the end of March an armistice was proclaimed, and the war came to an end.

So ended the great Crimea campaign, of which my narrative necessarily gives but a short and imperfect sketch. To the present generation it is now a mere matter of history, and few remain of all those who took part in a contest which, at the time, so deeply affected the people of this country, and, indeed, of the whole of Europe. The long siege, with its battles, vicissitudes, and sufferings, forms, however, a remarkable page in the annals of war. Of my own corps, 13 officers were killed[1] and 29 wounded. Altogether, no less than 10,508 officers and men of the Royal Artillery served during the campaign, of whom 1,520 died, either killed in action or from wounds and sickness.

Many weeks elapsed before the allied armies had altogether quitted the Crimea; and in the meantime we wandered about and formed acquaintances with the Russians, who were always civil and good-natured. At the end of the harbour of Sebastopol were extensive marshes, filled with frogs, which kept up an incessant croaking. The French soldiers were in the habit of catching and eating them in large quantities, but the English despised such food. It was said that the frogs, after a time, learnt to distinguish between the two nations, and that when our men appeared in their *red* coats the frogs chirped away merrily, but when they saw soldiers in *red* trousers approaching, down they went, and remained perfectly mute till the danger had passed away. *Se non è vero, è ben trovato.*

I did not leave the Crimea until June, and then embarked with a battery of Horse Artillery for

[1] Names of artillery officers killed: Brig.-General Strangways, Major Townsend; Captains Oldfield, Fitzroy, Childers, Dew, A. Gordon, and Snow; Lieutenants Cockerell, Walsham, Luce, Mitchell, and Asst.-Commissary Hayter.

home. The weather was beautiful, and, after passing through the Bosphorus and Dardanelles, we were steaming along past the Greek Islands when my servant one morning came into the cabin and said I had better get up. As it was only just daylight I did not take the hint. Presently, however, he looked in again, repeating his suggestion. On my asking why he disturbed me at such an early hour, he replied: 'I beg your pardon, sir, but the ship is on fire!' This altered the situation; I lost no time in jumping into my clothes, went on deck, where I perceived smoke coming up through the hatchways. Going on to the bridge I inquired of the captain, who informed me that the fire was in the powder magazine! It seems that having all the ammunition boxes and stores of a battery of Horse Artillery on board, the ordinary magazine was insufficient, and a temporary arrangement had been made on the lower deck. It is supposed that by some accident a box of lucifer matches had ignited, and set fire to the whole concern. Captain Dyneley, R.H.A., with a few men at once went below, and passing down buckets of water the fire was gradually extinguished, the boxes hauled up and laid on deck, several of them considerably burnt. It was a critical half-hour, but nothing could be more quiet and steady than the conduct of all on board. In the midst of our trouble the 'Charlemagne,' a French line-of-battle ship, came up close to us, crammed with troops, and offered help. We, however, explained that we had plenty of men on board, and in a short time we were able to say that all danger was at an end, and separated with three cheers from both vessels. That was my last adventure connected with the Crimean war.

CHAPTER XII

THE INDIAN MUTINY

In the early part of 1857 I was stationed at Cork Harbour in command of a few men on Spike Island, a period of tranquillity after all the anxieties of the great Crimean war. The tranquillity, however, was not destined to last very long. One day towards the end of May I crossed the harbour to call on a gentleman in the neighbourhood who had just returned from Cork, and on my asking if there was any news, he said that a remarkable telegram had been received from India that a native regiment at Meerut had killed its English officers and was marching on Delhi. That was the first news of the great Mutiny. It also stated that the natives in parts of India were passing chew-patties from village to village. What was a chew-patty? Nobody could tell us. It turned out to be a sort of pancake; but why the natives should specially pass round pancakes, and presumably eat them, as a signal of rebellion no one could explain. Week after week the news became more serious, and troops of all arms were sent off in large numbers round the Cape. Towards the end of July, being in London, I received information that the Duke of Cambridge had appointed me Assistant Adjutant-General of the batteries of Royal Artillery, then on their voyage; and about the middle of August I left *viâ* Egypt. There was, of course, no Suez canal in those days, and the railway from Alexandria only went as far as Cairo.

Generals Dupuis and Windham, and many other officers, were of the party; and from Cairo we had to cross the desert (about ninety miles) in uncomfortable carriages like bathing machines. There was no steamer at Suez, and we were detained a week at that dismal village of the desert, receiving occasional news that matters were becoming worse and worse in India. The only hotel was crowded with English officers, with little to eat and not a drop of water except what was brought in skins on camels from the Nile, nearly 100 miles away. At last, however, the 'Bentinck' arrived, carried us slowly down the Red Sea, with the thermometer at 96 degrees; in a week we were at Aden, thermometer still rising, and ten days afterwards at Galle. At Madras we heard of the fall of Delhi, and on October 5 our long voyage in the 'Bentinck' came to an end, and we steamed up the Hoogly to Calcutta. Several years afterwards, when inspecting the defences of the river with Sir William Mansfield, the Commander-in-Chief, we came across the wreck of the 'Bentinck' lying in a field at some distance from shore, and found that a short time previously she had been caught by a tidal wave called 'a great bore,' and was thrown up high and dry in the field. In the course of my career I have occasionally met a great bore, but never to be so completely stranded as was the case with the old steamer.

Matters were in a somewhat critical condition on our arrival at Calcutta, for although the fall of Delhi had given a severe blow to the mutineers, still we had no force of much strength to take the field; and the garrison of Lucknow under Outram and Havelock, with many women and children, were entirely surrounded, mere scraps of intelligence only arriving from them occasionally. I had several interviews with Sir Colin Campbell, who was very anxious to collect a sufficient force for the relief of Lucknow. During October troops of all arms arrived in quick succession after a three months' voyage round the Cape, but the great difficulty was transport. The railway extended to Raneegunge, 120 miles up country, but beyond that point our means only enabled us to push forward about 100 men a day, either in bullock carts or by march. Another difficulty was the provision of horses for the artillery. In fact, the whole of Central India from Delhi to Lucknow was practically in the possession of the mutineers, who fortunately had no generals to lead them, and were content for the most part to hover about and pillage as they could. Slowly, however, as our forces in a long thin line marched upwards towards Allahabad and Cawnpore, the tide began to turn, and on October 27 the Commander-in-Chief left Calcutta for the North.

The general conditions of the Mutiny campaign formed, indeed, a striking contrast to those of the Crimean war. In the latter case, the allied armies—English, French, Sardinian, and Turkish—amounting to nearly 200,000 men, had been virtually shut up in a corner, and compelled to fight a series of battles on the same ground, in order to gain possession of the Russian stronghold. In the present instance the circumstances were all the other way. A vast continent was in a great measure over-run, and its munitions and military stores were temporarily in the hands of a great mutinous army, more or less in sympathy with the inhabitants; whilst the English troops in small scattered detachments, often hundreds of miles apart, were fighting a succession of battles, with their communications precarious, and for the moment without the power of concentration.

To a stranger landing in India for the first time, knowing nothing of the language or the customs of the people, more especially in the middle of a revolution, there were many minor personal perplexities, especially about servants. Their very titles were embarrassing. Bearers, kitmagars, dhobies, durzees, bheesties, chuprassies, punkah-wallahs, hookahbadars, syces, and others. What were their duties? That was the point. Because in India, as we soon found, one man will only do his own mite of work, and scorns the idea of making himself generally useful. Any attempt to enlarge the sphere of their duties would lead, so we were told, to loss of caste. There were, of course, exceptional cases, such as that of the native servant who, on being asked by a new-comer as to his caste, replied, 'Same caste as master, drink brandy sahib.' Owing to the great influx of officers from home, all in a hurry to be off, servants were especially difficult to find. I was fortunate enough to get an old fellow whose name was Buktum Hassan to take care of me. He could not speak a word of English, and slept away his time on a mat outside my door. I believe he was a bearer, and a Hindoo, but he would not come near me at dinner time. Subsequently I procured another servant, who condescended to wait on me at dinner, but I was cautioned not on any account to eat ham in his presence. Curry and rice he did not object to. Two Sepoys, also, were appropriated for my service as orderlies. They were tall, dark, spare men, and all day waited patiently in the corridor in uniform, strictly buttoned up, with belts and boots. The first evening they said something, which being interpreted was that they wished to go home: they then proceeded to take off all their clothes, except a loin cloth, made them up into a bundle, and leaving them in a corner of my room, marched happily away.

The greater portion of the batteries from England having arrived, General Dupuis and his staff followed the Commander-in-Chief up country on November 12. The journey to Benares occupied five days, and from Raneegunge we were conveyed in dawk gharries about eighty miles a day, passing on the road every few hours detachments of troops of all arms, hurrying forward, some in bullock carts, some on the march. Portions of the road, especially near the river Soane, were unsafe from the vicinity of straggling parties of mutineers, and we had to be protected occasionally by an escort.

Remaining a few hours in a bungalow outside Benares, we found time to pay a hurried visit to this celebrated city. As an instance of the precarious nature of our long line of communications, it may be mentioned that although its inhabitants were in a restless, disaffected condition, the garrison only consisted of a weak company of infantry and two field guns. On the morning after our arrival I was informed that 'the elephant was at the door,' in readiness to take us into the city. It had no howdah, so we climbed up and sat on a large stuffed mattress. The environs consisted of tombs, temples, ruins, mosques, and gardens. The streets were crammed with people, and with little Brahminy bulls wandering about; in some parts the elephant was too wide for the narrow, tortuous passages, so that we had to dismount and walk. In one Hindoo temple which we visited, a fanatic, or possibly a lunatic, was seated in a niche. He was quite naked and covered with dust, but, oddly enough, had a fuschia flower lying on the top of his shaven head. He sat perfectly mute and still, and took no apparent notice of anybody, so that it was impossible to ascertain what object he expected to accomplish by so sedentary and monotonous an existence.

We were rather a large party at the hotel bungalow, some being officers newly arrived and others who had served for years in the country, and who were very good natured in giving us information. Colonel David Wood, of the Horse Artillery, was one of the new-comers, and had a habit occasionally of assuming ignorance on minor points which perhaps was not always genuine. During dinner he turned gravely to one of the old Indian officers and said, 'Can you tell me, what is a dhobie?' They all laughed, and it was explained that a dhobie was a man who washed your clothes. Wood, still quite grave, said: "Oh, that accounts for the difficulty. I told mine to clean my horse, and he refused. I will discharge him to-morrow.' The old Indian officer, however, assured him that a dhobie was absolutely necessary. Wood replied that he never required washing on active service. 'You must surely have your shirts washed,' was the rejoinder. 'Not at all,' said Wood. 'I always wear a flannel shirt in the field, and as soon as it gets dirty or worn out I throw it away and put on another.'

CHAPTER XIII

THE BATTLES AT CAWNPORE.

On November 19 we reached Allahabad, an interesting old fortress at the junction of the Ganges and Jumna; but important events were taking place, and we hurried on and reached Cawnpore on the 21st. On our arrival we found that Sir Colin Campbell, with nearly all the troops available, had left a few days previously for Lucknow, and that serious fighting had taken place there on the 16th and 17th; but the communications were subsequently interrupted by the mutineers in Oude, and for some days no further information could be obtained as to the progress of affairs. It was a critical period of the campaign. As already explained, the garrison of Lucknow, with many women and children, fifty miles distant, had been entirely shut up and surrounded by multitudes of mutineers for weeks past, and was running short of provisions, so that its relief had become a very urgent necessity. On the other hand, the great bulk of our troops, anxious as they were to reach the scene, owing to want of means of rapid conveyance, were still moving up in driblets along the 600 miles of road from Calcutta to Cawnpore. So that when the Commander-in-Chief had crossed the Ganges on his adventurous march to Lucknow, he was only able to take with him about 6,000 infantry and a moderate force of cavalry and artillery.

But that was not all. Cawnpore, his only base, was in a precarious, defenceless condition, and when Sir Colin had left and placed Windham in command of it, there were only 450 infantry remaining for its protection. The defences of Cawnpore were insignificant. A small incomplete earthwork had been made on the bank of the river with a view to protect the bridge of boats, and lying all round it were the ruins of burnt bungalows and a general scene of confusion and desolation; and beyond again, at a few hundred yards, stood the large city, composed, as usual, of a wilderness of narrow tortuous streets, and devoid of any external defences. So that it was not a favourable position to hold, even had a considerable force been available. The difficulties and dangers of the situation were indeed obvious. No sooner had the Commander-in-Chief crossed the Ganges and marched in one direction, than the Gwalior contingent—a well trained force which, joined by other mutineers, amounted to about 25,000 men—with a powerful artillery of 40 guns, field and heavy, was reported as advancing in several columns from Calpee forty-six miles distant on the other side.

The instructions given to General Windham were as follows. The force at his command for the time was estimated at about 500 men; and the detachments of troops as they arrived up country were to be sent on to Sir Colin Campbell at Lucknow. Windham was directed to strengthen the entrenchment, and also to watch carefully the movements of the Gwalior contingent; and should it indicate an intention of advancing, he was to make as great a show as possible by encamping his small detachments conspicuously outside the city, leaving a guard in the earthwork. If he should be seriously threatened, he was to communicate with the Commander-in-Chief as to detaining some of the troops arriving, to assist in the defence. From a military point of view, it is evident that, whilst Sir Colin's position was somewhat critical, that of Windham was far more so. The general, however, lost no time in carrying out his orders. The entrenchment was extended and strengthened with a few guns, and its glacis cleared. The troops were encamped outside; but whether this rather transparent artifice would have much moral effect on the enemy may be doubted, especially as they had ample means of obtaining correct information from their friends in Cawnpore. On the other hand, it was very difficult to procure accurate accounts of the movements of the Gwalior force. In the absence of cavalry, native spies were the only resource; but some of these were caught and mutilated by the enemy; besides which, under the circumstances of the general disaffection, their fidelity could not in all cases be relied on.

The duty of obtaining intelligence was entrusted to Captain Bruce, commonly called 'the intelligent Bruce,' an excellent officer who was also a magistrate. As all the prisons had been destroyed, the only punishments available for criminal natives were hanging and flogging, and in this horrible occupation he was engaged every day. He held his court in the open air in the yard of a ruined bungalow, surrounded by the *débris* of smashed furniture. Amongst others, he captured a native of rank, a friend of Nana Sahib's, and on threatening him with death, the native reluctantly gave information which led to the discovery of about £10,000 in money and a quantity of jewellery, &c., which had been looted and hidden away. I paid one or two visits to the bungalow, which had been the scene of the massacre, a few months previously, of the English women and children by Nana Sahib. The well into which their bodies were thrown had been filled up and closed; but on the walls of the house were still remaining some half-obliterated writing and stains of blood, and in the bushes of the garden, fragments of children's clothing.

Events were now hurrying on to a climax. General Windham, a few days after the departure of Sir Colin, sent a message informing him of the rapid approach of the Gwalior contingent, and obtained authority to detain some of the new arrivals, so that by November 26, when the first battle occurred, he had about 1,700 men and 10 guns drawn by bullocks at his disposal. But of these, four companies of infantry and a few artillerymen had to be left on guard in the entrenchments, so that his movable field force was still very limited. In the meantime, however, the road to Lucknow became closed, and for several days after November 19 no information whatever was received. On the night of the 23rd a tiny note, rolled up and concealed in a quill (which was the method commonly adopted), was brought in by a native from Lucknow. It proved to be from a commissariat officer, who asked for more provisions at once, but said he could give no opinion on military matters, except that they were complicated. The native who brought the note received 50 rupees (£5).

On the other side the mutineers from Calpee were now rapidly approaching in distinct divisions, and had arrived at several villages within a few miles of Cawnpore, and General Windham felt he could no longer remain inactive. On the 24th he advanced his camp a few miles along the Calpee road up to the Ganges canal, which runs across the country, and when its bridges were guarded it served as a wide wet ditch along his front. The Gwalior contingent, however, began to assume the offensive, and spies reported the advance of their main body from Akbarpore to Suchonlee, and that their leading division was on the Pandoo river, only three miles from the British camp. At daybreak on November 26 our men were under arms, and Windham, with ten men of the 9th Lancers and a few sowars, went forward to reconnoitre, and, finding that the mutineers were on the move, led forward his troops at once to the attack. His force consisted of about 1,200 men, being detachments of the 34th, 82nd, 88th, and Rifle Brigade. He also had eight guns, all drawn by bullocks; four manned by natives from Madras, the others by a few gunners of the Royal and Bengal Artillery and some Sikhs—a sort of improvised battery got up for the occasion. The British troops advanced cheerfully to the attack. When these reached the enemy's position, which was on the other side of the almost dry bed of the Pandoo river, the mutineers opened fire from some heavy guns, and poured in several rounds of grape, as we neared them. Our artillery at once replied. Nothing, however, could restrain the eagerness of our men, who came on with a rush, cheering as they went, crossed the river, and captured the position. The enemy retreated in haste, leaving three guns and some ammunition waggons in our hands. We followed them for some distance, and Windham, having halted for a couple of hours to rest his men, then withdrew, as he had intended, to his original position outside Cawnpore, taking the captured guns with him. The mutineers were evidently in considerable strength, and, notwithstanding their defeat, followed us at a distance as we withdrew. Our loss was rather severe, considering the rapidity with which the attack had been carried out. One young officer, Captain Day of the 88th, was killed, being struck by a round shot and knocked down a well.

Our total casualties were :—

Killed	1 officer	18 men	
Wounded	5 officers	78 „	
	6	86	= 92

General Windham on his return at length received the long desired letter from Lucknow. It was a short note from General Mansfield, chief of the Staff, saying that all was well and they were coming back at once to Cawnpore.

November 27 proved to be a very eventful day. Our small field force, as I have explained, was encamped outside the city, not far from the point where the great trunk road crossed that from Cawnpore to Calpee. General Windham naturally hoped that the successful blow he had delivered on the previous day would at all events so far tend to discourage the mutineers as to delay their movements and give time for the return of the Commander-in-Chief. The position, however, was critical. Whilst desirous of presenting a bold front and of protecting the city, it

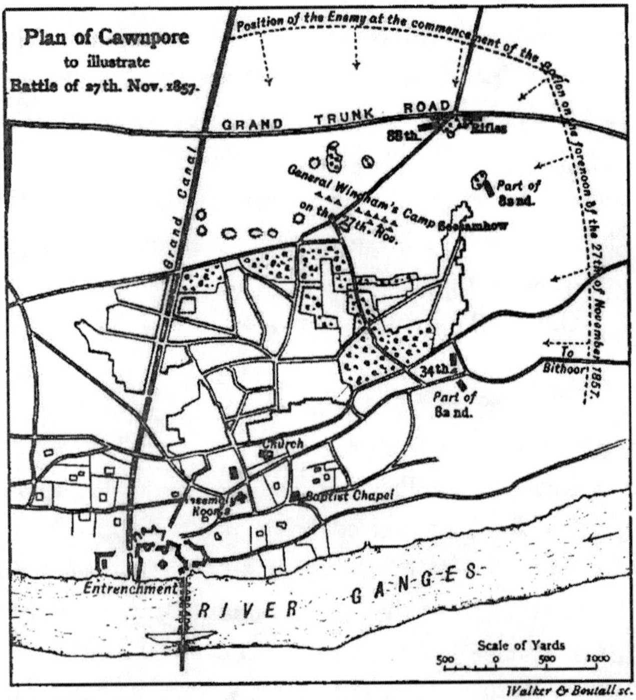

Plan of Cawnpore to illustrate Battle of 27th. Nov. 1857.

Walker & Boutall sc.

was evident not only that our force was insufficient, but that the right flank towards the Ganges was open to attack and liable to be turned. At daylight the troops were again under arms, and part of the 34th and 82nd regiments, with four Madras guns, were detached to the flank, to watch the road from Bithoor. Two 24-pounder heavy guns on travelling carriages, each drawn by a string of bullocks and manned by seamen of the 'Shannon,' under Lieutenant Hay, R.N., were brought out from the entrenchment to strengthen the position in front. Lieutenant Hay had a difficult duty to perform. In the first place, his guns were very heavy for field work; and the draught animals, though obedient to native drivers, were so timid that if an English soldier or sailor approached, they at once began to bolt, and became unmanageable. I remember discussing the matter with him in the morning, and suggested that in the event of a fight he should, if possible, bring his guns into action on the high road, as if he were to leave it, and get into heavy ground and were pressed, he might be in difficulties. He quite concurred, and during the battle, which lasted all day, he acted accordingly, and performed excellent service, he himself being twice wounded.[1]

About 10 A.M. a cannonade suddenly commenced away on the right, followed shortly afterwards by a similar demonstration in front. The mutineers were evidently determined to make a simultaneous attack on both points, and although for the time they held back their infantry, their artillery fire was very severe and

[1] This gallant officer was killed in action two years subsequently, in the New Zealand war, where he had command of the 'Harrier.'

continuous. Windham, conceiving that the flank attack might prove the more dangerous of the two, proceeded there himself in the first instance, but on his return to the front an hour afterwards, found that matters were becoming serious. Not only was the fire incessant, but there were indications that our left as well as our right was threatened—in fact, the enemy were in great strength (in a semicircle) all round us. The battle continued for several hours without signs of abatement, our ammunition was running short, and the bullock drivers began to desert.

Under these circumstances General Windham directed his troops to fall back a short distance, until they found a temporary shelter under cover of some mounds and remains of old brick kilns just outside the city. It seemed now that the position might be held. Still anxious about the right flank, late in the afternoon he sent an aide-de-camp to obtain information, and shortly afterwards directed me to ride through the streets and ascertain the state of affairs. Whilst threading the narrow lanes, I suddenly met the aide-de-camp coming back in haste, who informed me that the mutineers were in possession of the lower parts of the town and had just fired a volley at him. At this moment Windham himself joined us. Whilst deliberating on the critical position, two companies of the Rifle Brigade also appeared on the scene, as if they had dropped from the clouds. They had been marching all day up the trunk road, hearing firing in various directions, but unable to find anyone to give them information. Windham said a few words to them, and, placing himself at their head, away they went cheering, and soon cleared the streets of the enemy. It was, however, becoming dusk, and the general, feeling that it was impossible to remain in the exposed position outside the city, especially as his troops were exhausted and the ammunition running short, sent me to General Dupuis, who was for the moment in command at the front, with orders to withdraw the whole force and return to the entrenchment on the Ganges, as otherwise the position might be lost and the bridge of boats destroyed. The retirement through the streets was conducted without haste and in good order, and was not interfered with by the enemy. It was rather remarkable that although so closely hemmed in by the mutineers, they did not at first take the precaution of cutting the telegraph wires, so that messages were sent to Lord Canning at Calcutta of the results of each day's fighting. During the evening General Windham held a consultation with the senior officers with a view to a night attack on the mutineers, but in the absence of reliable information as to their position the idea was relinquished.

The chief officers of the staff were temporarily

accommodated in a bungalow outside the Fort; and late at night Windham came in and stated that one of the heavy naval 24-pounders had been upset somewhere in the streets during our retreat and had been left behind, and he requested me to go out and if possible recover it, giving me *carte blanche* to make any arrangements necessary for the purpose. It was rather like looking for a needle in a bundle of hay. I went to the entrenchment, obtained the assistance of some seamen under Midshipman Garvey[1] and a guard of 50 infantry, and, with a cart containing a triangle-gyn and the necessary tackle, we prepared to start. Most fortunately at the last moment we found one of the native bullock drivers, who said he knew the position of the lost gun, and on a promise of a few rupees agreed to conduct us to the spot; and so under his friendly guidance we marched off into the darkness. Our friendly native, however, instead of entering the city, led us for a considerable distance through its outskirts, along the banks of the Ganges canal, and some doubts arose as to whether he was not wilfully misleading and taking us into the enemy's camp. However, there was nothing for it but to go on, and at length, becoming very excited, he turned sharply into the town, and after wandering through some of

[1] This young officer was subsequently killed at Lucknow, in March 1858.

the narrow lanes, sure enough there was the gun lying upset against a small shop, with its wheel sunk in a narrow, deep, perpendicular drain. There were planks lying about, and indications that the enemy had been trying to extricate it. Small parties of the infantry were immediately placed at the corners of the adjacent streets, so as to isolate us from sudden attack. Their orders were to keep perfectly silent, but should an attempt be made to force their position they were to fire a volley and charge. As time was precious, and as mounting a gyn with its tackle, &c., in the dark would cause delay, it was decided to try and pull the gun out of its awkward position by main force; and, the seamen having fastened a rope to the trail and working with a will, the attempt succeeded, and so, withdrawing the infantry, we marched back to the fort in triumph. The coolie got his rupees and every man a glass of grog, and thus all ended well. On returning very late to the bungalow, the staff were all lying about asleep on the floor in the various rooms. The only one who woke was Colonel Charles Woodford, of the Rifles, to whom I mentioned our successful adventure. Poor fellow! he was out at daylight the next morning, engaged in the severe contest which took place, and was killed in capturing some guns from the mutineers in the open plain.

The fighting was incessant. On the morning of

the 28th it re-commenced on both sides of the city simultaneously, and for the third day in succession. Away on the left in the open plain, near the ruins of the 'old Dragoon lines,' the Rifles, with part of the 82nd and a battery, after a hard contested fight drove back the mutineers in a brilliant manner and captured two 18-pounder guns. On the right, along the Bithoor road, a second battle was going on at the same time, and continued all day. Brigadier Carthew, with parts of the 34th and 82nd regiments and the Madras battery, held a position somewhat in advance, between the city and the Ganges, and was attacked with overwhelming numbers, but maintained the position until sunset. Carthew was supported by a part of the 64th, commanded by Colonel Wilson, who during the day, in endeavouring to capture some of the enemy's guns, was killed, together with three of his officers and many men. Our losses during the three days' fighting were 9 officers killed, and upwards of 300 officers and men killed and wounded.

I have thus related as shortly and clearly as possible the general features of the battles round Cawnpore, at the end of November, as they came under my notice; because, in my opinion, much injustice was done at the time to General Windham, who was a brave soldier and an excellent leader, and whose difficulties were by no means understood and appreciated. General Windham, in anticipation of the

THE GARRISON OF LUCKNOW RETURNING TO CAWNPORE, NOVEMBER 1857

return of Sir Colin Campbell from Lucknow, had sent him several messages, pointing out the serious nature of the attack on Cawnpore; and on the evening of the 28th the Commander-in-Chief at length arrived, and with the chief part of his force encamped on the other side of the Ganges. What with the women and children, the wounded (amounting in all to 2,000 people), and the usual accumulations of camp equipage and stores which are inseparable from an Indian army in the field, his line of march extended for about twenty miles; and when the strings of elephants, camels, bullock waggons, palanquins, &c., began to cross the bridge of boats the following day, the scene was more like the emptying of Noah's ark than anything else.

The mutineers, who had now full possession of the city and its suburbs, brought some heavy guns to bear on the bridge, and struck the boats several times. However, on November 29 and 30 the whole force crossed the Ganges from Oude and encamped outside Cawnpore, near the 'old Dragoon lines.' Although all pressing danger was at an end on the return of Sir Colin's force, still the Commander-in-Chief had to proceed with considerable caution. His great anxiety, before assuming the offensive, was to provide for the safety of the women, children, and wounded. On December 3 they were sent under convoy down the road to Allahabad, and the

Commander-in-Chief at length was free to act against the mutineers, who, in the meantime, had harassed the camp by occasional demonstrations and artillery fire. Although the enemy were in full possession of Cawnpore, their main position was on the plain outside, and the Ganges canal between us acted as a wet ditch along their front. Sir Colin Campbell computed their numbers as about 25,000 men with 36 guns.

On the morning of December 6 the British camp was struck, and about noon the whole force, consisting of 5,000 infantry, 600 cavalry, and 35 guns, advanced across the open to the attack. The cavalry and horse artillery made a detour to the left, so as to pass over the canal by a bridge a mile and a half distant, and threaten the enemy's flank. The brigades of infantry supported by the artillery, advanced steadily in line across the plain, but were somewhat delayed at the Ganges canal owing to there being but one bridge within reach. This obstacle and the necessary crowding once overcome, they rapidly regained their formation, and, spreading out like a fan, soon drove the enemy back, and ran into their main camp at 1 P.M., Sir Colin, fine old soldier as he was, riding in front with his helmet off, cheering on his panting troops. The mutineers were disorganised, the retreat became a rout, and they fled in all directions, being pursued by Sir Colin and staff with the cavalry and horse artillery up to the fourteenth mile-stone along the

Calpee road, every gun and ammunition waggon which had gone in that direction falling into our hands. Heartily tired, we returned and bivouacked that night in the plain outside Cawnpore. I could not help admiring the toughness of old Sir Colin, who rolled himself up in a blanket, lay down to sleep in a hole in a field, and seemed to enjoy it. The following day Brigadier-General Hope Grant, with the cavalry and horse artillery, followed up such of the mutineers as had retreated by the Bithoor road, caught them just as they were about to cross the Ganges, capturing the remainder of their guns without any casualties on our side. That was the end of the Gwalior contingent as a fighting force.

The loss of the British troops on the 6th was about 100, and 37 guns[1] in all were taken, besides quantities of munitions and stores.

The following is a translation of a Hindostani document issued by the Gwalior contingent, and found on the field of battle outside Cawnpore:

'Cawnpore. By order of the great rajah—the leader.[2] May his shadow never be less. Let all the

[1] Guns captured from the Gwalior contingent—

By General Windham, November 26 . .	3
" " " " 28 . .	2
Battle of December 6	17
By Sir Hope Grant	15
Total	37

[2] Probably the Nana Sahib.

lords of the manor and the rajahs of this country know that a dromedary rider, for the purpose of finding out all about the roads, and defiles, and ferries, is about to be sent, in consequence of the departure of the Gwalior contingent towards Cawnpore; that no person is to molest or hurt in any way the above-mentioned dromedary rider; and let them, in fact, assist him to the best of their power . . . It is written on the 3rd of the month of Suffer, and it corresponds with 1274 of the year of the Flight.'

CHAPTER XIV

CAUSES OF THE MUTINY AND POLICY OF LORD CANNING

The fall of Delhi in September, the relief of Lucknow in November, and the severe conflicts round Cawnpore, had shattered, as it were, the main force of the Mutiny; and although during 1858 active military measures were carried out in various parts of the country, still in reality the great crisis was past. The absence on the part of the natives of any men of military genius to lead them, the want of mutual confidence amongst their widely dispersed forces, and their tendency to marauding expeditions rather than to combined operations, all led to their final defeat in detail. On the other hand, the vigour of our movements, and the large reserves of men, arms, and munitions brought from England, at length restored our shaken power, and enabled us gradually, but firmly, to re-establish our authority throughout the numerous provinces under our rule.

Owing to the wide distribution of the large force of artillery which had arrived from home, it was considered necessary, for administrative purposes, that General Dupuis and his staff should return to the seat of Government at Calcutta; and therefore, after the battles at Cawnpore in November and December, I took no further active part in operations in the field. Residence in India, however, was full of interest at that time, when the causes of the revolution, together with the military changes which ensued, were matters of constant discussion and consideration. The idea that the serving out of greased cartridges to the native soldiery was a dominant factor in the crisis is of course a mere exaggeration of a minor ultimate detail. It may possibly have been the final exciting cause, in the same way that a lucifer match suddenly lighted in a powder magazine may lead to a great explosion; but the causes which conduced to the revolution had been accumulating long before 1857, and were partly political, partly military; and it will be interesting to quote briefly the opinions of various statesmen and high authorities who took part in and studied the history of our conquests, and who traced the results caused by our gradual absorption of the kingdoms, principalities, and provinces into which, until our advent, the vast peninsula of India was divided.

Sir John Malcolm, in his 'Political History of India,' in 1826, wrote: 'The great empire which England has established in the East will be the theme of wonder to succeeding ages. That a small island in the Atlantic should have conquered and held the vast continent of India as a subject province, is in itself a fact which can never be stated without exciting astonishment. But that astonishment will be increased when it is added that this great conquest was made, not by the collective force of the nation, but by a company of merchants, who, originally vested with a charter of exclusive commerce and with the privilege and right to protect their property by arms, in a few years actually found themselves called upon to act in the character of sovereigns over extended dominions before they had ceased to be the mercantile directors of petty factories.'[1] Sir John goes on to show that our rapid progress was due in a great measure to two leading causes: one, that coming originally as unpretending traders, we disarmed suspicion, and were, indeed, welcomed by the natives; the other, that the gradual rise of our power was coincident with the decline of the Mogul empire.

General Sir Thomas Munro—an officer who entered the Madras service of the East India Company as a cadet in 1780, and who by his genius and statesmanlike qualities rose to be Governor of that Presidency—writing in 1817 to the Governor General on the effects of our policy, said: 'The strength of

[1] *Political History of India*, Major General Sir John Malcolm, K.C.B. (John Murray, 1826.)

the British Government enables it to put down every rebellion, to repel foreign invasion, and to give to its subjects a degree of protection which those of no native power enjoy. Its laws and institutions also afford them a security from domestic oppression unknown in those States; but these advantages are dearly bought. They are purchased by the sacrifice of independence of national character, and of whatever renders a people respectable. The natives of the British provinces may without fear pursue their different occupations as traders, meerassidars, or husbandmen, and enjoy the fruits of their labours in tranquillity; but none of them can aspire to anything beyond this mere animal state of thriving in peace, none of them can look forward to any share in the legislation, or civil or military government of their country.'[1] . . . 'It is from men who either hold, or are eligible to hold, public office that natives take their character; where no such men exist, there can be no energy in any other class of the community. The effect of this state of things is observable in all the British provinces, whose inhabitants are certainly the most abject race in India. No elevation of character can be expected among men who, in the military line, cannot attain to any rank above that of subadar, where they are as much below an ensign as an ensign is below the Commander-in-Chief, and

[1] Gleig's *Life of Sir Thomas Munro, Bart, K.C.B.*

who in the civil line can hope for nothing beyond some petty judicial or revenue office, in which they may, by corrupt means, make up for their slender salary. The consequence, therefore, of the conquest of India by the British arms would be, in place of raising, to debase the whole people. There is, perhaps, no example of any conquest in which the natives have been so completely excluded from all share of the government of their country as in British India.'

Again in 1818, in a letter to Lord Hastings, he says: 'Our Government will always be respected from the influence of our military power, but it will never be popular while it offers no employment to the natives that can stimulate the ambition of the better class of them. Foreign conquerors have treated the natives with violence and often with great cruelty, but none has treated them with so much scorn as we; none has stigmatised the whole people as unworthy of trust, as incapable of honesty, and as fit to be employed only when we cannot do without them. It seems to be not only ungenerous, but impolitic, to debase the character of a people fallen under our dominion.' Again in 1824: 'With what grace can we talk of our paternal government if we exclude them from every important office, and say, as we did till very lately, that in a country containing 150,000,000 of inhabitants no man but a European shall be trusted with so much authority as to order the punishment of a single stroke of a rattan? Such an interdiction is to pass a sentence of degradation on a whole people for which no benefit can ever compensate. There is no instance in the world of so humiliating a sentence having ever been passed upon any nation. . . .' 'The advocates of improvement do not seem to have perceived the great springs on which it depends; they propose to place no confidence in the natives, to give them no authority, and to exclude them from office as much as possible; but they are ardent in their zeal for enlightening them by the general diffusion of knowledge. No conceit more wild and absurd than this was ever engendered in the darkest ages, for what is in every age and every country the great stimulus to the pursuit of knowledge, but the prospect of fame, or wealth, or power?' . . . 'In proportion as we exclude them, we lose our hold upon them; and were the exclusion entire we should have their hatred in place of their attachment, their feeling would be communicated to the whole population and to the native troops, and would excite a spirit of discontent too powerful for us to subdue or resist. . . .' 'It would' (he says) 'certainly be more desirable that we should be expelled from the country altogether than that the result of our system of government should be made a debasement of a whole people.' The above are wise and weighty words, and it would be well perhaps, even in these days, if more heed were taken of these outspoken opinions of Sir Thomas Munro.

There is, however, another and more recent authority, greater perhaps than any; one who, year after year, and not long before the Mutiny, urged that we should give opportunities to the natives, and enable them to rise to power, civil and military; and who predicted that unless this were done our system must collapse, either in a mutiny or in general despair. That authority is Sir Henry Lawrence, who fell at his post in the Residency of Lucknow, killed by the mutineers in the very crisis which he had, as it were, foretold. Writing in 1855 [1] he pointed out that the natives had no outlet for their talents and ambition as of old, and said: 'These outlets for restlessness and ability are gone; others are closing. It behoves us therefore now, more than ever, to give legitimate rewards, and as far as practicable employment, to the energetic few, to that leaven that is in every lump—the leaven that may secure our empire, or may disturb, nay even destroy, it.' Again, he says: 'Legitimate outlets for military energy and ability in all ranks and even among all classes must be given. The minds of subadars and resseldars, sepoys and sowars, can no more with safety be for ever cramped, trammelled, and restricted as at

[1] *Essays*, by Sir Henry Lawrence, 1859.

present than can a twenty-foot embankment restrain the Atlantic. It is simply a question of time. The question is only whether justice is to be gracefully conceded or violently seized. Ten or twenty years must settle the point.'

Leaving for the moment the political results of our conquests in India, it will be well now to consider its military aspects; to trace the formation and services of our native armies, and to watch the signs of their gradual decline both in efficiency and loyalty; and I will again give short quotations from the writings of recognised authorities as conveying clear outlines of this interesting and important subject.

Sir John Malcolm, writing of our early levies, said: 'A jacket of English broadcloth made up in the shape of his own dress, the knowledge of his manual exercise and a few military evolutions, constituted the original Sepoy.' He goes on to tell us that the only English officers were a captain and adjutant per battalion; that the native officers were treated with great kindness and consideration, were often in high command, and that many of the oldest regiments were known by the names of their former native commandants. After dwelling on the efficiency of our original native corps, he points out that their constitution was gradually changed by the increase of European officers, involving alterations of dress, more rigid rules, and with so-called improvements in discipline, until at length in 1796 they were organised like the king's regiments, with the full complement of officers, and with the expectation of greatly increased efficiency—an expectation which was never fulfilled. He wrote in 1826: 'In the native army, as it is at present constituted, no native can rise to the enjoyment of any military command.' Again, he says, the danger lies in 'confiding too exclusively in our European troops and altogether undervaluing and neglecting our native army. From the day of that fatal error we may date the downfall of our Eastern empire.'

Sir John Kaye, in his history of the Mutiny, says[1]: 'Our first Sepoy levies were raised in the Southern peninsula, where the English and French powers were contending for the dominant influence in that part of the country. They were few in number, and at the outset commonly held in reserve to support our English fighting men. But little by little they proved that they were worthy to be entrusted with higher duties; and once trusted they went boldly to the front. Under native commandants, for the most part Mohammedans or high-caste Rajpoot Hindoos, but disciplined and directed by the English captains, their pride was flattered and their energies stimulated by the victories they gained.

[1] Kaye's *Sepoy War*, 1865, vol. i.

All the power and all the responsibility, all the honours and rewards, were not then monopolised by the English captains. Large bodies of troops were sometimes despatched on hazardous enterprises, under the independent command of a native leader; and it was not thought an offence to a European soldier to send him to fight under a black commandant. That black commandant was then a great man in spite of his colour. He rode on horseback at the head of his men, and a mounted staff officer, a native adjutant, carried his commands to the subadars of the respective companies. And a brave man or a skilful leader was honoured for his bravery or his skill as much under the folds of a turban as under a round hat.' Again he writes: 'The founders of the native army had conceived the idea of a force recruited from among the people of the country, and commanded for the most part by men of their own race but of a higher social position. . . But it was the inevitable tendency of our increasing power in India to oust the native functionary from his seat, or to lift him from his saddle, that the white man might fix himself there, with all the remarkable tenacity of his race. . . . So it happened in due course that the native officers who had exercised real authority in their battalions, who had enjoyed opportunities of personal distinction, who had felt an honourable pride in their position, were pushed aside by an incursion of English gentlemen who took all the substantive power into their hands. As the degradation of the native officer was thus accomplished, the whole character of the Sepoy army was changed. It ceased to be a profession in which men of high position accustomed to command might satisfy the aspirations and expend the energies of their lives. . . . Thenceforth, therefore, we dug out the materials for our army from the lower strata of society.' Captain Macan, an officer who had long experience and knew the Sepoys well, gave evidence before a Parliamentary Committee in 1832, and declared that 'in all the higher qualifications of soldiers, in devotedness to the service, cheerfulness under privation, confidence and attachment to their officers, and unhesitating bravery in the field, the native soldier is allowed by all the best informed officers of the service, and by those who have most experience, to have infinitely deteriorated.'

The late Rev. Mr. Gleig, in a remarkable article in the 'Edinburgh Review' in 1853, wrote: 'The original native army consisted chiefly of infantry, who, though drilled after European fashion, worked both in peace and war under chiefs connected with the men by ties of consanguinity and friendship.' He goes on to point out that the English element gradually increased until 1784, when a European subaltern was allotted to command each company, and he says: 'Though the subalterns thus disposed of were carefully selected, and the feelings of the subadars spared as much as possible, the native gentleman could no longer disguise from himself or from his men that his shadow was growing less. He supported himself, however, tolerably well till the tide which had begun to set in against him acquired greater force. In 1790, and again in 1796, the European element became still stronger, and then, and not till then, the spirit of the native sank within him. The effect produced by these changes upon the native officers, and ultimately upon the service at large, has been deplorable.' Mr. Gleig's article—written, be it borne in mind, in 1853, shortly before the Mutiny—concludes as follows: 'We have won an enormous empire with the sword, which is growing continually larger. We have established a system of civil administration there which protects the peasant and disgusts all the classes above him . . . With a large body of discontented gentry everywhere, and whole clusters of native princes and chiefs interspersed through our dominions, it is idle to say that the continuance of our sovereignty depends from one day to another on anything except the army. Now the army is admitted by all competent judges to be very far in many respects from what it ought to be.'

The extracts which I have quoted of the opinions

of various authorities all appear to point in the same direction, and to prove that both in a political and a military sense the various races under our rule in India were gradually becoming degraded and demoralised, and that these results were observed years before the crisis came, and when our power was, for the time, subverted by the general Mutiny of 1857. Our intentions throughout were doubtless good. We introduced sound laws for the people, though not perhaps always in accordance with their customs and prejudices. We also gave them security of life and property, such as they had not enjoyed for centuries; and to some extent we promoted education and commerce and more general prosperity. These benefits are by no means to be ignored. But, on the other hand, in our advance across the great continent we had dethroned kings, upset hereditary princes, and had removed from positions of authority not only men of high rank, great possessions, and ancient lineage, but also men of vast influence, religious and other, and often of great ability and courage. These all found themselves pushed aside and superseded; whilst the various races of people, Hindoo and Mohammedan, not only perceived that their ancient leaders were gone, but that their new governors were aliens in race, religion, language, and customs. All these considerations cannot be carelessly disregarded. The situation is undoubtedly difficult. There is, indeed, one solution, and one only, which must ever be kept steadily in view—namely, that men such as I have indicated must gradually be admitted to positions of responsibility and power, both civil and military; that the people of all ranks, classes, and religions may feel that a career is open to them, and that they are to be allowed to participate in the government of their own country. I do not urge that the time has by any means arrived when the natives should be admitted to the public service by competitive examinations. It is not a system adapted to the circumstances. That, however, is comparatively a minor detail; but there are many other and better modes by which they can and ought to be selected for service under the Government.

In the ultimate reorganisation of the native armies after the Mutiny, the number of English officers to each regiment was restricted to six, so that in some degree the influence of native officers was recognised; but the restriction did not amount to much, and the apparently inevitable tendency is to an augmentation of the English element, the present number being eight. It is also to be observed that there is no instance of a native regiment commanded and led entirely by officers of their own race and faith, so that no opening exists for the many brave and loyal chiefs, men of ability and influence, to serve in the army.

Whether under such circumstances we can hope to maintain the military virtues of our Indian troops is a grave question on which opinions differ. Judging by the history of the past, by the views of the soldiers and statesmen which I have quoted, and by the culminating experience of the Mutiny, it seems to me that our policy is rather timid and retrograde, and that we can only govern successfully by gradually entrusting power to the natural leaders of the people.

There is yet another consideration, which relates specially to India of the present day. Education and enlightenment are progressing all over the country, not only by means of schools and colleges, but also by the establishment of railways, roads, and river communications, so that the people now move about freely and exchange ideas to a degree formerly unknown. Literature and the press, the telegraph and the post office, are also exercising increasing influence; and these various causes are somewhat rapidly undermining many ancient prejudices and superstitions. All these are, doubtless, beneficial influences in themselves, and are likely to produce great results, but they require watching, as they inevitably will tend to increase the legitimate desire of the people for more self-government. We cannot stand still.

I have heard it said sometimes that such principles

as I advocate would, if carried out, cause to us the loss of the Empire of India; and my reply is, that if such principles are *not* carried out, we shall not only lose India, but shall deserve to do so. Others talk of the people of India as being composed of inferior races. I am not aware that God has created any races of men who are inferior; but at all events in India, we know that centuries ago they were civilised and distinguished in arts and sciences, in government, and in war—long, indeed, before we had become so. We hear a great deal nowadays of the depreciation of the rupee; but in our government of India, unless we act on the principles which I have endeavoured to illustrate, by quotations from the writings of statesmen of the highest authority and experience of India, we may find in the days to come that we have a far more dangerous result to face, and that is the depreciation in the character of the millions under our rule. Sir Henry Lawrence wrote: 'We cannot expect to hold India for ever. Let us so conduct ourselves in our civil and military relations, as, when the connection ceases, it may do so not with convulsions, but with mutual esteem and affection; and that England may then have in India a noble ally, enlightened, and brought into the scale of nations under her guidance and fostering care.'

Finally, before leaving this part of the subject I

will quote extracts from the noble proclamation issued by the Queen in 1858, on the termination of the Mutiny, and which should ever be considered as the Magna Charta of the people of India: 'We declare it to be our Royal will and pleasure, that none be in any wise favoured, none molested or disquieted, by reason of their religious faith or observances, but that all shall enjoy the equal and impartial protection of the law . . . And it is further our will that, so far as may be, our subjects of whatever race or creed be freely and impartially admitted to offices in our service, the duties of which they may be qualified by their education, ability, and integrity duly to discharge.' It is often said that India has been won by the sword, and must be governed by the sword. The first statement is in a great measure true; but to the second, as laying down a principle of government, I demur. No nation can be permanently or successfully governed by the sword.

As the crisis of the Mutiny gradually passed away, and as the people of the various provinces, though still violently agitated, began to realise that the British authority was being firmly re-established, it became evident to the Viceroy that the time had arrived when the summary powers which had been exercised, and the severe punishments which had been inflicted, all over the country, must be modified, and that a policy of conciliation should gradually replace that of stern repression. These views of Lord Canning were, however, by no means in accord with the general sentiments of the European population, and of the Press of Calcutta at the time, and his policy was strongly condemned. This feeling on their part is perhaps not altogether surprising. The terrible scenes which had been enacted in so many parts of the country on the outbreak of the Mutiny—the cruel murders, and the atrocious conduct of the natives, not only to men, but to innocent and defenceless English women and children—all these sad events had naturally roused feelings of intense anger; and the idea of conciliation was repugnant to the minds of the great majority. So much was this the case, that even at the end of 1857 the Europeans of Calcutta and Bengal sent home a petition to the Queen, urging that, owing to the weakness of the Government and in disapproval of the views of the Viceroy, he should be recalled. Lord Canning, however, fully convinced that a policy of vengeance was not only wrong in principle, but impossible, was by no means persuaded or moved from his purpose. Writing to the Queen in September 1858,[1] he said: 'There is a rabid and indiscriminate vindictiveness abroad, even among those who ought to set a better example.' Again, to Lord Granville he wrote: 'As

[1] *Rulers of India: Earl Canning*, by Sir H. S. Cunningham, K.C.S.I.

long as I have breath in my body, I will pursue no other policy than that I have been following. . . . I will not govern in anger. . . . Whilst we are prepared, as the first duty of all, to strike down resistance without mercy wherever it shows itself, we acknowledge that, resistance over, deliberate justice and calm patient reason are to resume their sway; that we are not going, either in anger or from indolence, to punish wholesale, whether by wholesale hangings and burnings, or by the less violent, but not one bit less offensive, course of refusing trust and countenance and favour to a man because he is of a class or a creed.'

The violent opponents of the Viceroy at the time were in the habit of calling him 'Clemency Canning' as a term of reproach. They did not seem to be aware that, under the circumstances, it was the highest honour they could pay him. In my opinion, Lord Canning proved himself to be a wise and courageous Viceroy, and in a period of great difficulty and danger rose superior to the violence of many of those by whom he was surrounded.

When the Mutiny was at an end a thanksgiving service was held in the cathedral at Calcutta, and a special collection made for some charitable purpose to commemorate its termination. There was at that time, and probably is now, a peculiar system of collecting subscriptions at the church services there.

It was not the custom to carry money in your pocket. I asked the reason, and was told that the climate was too hot. The consequence was that when a collection was made, the persons who carried round the plates also brought packets of small pieces of paper and bundles of pencils, and each person had to write down and sign the amount of their gift. It was a tedious, but possibly an advantageous, process from a charitable point of view. The following day the collectors went round and called for the amount subscribed. On the occasion in question Lord Canning's secretary informed me that when the collector presented his paper at Government House, the sum inscribed was so large that, imagining there was an error, he took it to the Viceroy, who, however, merely remarked that the occasion was a memorable one, and the amount was paid accordingly. It was for 10,000 rupees (1,000*l.*). I doubt whether many instances can be given of such a sum having been put into the plate at a church collection.

During my residence at Calcutta I became acquainted with an English official who appeared to possess an extraordinary amount of intuitive knowledge. Whatever the subject discussed, he was always at home, and could lay down the law, and did so. It is not, perhaps, agreeable to find yourself always in a position of ignorance and inferiority. Still, on the whole, society, it may be presumed, benefits. I inquired of an old Indian officer what position this exceptional person held. 'Oh!' he replied, 'that's what in India is called a "sub-janta" —a man who knows everything better than anyone else—be careful not to contradict him.' However, I found that you must have been thirty years in the country and speak all the languages before becoming qualified for the position, so that, fortunately, there are very few sub-jantas to be found.

I occasionally received invitations from natives of rank at Calcutta to be present at family festivities, and the following is a copy of one of them: 'Wedding Party. Cowar Kallykissen Bahadoor presents his respectful compliments to Colonel Adye and requests the favour of his company to a dinner at 7.30 P.M., and a nautch and fireworks at 8.30 P.M., in honour of his daughter's marriage, on Monday, February 22, at Rajah Badinath Bahadoor's garden house at Cossipore.'

On one occasion I paid a visit to the celebrated Chinese Commissioner Yeh, who was a state prisoner at Calcutta, and lived in a large house in the environs. He was dressed in loose white Chinese clothes, with wooden shoes, and was very polite but extremely cautious. We conversed by means of an interpreter. Nothing would induce Yeh to leave his house, although a carriage and horses were kept for him. My efforts to interest him in various subjects entirely failed. I asked if he liked the Indian climate, and he replied that he had not turned his thoughts in that direction. I described the bazaars and shops, and recommended him to go out in his carriage and visit them; but he only said he had heard about them, and would send his secretary to make a report. He told me he was much occupied, and on my asking what he did, he replied that he liked to 'sit down.' He was offered books to be translated to him, but remarked that the contents of all the best ones were already in his stomach, so that he did not require them. He died soon afterwards, presumably of indigestion.

In the early part of 1859 another serious and untoward event occurred, in the discontent of the men of the local European forces at many of the large stations all over the country. Hitherto, in each presidency, the artillery and three regiments of infantry consisted of men recruited at home, but who served continuously in India—in fact, a local European army distinct from the Queen's troops. In the years gone by, and during the Mutiny, they had performed great services, and were deservedly held in high esteem. When, however, in 1858 the rule of the old East India Company came to an end, the great majority of these men considered that, as the Queen had assumed direct authority over the local armies, they were entitled either to their discharge, or, at all events, to a bounty on the transfer of their services to the Crown. Their claims were referred to England for consideration, but were ultimately refused by the Home Government; and, as a consequence, serious disaffection, combined in some cases with violence and a refusal to perform their duties, ensued. It may perhaps be conceded that the curt refusal of their claim was not altogether judicious, but in reality the causes of discontent lay deeper and had been accumulating for some time. The Commander-in-Chief, who was ill at Simla, was much impressed with this unfortunate state of affairs, and was in frequent communication with Lord Canning at Calcutta. Writing in May 1859, he said:[1] 'I am irresistibly led to the conclusion that henceforth it will be dangerous to the State to maintain a European local army. . . . We cannot afford to attend to any other consideration than those of discipline and loyalty, which may be constantly renovated by the periodical return to England of all the regiments in every branch of the service.' The Viceroy was much pressed by some authorities at the time to grant the bounty, notwithstanding the refusal of the Home Government; but to have done so and to have given way to violence would have been a virtual abnegation of authority, and would not in reality have removed the disaffection. In this dilemma, Lord Canning at

[1] Shadwell, *Life of Lord Clyde*, ii. 419.

length gave a free discharge and passage home to all who wished it, and about 10,000 men then left for England. The cost is said to have been a million sterling. Many of these men, after a short holiday at home, re-enlisted in various Queen's regiments and returned to India. The general result, however, was that ere long the local European troops ceased to exist as a separate force, and became merged in the army of the Empire.

CHAPTER XV

RECOLLECTIONS OF THE MADRAS PRESIDENCY

In May 1859 I left Calcutta, having been appointed to command the Royal Artillery in the Madras Presidency. Speaking generally, the affairs, both civil and military, of Southern India had remained for many years in a condition of comparative inaction and tranquillity. Indeed, ever since the great campaigns towards the close of the last century, ending with the fall of Seringapatam and the death of Tippoo Sahib, the tide of war had drifted away to the north-west, and the Madras army had thus been deprived of much active experience in the field. Fortunately, even the Mutiny had failed to entangle the southern native troops in its disastrous meshes. As a term, perhaps, of undeserved reproach, Madras was often called the benighted presidency. Shortly before my arrival a new Governor, Sir Charles Trevelyan had been appointed, and being a man of great energy and ability, soon succeeded in temporarily galvanising the administration into unwonted life and activity. His somewhat abnormal qualities were not, however, generally appreciated. One of his first efforts was to improve the sanitary condition of the large native city, which stretches for a mile or two along the flat, sandy, surf-beaten shore. During the latter years of the last century the city had been enclosed on its land front with a series of old bastions and curtains and a continuous stagnant ditch—works which were intended as a defence against the hordes of Mahrattas and Pindarees who were then in the habit of swooping down on our cities and settlements. But these hostile races had long ceased their swoopings and lootings, and the decaying fortifications were not only obsolete, but by their existence prevented a due circulation of light and air, and were highly insanitary. Sir Charles accordingly decided on their entire removal, and the conversion of the vacant space and of the ancient glacis into a People's Park. The idea was received with considerable scorn. Few people in Madras had ever heard of people's parks in those days. I, however, had the satisfaction of being present at the destruction by successive explosions of the old, useless bastions, and in my opinion the Governor conferred a great benefit on the city by his enlightened policy. More serious events, however, soon followed.

When the Mutiny came to an end, its financial bearings and the enormous expenditure incurred, not only on account of the large reinforcements from home, but also in the arrangements which had been necessary for the due prosecution of active operations all over the country, pressed heavily on the Government of India; and it became an urgent duty to meet the financial deficit, which amounted to several millions sterling. Amongst other measures it was decided to introduce an income tax. Sir Charles Trevelyan, backed by his council, protested against such a policy. In his opinion, an income tax, in the condition of the native feeling, was likely to revive dangerous discontent; further than this, he argued in successive despatches to Calcutta that, as the Mutiny was over, the proper way of meeting the deficit was by a reduction not only of the English reinforcements, but also by disbanding many of the new native regiments which had been hastily and temporarily raised during the crisis. Finding that his remonstrances were in vain, he at length published the entire correspondence in one of the Madras daily journals. As Governor of a presidency containing fifty millions of people, he considered it his duty that his views should be made public. The result was that in a few days he received a message by telegraph from Sir Charles Wood, the then Secretary of State for India, announcing his recall. Whether the Governor acted with due discretion in the measure he took to ensure publicity for his views, may be questioned; but, in my opinion, he was perfectly right in his main principle that, the crisis being over, the financial equilibrium could best be attained, not by unusual and obnoxious taxation, but by a reduction of the enormous military expenditure, the necessity for which had passed away, and which was eating up the resources of our empire in the East. His recall was a public misfortune.

Soon after my arrival in Madras I made the acquaintance of an old colonel, who had served many years in the country and was an excellent officer, but who, owing to absence of mind or partial loss of memory, had great difficulty in correctly remembering people's names. For instance, one morning he came into the club, and told us that he had just met Sir John Trelawney taking a walk in the park. As there was no one of that name in Madras we were rather puzzled, but on inquiry found he alluded to the Governor, Sir Charles Trevelyan. That was harmless enough, but on another occasion he fell into a more serious error. It occurred in the Neilgherries. There was a lady residing there, a Mrs. Coffin, the wife of a general officer. It is the fashion up in the hills for ladies to be carried about by coolies in a sort of sedan chair, called a tonjon. One afternoon, the general's wife was paying a visit to a neighbour, where she met the colonel, and on her rising to take leave the old officer jumped up, and, meaning to be extremely polite, said, 'Mrs. Tonjon, allow me to hand you to your coffin!'

Military service in the tropical climate of the

Madras Presidency in time of peace, and with the thermometer never below 80 degrees, is not an exhilarating experience. There were no railways to speak of in those days, and no bridges over the rivers, so that during tours of inspection I had constantly to pass many weary days and nights in travelling hundreds of miles, along bad roads, over dusty plains, in what is called a bullock bandy, at the rate of two miles an hour, not including accidents, and probably without meeting a single Englishman. On one occasion, I went from Madras northwards by steamer along the coast to Masulipatam, on my way to the Deccan, and found the tomb of an old Dutch admiral, the inscription on it being as follows: [1]

HIER LEYT BEGRA
VEN DEN. E. JACOB
DEDEL

IN SYN LEVEN RAET VAN
IN DIEN ENDE OPPER
HOOFT TE WATER ENDE
TE LANDE OVER DE NEDER
LANTSE NEGOTIE DE SER
CUST CORMANDEL. OVER
LEDEN. DEN. 29. AUGUSTY
ANNO. 1624.

[1] Here lies buried E. Jacob Dedel, in his lifetime Councillor of the Indies, and Commander-in-Chief on sea and land, over the Dutch Company of the Coromandel Coast. Died, 29th August, 1624.

During 1862 I was in command of the artillery at Secunderabad, a large station near Hyderabad in the Deccan, the latter city being supposed to contain a somewhat turbulent dangerous population, but who in reality gave no trouble. The monotony of life was occasionally varied by hunting wild animals in the hills and jungles. Although a very bad shot, I took part in the sport on two special occasions. The one was in pursuit of a bear, and the other of a tiger. In the first case we rode by night to some distant hills, and were posted in the dark behind rocks by the shikarree; and, being a novice, I was given the place of honour, the native kindly remaining at my side, and explaining that the cave of the bears was just above and behind me, and that at daylight I should find several coming straight up the hill on their way home. Sure enough, as day dawned, two large black objects appeared leisurely crossing the plain, snuffing about, as they slouched along, and presently they began the ascent. The critical moment had arrived, and, on a signal from the shikarree, I fired, and the bears immediately bolted. The shikarree threw up his hands, and, much disappointed, said that my shot had missed. It was not so, however, for on going to the spot we discovered traces of blood, and were able to track the wounded animal up the hill to his home—a dark, narrow, steep cleft in the rock. Here a consultation was held, and it was decided by the experts that we must follow up the track, and enter the den. A procession was formed accordingly. First came a coolie with a long lighted torch, which he waved about and pushed into the crevices; then I followed, crawling on all fours with a gun on full-cock ready for all emergencies. Two or three companions came on similarly prepared. All at once we heard a scream and a rush, and I was about to fire at anybody or anything, and should probably have killed the coolie, when it turned out to be merely a bat fluttering against the lighted torch. The smell of bears, bats, rats, and other creatures was horrible. Still we struggled on, until the narrow tortuous passage gradually ramified into large fissures, and we then discovered that the bear had passed out of its home by another opening, and so escaped. The adventure ended, and we were glad to crawl back into the open air again.

The other expedition was also exciting in its way. In hunting tigers in Bengal it is the custom to be seated in a howdah on the back of an elephant, so as to stamp through the jungle and shoot the animals from a commanding position in comparative safety. In Madras, however, it is considered fairer to advance on foot, on the principle, I presume, of giving both sides a chance. One afternoon we were again conducted by the shikarree to a distant hill, and on an elevated plateau were all posted in a large

N

semicircle, each hidden behind a rock, and in the centre a young kid was tied to a stone. The expectation was that the tiger would come to eat the kid, and then we were all to fire and kill the tiger. As this was my first experience, I inquired, with some interest, whether possibly the animal might not approach from behind, and begin to eat me instead of the kid. The suggestion, however, was scouted, and I was assured that it would much prefer the latter. So we took up our positions, and remained on watch. After a time the young goat, finding the entertainment dull, laid down and tried to go to sleep; but the shikarree advanced and with a knife cut a small slit in its ear, which made it bleat piteously; and this, it was hoped, would afford an additional attraction. Again we waited, and I could not refrain from occasionally looking over my shoulder, to assure myself that the expected wild beast was not surreptitiously altering the programme. It was getting dark when a breathless coolie arriving from a distant hill, brought the news that the tiger was asleep in a cave a long way off; so the kid escaped, and we all went home. I thought the sequel rather flat.

Society at Secunderabad was occasionally enlivened by amateur theatricals in the assembly rooms, and, being fond of painting, I was induced on one occasion to produce a drop-scene for the stage.

One afternoon I was seated accordingly, in some old clothes, on the top of a step-ladder, with a large brush and a bucketful of sky-blue, attempting to produce some lovely cloud effects, when a private soldier of the 18th Royal Irish strolled in smoking his pipe. After admiring the scenery for some time, and evidently taking me for a professional, he remarked: 'I say, guv'nor, is that a good business out here?' My reply was, 'No, it isn't a very permanent affair, but I like it.' Then he went on, 'I think I've seed you afore' (which was probable). 'Was you ever engaged at the Surrey in London?' I said that I had been at that theatre, but had never been engaged. 'Well, then, I *have* seed you afore,' he continued; 'you was acting the part of Belphegor.' What play he was alluding to I had no idea, or who Belphegor was, but unfortunately at that moment a brother officer casually looked in and said, 'Well, Colonel, how are you getting on?' The soldier at once took in the situation, stood up, saluted, and saying, 'I'm thinking I'm in the presence of my supariors,' faced about and left the room. The drop-scene was finished, and was considered a great success.

CHAPTER XVI

RETURN TO BENGAL—AMALGAMATION OF THE ARTILLERY REGIMENTS

TOWARDS the end of 1862 I left the Deccan on a pleasant visit to Sir William Denison, then Governor of Madras, and in February 1863, having served upwards of five years in India, was on the eve of embarkation for England when a telegram came from Sir Hugh Rose, Commander-in-Chief, inviting me to return to Bengal to become Adjutant-General of all the artillery in India. My plans were therefore entirely altered, and I embarked for Calcutta instead of England, and, after a long journey up to Meerut, joined Sir Hugh, and went with him to Simla in the Himalayas.

At this time great changes had become necessary in the army in India in consequence of the Mutiny of 1857, and of the subsequent discontent of the local European forces in 1859. In fact, the whole administration, both civil and military, was undergoing revision and reform. The direct assumption of the government of India by the Crown, and the disappearance of the old East India Company, though a beneficial change in itself, still naturally caused some confusion and revived old controversies. Hitherto there had been two armies in the country, serving side by side, with two separate staffs, with somewhat different sentiments, and not devoid of feelings of jealousy. The artillery were specially affected by the contemplated changes. Although in the early days of the East India Company a battery or two from England had occasionally served in India, still they were exceptions, and for many years each presidency had maintained a regiment of its own, partly English, partly native; and as we gradually conquered one province after another, they took part in many campaigns, performing distinguished services, and were deservedly held in high esteem. Therefore, when it became evident that unity of administration must be introduced as regards our military forces, and when, in the autumn of 1862, the three regiments of Indian artillery were incorporated with the Royal—losing, as it were, their separate individuality—it was only natural that the officers and men of all the four corps should have felt some regret at an arrangement which, however necessary it might be, was not in accord with old feelings and sentiments. All organised bodies may be said to be conservative, in so far that they dislike change.

The foregoing remarks may be sufficient to

indicate the general conditions of the artillery problem when I was invited to become the chief staff officer, and to carry out the amalgamation. There were not only sentimental feelings and differences to be considered, but the systems of training, discipline, and even the *matériel*, were all to some extent different. Still, all these were comparatively minor and transient questions; and I fully recognised in the first place that whilst the batteries of old Royal Artillery would benefit by the wide experience of service in India—from which, previous to the Mutiny, they had been debarred—those of the local regiments would, on the other hand, benefit even more largely by periodical return to England, especially in these days of constant change and progress in the science of artillery. It was with these views that I entered on the somewhat difficult task of producing unity of system and of feeling in the hundred and four batteries which at that time were serving in India. Sir Hugh Rose, the Commander-in-Chief in India, and H.R.H. the Duke of Cambridge, the head of the Army at home, were in full accord in these matters; and notwithstanding certain differences of opinion, I also received loyal support from the officers of artillery all over the country, so that in the course of 1863 all real difficulties gradually disappeared. My great desire was, as far as possible, to respect the interests of all, and to promote unity, not only as good in itself, but also as conducing to the efficiency of the regiment and to the advantage of the State. It was not altogether an easy task, but I was amply rewarded by the generous confidence of my brother officers. Reminiscences of the bygone system of the East India Company still, however, prevailed more or less in the councils of the Government of India, and nothing could be more difficult than the position of Sir Hugh Rose at that period of change; and it was a pleasure to me to serve under, and if possible to assist, so distinguished a soldier and one with whom I had been in frequent association during the Crimean war. Lord Elgin was at that time Viceroy, and I had one or two conversations with him regarding the alleged danger from the turbulent population of Hyderabad, and gave my opinion that these fears were exaggerated, and that, especially with a Prime Minister such as Salar Jung, there need be no real apprehension of an outbreak.

It is sometimes supposed that red tape is peculiar to official departments at home, but that is an error. There are large consignments of it sent to India, and I will give an instance. One day at Simla an old artillery officer called and requested me to give him a certificate of his being alive, as the audit office refused to give him his pay without it. He seemed to be well and lively, and I therefore complied at once; and as his visit was in August, dated it accordingly. On looking at it, he remarked: 'Ah, you have dated it August. That is of no use. I have already sent them one of that kind, but what they require is a certificate that I was alive in July.' This opened out a new aspect of the case, but, after consideration, I certified that to the best of my belief he was living the previous month. Whether he ever received his pay, I am not sure.

CHAPTER XVII

FRONTIER CAMPAIGN IN THE AFGHAN MOUNTAINS—ITS ORIGIN—POLITICAL AND MILITARY DIFFICULTIES

In the autumn of 1863 our somewhat tedious devotion to military administration in all its complicated details was suddenly interrupted by the outbreak of hostilities on the north-west frontier, which rapidly and unexpectedly developed into a war of considerable magnitude in the Afghan mountains. Its origin was of a rather singular and exceptional character. For many years previously a number of violent fanatical outlaws, chiefly from the lower provinces of Bengal, hundreds of miles away, had fled from our territories, and settled amongst the independent Afghan tribes who live in the countries across the border. These outlaws, occasionally reinforced by disaffected Mohammedans from the plains, lived chiefly in a village called 'Sitana' on the lower slopes of the Mahabun mountain, about forty miles north of the old Mogul fortress of Attock, and on the western side of the Indus—hence their name of Sitana fanatics. Their ordinary occupation consisted of incursions into the plains of Eusofzye, and in robbing and murdering peaceful traders in our territories. In 1858 the late Sir Sydney Cotton led an expedition against them and burnt some of their villages; but as they were harboured, and probably to some extent encouraged, by their Afghan neighbours, and as the country of their adoption was devoid of roads and almost inaccessible, they soon re-established themselves in the

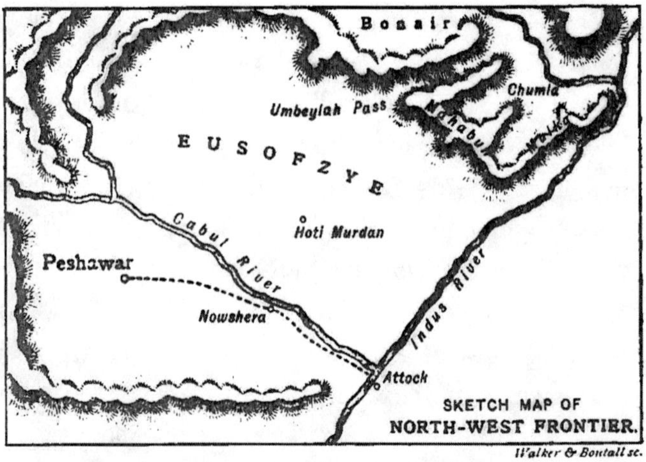

SKETCH MAP OF NORTH-WEST FRONTIER

large new village of Mulka, high up on the slopes of the mountain, and recommenced their depredations. It was under these circumstances that a fresh expedition was determined on; and as, from causes which were not foreseen at the outset, it rapidly developed into a considerable campaign, it will be interesting to take a short survey of the conditions, military and political, of our north-west border.

A glance at the map will show that our frontier in that part of India is composed of great rugged mountain ridges which, radiating southerly from the Hindoo Koosh, terminate somewhat abruptly in the plains, and form, as it were, a great natural boundary of the Empire. These mountains are inhabited by tribes who, though Afghan in language, religion, and race, are for the most part independent of the ruler at Cabul. They are poor but brave, fanatical, and half civilised, and are governed by native 'jirgahs' or councils; and, although turbulent and difficult to deal with, still have a great love of their country and cherish its independence, possessing qualities that we admire in ourselves, and which deserve consideration and respect. Except in the narrow and secluded valleys there is little cultivation, and the whole country is almost devoid of roads, beyond mere goat paths. Military operations are therefore difficult. The Commander-in-Chief, when the expedition was under consideration, pointed out that the season was late, as snow falls in November, and that to march a force through such a country of scant resources would necessitate careful preparations and ample transport, and he advised postponement until the following spring; but his views were disregarded by the Punjab Government, who entered into the campaign in a somewhat heedless, lighthearted fashion, which speedily brought its own punishment. It is further to be remembered that in those days our line of frontier for hundreds of miles was guarded chiefly by the Punjab Irregular Force, consisting of about 10,000 men of all arms recruited from the martial races within our border, many of whom were really Afghans in religion and race. Strange to relate, also, this army was under the orders of the Punjab Government, and altogether independent of the Commander-in-Chief. To guard a long and exposed frontier by native levies raised on the spot, and to the almost total exclusion of English soldiers, was a bold and possibly a dangerous policy; but to increase the risk by a complex division of military authority appears to be a violation of all commonly received maxims of war.

The force decided on for the Sitana expedition consisted of about 6,000 men, chiefly of the Punjab force just mentioned, to which, however, was added the 71st Highlanders, the 101st Bengal Fusiliers, and a battery of Royal Artillery, with its field guns carried on elephants. The Government were fortunate in one respect, that the expedition was placed under the command of Sir Neville Chamberlain, an officer of long experience and of the highest ability and courage. Indeed, it was a happy circumstance that in the serious complications and hard fighting which ensued a man of such great qualities should have been at the head of affairs; and although he was struck down and severely wounded before the operations came to an end, still it may be admitted, without disparagement of his successor, that the neck of the confederacy had been broken by his vigorous measures, and that the tribes were sick at heart and weary of the combat.

In entering on a campaign against the Sitana fanatics, who doubtless were tolerated and harboured by the inhabitants, it must still be borne in mind that in crossing the border we were entering upon foreign territory; and a question therefore arose as to the light in which our suspicious Afghan neighbours would regard our advance. There was also another important point which must not be overlooked. In determining the exact direction of our march, it was considered, as a matter of strategy, that instead of moving straight up the mountain, towards the enemy's stronghold, we should enter the country by the Umbeylah Pass, a narrow gorge to the west of the Mahabun, and proceed through the Chumla Valley on its north side (see map); and thus by a flank march, as it were, attack the fanatics in rear and cut off their line of retreat. Our intentions in this respect were kept secret. In a military point of view the proposal had advantages, but politically it had quite another aspect—it being evident that we were thus entering the territory of neighbours, many miles distant from the real object of the expedition, who might, and indeed did, at once take violent exception to our proceedings. Official documents published afterwards explain this clearly. Speaking of the intended march through the pass, Colonel Taylor, the commissioner with the expedition, wrote: 'It was, under the circumstances, impossible to examine the proposed route by questioning those of our own territories best acquainted with it, without raising suspicions as to the line we proposed to take in entering the hills.' Again, General Chamberlain's first despatch after the advance of the force, on October 20, said: 'I should here mention that on the afternoon of the 19th,[1] when it would be too late for the Chumla or other tribes to make any preparations on a large scale for impeding the march of the troops through the Umbeylah Pass, a proclamation was forwarded by the commissioner, to the Chumla and Bonair tribes, stating the object with which the force was about to enter the Chumla Valley, and assuring them that it was with no intention of injuring them, or of interfering with their independence; but solely because it was the most convenient route by which to reach the Hindostanee fanatics, and to effect their expulsion from the Mahabun.'

But the question was, in what light were the Bonairs and others likely to regard our sudden and

[1] October 19, 1868.

unexpected arrival at the door of their house, our purpose having been carefully hid until the time for their objecting or defending themselves had passed away? The late Major James, who was the commissioner when peace was made, alluding to these circumstances, makes a significant remark: 'Even supposing, therefore,' he says, 'that the proclamations actually reached their destination, was it likely that a brave race of ignorant men would pause to consider the purport of a paper they could not read, when the arms of a supposed invader were glistening at their doors?' It so happened, also, that the fanatics, when they heard of the assembly of our troops in the plains and became aware that we were about to call them to account, although not cognisant of our exact plan, nevertheless wrote a very crafty letter to their neighbours, which subsequently fell into our hands, as follows: 'The evil-doing infidels[1] will plunder and devastate the whole of the hilly tract, especially the provinces of Chumla, Bonair, Swat, &c., and annex those countries to their dominions, and then our religion and worldly possessions would entirely be subverted. Consequently, keeping in consideration a regard for Islam, the dictates of faith, and worldly affairs, you ought by no means to neglect the opportunity. The infidels are extremely deceitful and treacherous, and will by

[1] Meaning the English.

whatever means they can come into these hills, and declare to the people of the country that they have no concerns with them, that their quarrel is with the Hindostanees, that they will not molest the people, even as much as touch a hair of their heads, but will return immediately after having extirpated the Hindostanees, and that they will not interfere with their country. They will also tempt the people with wealth. It is therefore proper for you not to give in to their deceit, or else, when they should get an opportunity, they will entirely ruin, torment, and put you to many indignities, appropriate to themselves your entire wealth and possessions, and injure your faith.'

From the foregoing remarks it will, I think, be evident that our policy was not only somewhat rash, but was not altogether straightforward. In the first place, we undertook the expedition with an inadequate force, chiefly comprised of native troops, raised on the spot, at a late season of the year, and without sufficient preparations as to supplies and transport; in the next, we attempted to march through a country inhabited by tribes with whom we had no cause of quarrel, and from whom we carefully concealed our intentions. The result of the first day's march (October 20) brought matters to a climax, and instead of being able to cut off the 'Sitana' fanatics, we found ourselves face to face with the Bonair and other tribes, whose territory we had invaded, and who, scoffing at our professed strategy, at once united and determined if possible to drive us out of their country. The whole condition of affairs was thus entirely altered, and General Chamberlain found himself holding the end of a narrow gorge, with steep mountains running up several thousand feet on either side, and attacked incessantly day and night, not only in front, but on either flank.

In the meantime another unfortunate circumstance had occurred. It so happened that towards the end of October both the Viceroy and Sir Hugh Rose had left Simla, on short expeditions towards the distant ranges of the Himalayas. Accidentally I had seen Lord Elgin when he started, and he appeared to be in good health; soon afterwards, however, owing, it was supposed, to his having ascended and crossed some high passes, or whatever the cause, he suddenly became dangerously ill with an affection of the heart, and when he arrived at Drumsala in the Kangra Valley, his case was deemed hopeless. Sir Hugh also, for the moment, was almost out of reach, but on hearing of the untoward development of the military operations, he at once proceeded to Lahore, where his staff joined him in November. The successive despatches of General Chamberlain give a clear account of the altered condition of affairs.

Writing on October 23, he said: 'The Bonair people having thus taken a hostile part against us is extremely serious, and has altered our whole position and probably our plan of operations.' He then goes on to explain the necessity of guarding his communications through the pass, and asks for reinforcements. Again, on October 25, he writes: 'There appears to be reason to believe that the Bonair people have applied to the Akoond of Swat for aid, and should they succeed in enlisting him in their cause—which is not improbable, as they are his spiritual followers—the object with which this force took the road to the Chumla Valley would be still more difficult of attainment.'

CHAPTER XVIII

HARD FIGHTING IN THE MOUNTAINS

General Chamberlain now took steps to clear himself of encumbrances, and to prepare for hard fighting. The sick, the baggage, and spare transport animals were sent back to the plains, and the road was improved. A breastwork was thrown across the front of the camp and flanked with guns; the steep slopes on either side were occupied by strong pickets, stockaded and entrenched. Still the position was weak. Far above on the extreme left our troops held a post called the 'Eagle's Nest;' and opposite, on the right, another named the 'Crag Picket,' a commanding pinnacle of rocks scantily clothed with pines and towering up into the sky. Both were vital points to hold, for they entirely overlooked the lower defences. But high as they both were, there were other ridges and dominant points still far above, and our troops were thus exposed to sudden overwhelming attacks, from enemies who could collect unseen at their leisure and choose their time for an assault.

The men of the tribes were brave and worthy foes. These bold mountaineers, ignorant of what is termed discipline, or of any regular art of war, armed only with old matchlocks and short swords, nevertheless, by a kind of rude instinct, discovered at once our weak points; and by feints at the centre, combined with furious assaults on the isolated flanks, not only inflicted heavy loss upon us, but succeeded occasionally in endangering the whole position. The Crag Picket alone fell three times into their hands by direct assault in open daylight, at different periods of the campaign, although in each case we drove them out again. The despatches received day after day, though hastily written, gave a vivid reality to the scenes depicted, and extracts from them will perhaps convey the best idea of the fierce nature of the contest and of its vicissitudes. On October 24 large bodies of men, with numerous standards, appeared in the Chumla Valley, and were ascertained to be arrivals from some of the minor hill tribes, and a portion of the fanatics under Mobarik Shah. At daylight the next morning they appeared above our right defences on the Mahabun, but were driven off by Major Keyes,[1] who chased them along the ridges and forced them back precipitately into the valley.

The events of the following day (October 26) were serious. Chamberlain, having some reason to

[1] Now General Sir Charles Keyes, G.C.B.

apprehend an attack on the Eagle's Nest, reinforced the troops on the mountain, sending up 200 of the 71st Highlanders, the 5th and 6th Punjab regiments, and a mountain battery. The Eagle's Nest itself was held by 230 men under Major Brownlow.[1] The enemy, who had established a breastwork of their own on the heights above and were in great strength, no sooner observed our preparations for battle than they joyfully accepted the challenge. The scene is well described by Colonel Vaughan, who was in command: 'The troops were hardly in position when a very large body of the enemy rushed down the steep slopes, and, with loud cries, attacked at once the picket and the troops. The mountain train guns fired upon them with shrapnel, common case, and round shot, and this fire checked those advancing against the troops in position, but not those advancing against the picket. The latter were attacked with the greatest determination, and two of the enemy's standards were planted close under the parapet. All the efforts of the picket failed to dislodge them for some time, notwithstanding that the direct fire from the picket was aided by a flanking fire from the mountain train guns and from the Enfield rifles of the 71st. . . . When the enemy had been checked by the guns, they were charged by the 6th Punjab Infantry, but the regiment was unfortunately carried too far in the ardour

[1] Now General Sir Charles Brownlow, G.C.B.

of pursuit, and lost heavily before it could regain the position.' Major Brownlow, who was standing at bay in the Eagle's Nest, gives a simple and vivid account of the attack upon him. 'About 12 o'clock (noon) the Bonairwals commenced to move down from their position, matchlock men posting themselves advantageously in the wood, and opening a very galling fire upon us, whilst their swordsmen and others advanced boldly to the attack, charging across the plateau in our front, and planting their standard behind a rock, within a few feet of our wall. The steady fire, however, with which they were received rendered their very gallant efforts unavailing, and they were driven back and up the hill, leaving the ground covered with their dead.'

Our casualties on this occasion were as follows:

	Killed	Wounded	Total
English officers . .	2	2	4
Native officers . .	1	9	10
Men	28	129	157
	31	140	171

The great losses incurred by the native corps in this as in every action during the campaign, are proofs of the loyalty of the men to our cause. General Chamberlain, in his despatches, bears warm testimony to their devotion; and points out that although there were men in the native regiments of almost every tribe on the frontier, including those which were fighting against us, still there were no desertions, nor was there any instance of backwardness in engaging the enemy.

After the 25th there was a lull for a few days, but the storm soon gathered again, and important events followed each other in rapid succession. General Chamberlain, in his despatch of October 31, reports 'that the Akoond has joined and has brought with him upwards of 100 standards from Swat, each standard representing probably from twenty to thirty footmen.' Other distant tribes had also been summoned, and in fact there was a general combination all along the border against us. He goes on to say: 'It is necessary that I should place the state of affairs thus distinctly before His Excellency, in order that he may understand how entirely the situation has altered since the force entered the Umbeylah Pass.' And he goes on to explain that with his present numbers he could only stand on the defensive. During the early part of November vigorous efforts were made to strengthen our outposts and to improve the communication to the plains of Eusofzye; but the confederate tribes jealously watched our movements and incessantly attacked us day and night; and on the morning of the 13th succeeded a second time in capturing the Crag Picket. General Chamberlain in his despatch said: 'I was in the camp when the picket fell into the hands of the enemy, and my attention having been accidentally drawn to the unusual dust and confusion caused by the rush of camp followers down the hill, I felt convinced that some reverse had occurred, and immediately sent forward Her Majesty's Royal Bengal Fusiliers.' Lieutenant-Colonel Salisbury[1] was in command of the regiment, and his orders were to push on and retake the position at any cost. The ascent was long and steep, but the Fusiliers never halted, and in five-and-twenty minutes the key of the position was recovered.

An important change was now made in the disposition of the force. As already explained, the prolonged halt in the pass was due to unforeseen causes, and the general had to make the best of it, its great weakness consisting in the isolation of its flanks. As some delay must occur before sufficient reserves could arrive, so as to enable Chamberlain to resume the offensive, he determined to abandon the gorge and also the pickets on the mountain to his left, and to concentrate his whole force on the slopes of the Mahabun. In a military point of view this was a judicious arrangement. Instead of holding a series of straggling posts, perched upon rocks, on two separate mountains, and with his main body far down in a hollow gorge, our troops would thus be concentrated and able to reinforce any point required. The movement was quietly carried out

[1] Now General Salisbury, C.B.

during the night of November 17. The vigilance of the tribes for once failed them, and when daylight broke on the 18th, to their astonishment the Eagle's Nest and all the pickets on that side were silent and empty. Exasperated by the success of our manœuvre, and imagining probably that it was the precursor of a general retreat, the enemy swarmed up the Mahabun ridges, and before our troops were well settled in their new positions, attacked them fiercely, and for the moment with some success, but were finally driven off. General Chamberlain, writing at the time, said: 'The troops have now been hard-worked both day and night for a month, and having to meet fresh enemies with loss is telling. We much need reinforcements. I find it difficult to meet the enemy's attacks, and provide convoys for supplies and wounded sent to the rear. . . . This is urgent.'

The confederate tribes, consisting of the fanatics, the men of the Mahabun, of Bonair, Swat, Bajour, and of other distant secluded valleys, joined also by a sprinkling of men from our own border villages, were now in such numbers that the hill sides literally swarmed with them; and although they had failed in their efforts to capture the position they had not lost heart, but again made a vigorous effort; and on November 20 advanced on the Crag Picket, coming boldly up, with their standards flying, to within a few feet of our breastworks; and at length, after a desperate hand-to-hand encounter, for the third time took possession, amidst shouts of triumph from the Afghans on the hills all round. Victory, however, did not long remain with them. The 71st Highlanders, who had taken a full share in every action of the campaign, were selected, with a regiment of Goorkas, to retrieve the fortunes of the day, and they were not wanting in this hour of need. Whilst the troops were being assembled for the assault of the captured work, the field and mountain guns were turned on the enemy, who were thus forced to lie close under cover of the rocks. Under a perfect storm of matchlock balls and of stones hurled from the summit, Colonel Hope, the gallant leader of the Highlanders, deliberately formed his men at the foot of the Crag; and sending the Goorkas to turn the flank, he placed himself at the head of his corps, and, with a cool determination which excited the admiration of every soldier of the force, proceeded to march up the rocky height. The mountaineers throughout the war had shown themselves ready to do and to dare a great deal, but they were not quite prepared for the direct assault of a Highland regiment which in open day, with its colonel at its head, was steadily approaching, and would infallibly in a few seconds close upon them, with a volley and a bayonet charge. The storm of shells which had been raining on them for the preceding half hour, shattering the rocks and trees, had somewhat shaken their confidence; and almost as soon as the Highlanders reached the summit the mountaineers evacuated the position, and were chased along the ridges. Sir Neville Chamberlain, ever foremost in danger, having felt it his duty to accompany the troops in so critical an attack, was unfortunately severely wounded, and Colonel Hope was also dangerously wounded in the thigh. Our lost ground was thus recovered, but at the cost of two distinguished men, the first and second in command, who were rendered unable to take any further part in the war. Our losses up to this time had been considerable; no less than 14 English[1] and 4 native officers, with 213 men, had been killed, whilst 15 English, 17 native officers, and 468 men were wounded, making a total of 731 casualties, and so far as the original object of the war was concerned, we had as yet really accomplished nothing.

[1] The following officers were killed: Lieutenant Gillies, R.A., Captains C. Smith and Aldridge, and Ensign C. Murray, 71st Highland Light Infantry; Lieutenants Dougal and Jones, 79th Highlanders (doing duty with 71st); Lieutenant H. Chapman, Ensign A. Sanderson, and Surgeon Pile, 101st Bengal Fusiliers; Lieutenant J. Davidson, 1st Punjab Infantry; Lieutenant Clifford, 3rd Punjab Infantry; Lieutenant W. Moseley, 14th Ferozepore Regiment; Lieutenant Richmond, 20th Native Infantry, and Major G. Harding, Bombay Staff Corps.

CHAPTER XIX

POLITICAL COMPLICATIONS—END OF THE WAR

THE preceding remarks will be sufficient to give a general idea of the difficulties, both military and political, which had ensued on our crossing the border. The situation was undoubtedly grave. Major James, the commissioner, wrote, that it was a truly formidable and dangerous combination, and that immediate action was necessary to save the Government from a war involving us not only with all the tribes on the border, but also in all probability with Afghanistan. The Lieutenant-Governor of the Punjab, Sir Robert Montgomery, had doubtless long and anxiously considered the untoward aspect of affairs; and at length, when the telegrams arrived announcing the severe actions just described, he looked upon the matter as so serious, that he was actually prepared to order an immediate withdrawal of the whole force to the plains; and in this view he was supported by some members of the Viceroy's Council; in fact an order to that effect was sent to the Commander-in-Chief. What Sir Hugh Rose thought of the proposition is plain enough. In the first place he remonstrated against the withdrawal, pointing out the danger of such a policy and the loss of prestige which would result. In the next he ordered large reinforcements to proceed by forced marches to the frontier, so that the great northern road from Lahore to Peshawur was crowded with cavalry, artillery, and infantry, all hurrying upwards. At the beginning of December there were five-and-twenty thousand men north of the Jhelum.

Soon after my arrival at Lahore in November, I had written to my old friend Sir William Denison at Madras, giving him a short description of the state of affairs.[1] On November 20 Lord Elgin died, and Sir William, as the senior governor present in India, was summoned by telegraph to Calcutta, and assumed temporarily the functions of Viceroy. His reply to my letter is dated Calcutta, December 7, and is interesting as giving his views on the situation.

It is as follows:—

'My dear Adye,—Thanks for your letter. I got the whole of the papers relating to the business in the North-west on my way up the river, and spent my time in reading them and making notes. It is hardly worth while to say anything about the commencement of the affair beyond this, that if any

[1] My letter was published *in extenso* in *Varieties of Viceregal Life*, by Sir W. Denison. 1870.

move was to have been made at all, the plan proposed by Sir H. Rose was clearly that which should have been adopted. With reference, however, to the future, I trust I have been in time to check further evil. . . I found an order had been sent to the Commander-in-Chief, telling him that their wish was that the force should be withdrawn, thrusting upon the Commander-in-Chief the responsibility of deciding not only the mode of doing this, and the time, but also that of determining whether such a move would peril our reputation. The first step I took was to press for a modification of the order. I pointed out that it was unfair to the Commander-in-Chief; and that, as we had a sufficient force, it would be decidedly impolitic to withdraw, until we had accomplished the design for which we had made our inroad into the country. Alter a good deal of talk, I carried with me the majority of the council, and it was decided to bring the Bonairs to terms before withdrawing the troops. To leave without doing this would almost insure another campaign in the spring, and this would be expensive and useless. I trust that our orders may arrive in time to prevent any hasty move to the rear.'[1]

Many days, however, before I received Sir William's

[1] Sir Hugh Rose, in writing to me from Lahore on the same date as Sir William Denison (Dec. 7), said that the Governor General had entirely approved of his not consenting, although hard pressed, to give up the Umbeylah Pass and retreat to the plains.

GOING TO THE WAR. CROSSING THE INDUS AT ATTOCK, NOVEMBER 1863

letter, circumstances had occurred at Lahore which led to my making a long and rapid journey of several hundred miles northwards, and joining the force in the mountains during the remainder of the war.

On November 19 Sir Hugh spoke to me of his difficulties and of the suggested retreat, which seemed both impolitic and unnecessary. The letters and telegrams received from the front were, however, necessarily somewhat short and hasty, and did not give full details of the position; and I offered my services as a staff officer, to pay a rapid visit to Chamberlain, hear his views, take a personal survey of the country, and then return. The Commander-in-Chief accepted my offer, and also selected Major Roberts,[1] who knew the people and the language, to accompany me. He was a delightful companion. On the evening of the 20th we left Lahore on the mail cart, placing the driver behind, and ourselves driving each stage alternately. We galloped up the trunk road all night, and all the next day, crossing the Ravee, the Chenab, and the Jhelum, and were nearly done up from want of sleep, when we fortunately drove into the camp of a battery of Horse Artillery and obtained a few hours' rest. Before daylight we were off again, passed through Rawul-Pindee, and in the afternoon crossed the Indus by a bridge of boats close under the old Mogul fortress of Attock; and at

[1] Now General Lord Roberts, G.C.B.

sunset on the second day our long drive of nearly 300 miles came to an end at Nowshera, on the Cabul river, where the officers of a battery under Captain Nairne, R.A.,[1] hospitably received us. Until our arrival at Nowshera, we had not heard of the latest fight at the Crag Picket, and that Chamberlain and Hope were severely wounded. In the meantime horses had been laid out for our use across the plains of Eusofzye; and, crossing the Cabul river, we galloped about thirty miles, passing numerous detachments of Seiks and Pathans, with elephants and camels, and on the evening of November 23 reached the camp of Major Probyn,[2] in command of a native cavalry regiment at the foot of the mountains. The weather was fine but cold, and altogether the long journey was very enjoyable.

Sir Neville Chamberlain's force was about ten miles distant on the heights of the Mahabun, whose ridges run up to 8,000 feet. Our instructions were urgent, and we were very anxious to be off. Probyn, however, whose troops were patrolling the frontier, pointed out that the communications were uncertain, and that the road, such as it was, was only opened occasionally by armed convoys taking up food and munitions to the front. However, as delay was unadvisable, after considering the matter, he said:

[1] Now General Nairne, C.B., Commander-in-Chief, Bombay.

[2] Now General Sir Dighton Probyn, V.C.

'You can, if you like, go up with the "catch-em-alive-ohs."' I inquired who these interesting people were, and his reply was that they were Afghans—in fact, the same people we were fighting against; but he added that these were friendly and in our pay, and would take care of us. He had them paraded for our inspection. These 'catch-em-alive-ohs' were a rough, handsome, picturesque lot of fellows, armed with old matchlocks, shields, and short knives, and seemed very good-natured and friendly; so, in default of better, we determined on accepting their escort, and away we went, accompanied by the Reverend Mr. Cowie, afterwards Bishop of New Zealand. The mountain was steep and rugged, and the route a mere goat path, so that our progress was slow. After climbing for some miles, we suddenly observed a large number of people on a high, distant ridge, but whether friends or enemies was not so certain. The body of a native just killed was lying in the path. At that moment a messenger ran up bringing me a small note in pencil, and reading it hastily I made it out to be 'the road is *now* safe, push on as fast as you can.' This was satisfactory, but on looking more carefully we found the message really was, 'the road is *not* safe, push on,' &c. This rather altered the conditions; but fortunately the men we had observed on the heights were a party of Goorkas, and the note was from the officer in command, who was looking out for us, so that our journey soon came to an end, and we arrived safely in camp.

The next morning I paid a visit to Chamberlain. We had been cadets together many years before at Woolwich, but he left the Academy before obtaining a commission, joining the Bengal army, and we had never met since those early days. His wound, however, was severe and his condition serious, so that I was unable to discuss the position of affairs with him, as had been intended, and in a few days he was carried down to the plains. I found a strong and unanimous feeling amongst the officers against any withdrawal. Although the tribes were in great force in the valley, with their standards flying, it was evident that we only required reinforcements; and that a movement in advance would soon scatter the brave but badly armed, undisciplined hosts of our mountain foes. I lost no time in sending day by day, detailed reports, sketches, and plans of the position to Sir Hugh Rose, urging also the necessity for an early forward movement, and in reply received an order by telegraph, to remain with the force until the termination of the war.

The scenery all round us from our elevated camp was very varied, and had many elements of grandeur. Looking back to the south through the dark defiles of the pass, we could see the fertile plain of Eusofzye stretching away to the Indus and Cabul rivers, whilst in front the sheltered Chumla valley and the village of Umbeylah were lying beneath us; and away in the distance to the north, high ranges of mountains, capped by the snowy peaks of the Hindoo Koosh, closed in the horizon. Owing to the success which had been achieved on several occasions by the tribes in capturing our outlying breastworks—due, perhaps, in some cases, to want of vigilance on our part—strict instructions had been given that our pickets were to hold their ground at all hazards; and on one occasion a soldier coming on duty was heard to say to his comrade, 'Well, Jim, what's the orders at this post?' and Jim replied, 'Why, the orders is, you're never to leave it till you're killed, and if you see any other man leaving it, you're to kill him.'

Our life was a very open-air kind of existence, a sort of prolonged picnic, and we lived partly in small tents and partly in caves, always sleeping in our clothes; our dinners such as they were, being cooked and laid out on the rocks. The Afghans perched themselves about, and now and then made long shots at us with their matchlocks. One old fellow took up his position every day on an elevated spot, on the other side of the pass, at a distance, and watched the proceedings. Our men frequently fired at him, but apparently without effect; so at last they gave it up, and nicknamed him 'Oh! Willie, we have missed you.' There was another peculiarity amongst the tribes which is, perhaps, unusual in warfare. Some of our native troops, when on isolated pickets at night, used to pass away the dreary hours by singing some of their national airs; and the enemy, apparently not wishing to be left out, would cheerily join in the chorus.

At the end of November General Garvock[1] arrived, taking command of the expedition; and during the next few days considerable reinforcements marched up from the plains, including amongst others the 7th Fusiliers, the 93rd Highlanders, and Probyn's Horse, 400 strong. Our total force was over 8,000 men, with 16 light guns, some carried on elephants and the rest on mules. The men of the tribes, no doubt, were quite aware of these accessions to our strength; and although Guzzhan Khan, from the distant province of Dher, had joined them with 6,000 followers, they hesitated to attack our position, which was now strongly entrenched and vigilantly guarded. Early in December a small deputation of Bonair chiefs came into camp to confer with Major James, the commissioner, with a view to peace; and after a parley withdrew to consult the other tribes as to the terms we offered; which were the destruction of Mulka, and that the fanatics should no longer be harboured and protected by the Afghans. We could hardly demand less. It was understood that there were

[1] The late Sir John Garvock.

AFGHAN FRONTIER CAMPAIGN. STORMING THE CONICAL PEAK, DECEMBER 1863

considerable dissensions amongst the native chiefs, and on the afternoon of December 14 a solitary messenger returned, stating that our proposals were rejected. It was also known that an attack by the combined tribes was imminent on the morrow.

The moment of action had at length arrived. General Garvock, forestalling the intentions of the enemy, assembled a force of 5,000 men, including the 7th and 101st Fusiliers, at daylight near the Crag picket, leaving the remainder to guard the camp, and at 8 A.M. led off his troops along the ridges to the attack. About two miles beyond the Crag stood the small village of Laloo, and a few hundred yards in front of it, one of the great spurs running up from the Chumla valley, terminated in a lofty peak dominating the whole ridge. On this natural stronghold the men of the tribes had established themselves in great force, flying their standards, and prepared to abide the last issues of war. The ordinary difficulties of the ascent had been increased by numerous 'sungas' (breastworks), so that it was a formidable position to take by assault. Our skirmishers, who had easily driven in the outlying mountaineers, then halted about 600 yards in front of and looking up at the conical peak, and, supported by the mountain guns, waited for the arrival of the main body..

These mountain batteries rendered great service during the war. Their light ordnance, carriages, and ammunition being all carried on mule back, they are thus independent of roads, can accompany infantry over any ground, and come into action on the most restricted space. As the several regiments came up they sought a momentary shelter in the broken ground, and when all was ready, General Garvock sounded the 'advance.' At that signal 5,000 men rose from their cover, and with loud cheers and volleys of musketry, rushed to the assault; the regiments of Pathans, Seiks, and Goorkas vieing with the English soldiers as to who should first reach the enemy. From behind every rock and shrub at the foot of the peak small parties of mountaineers jumped up, and fled as the advancing columns approached. It took but a few minutes to cross the open ground, and then the steep ascent began, our men having to climb from rock to rock, and their formation necessarily becoming much broken. Foremost among the many could be distinguished the scarlet uniforms of the 101st Fusiliers, who, led by Colonel Salisbury, steadily swarmed up the mountain and captured the defences in succession at the point of the bayonet, the enemy's standards dropping as their outworks fell; whilst here and there the prostrate figures of our men scattered about the rocks, proved that the hill-men were striking hard to the last. Nothing, however, could withstand the impetuosity of the assault, and ere many minutes had elapsed the conical peak from foot to summit was in the possession of British soldiers. I had the misfortune during the assault to fall over a large rock, seriously injuring my right knee and tearing the ligaments, becoming for the moment incapable of climbing; but by the help of a mule, lent from one of the batteries, managed to reach the crest of the mountain. Our panting troops still pushed on, captured the village of Laloo, and the mountaineers were then driven headlong in thousands, down the steep glades, through the pine forests to the Chumla valley, many hundred feet below.

This was the first general defeat the enemy had experienced, and they were not left long to recover from its effects. At daylight the next morning our troops were again in movement; one brigade marching down direct on Umbeylah, accompanied by Probyn's cavalry, who, however, had to lead their horses down the precipitous slopes until they reached the valley. In the meantime the other brigade descended from Laloo and deployed at the foot. The tribes, although at first they seemed inclined to make a stand, gradually fell back. The brigade from Laloo followed them up, passed the village of Umbeylah, and approached the hills leading to Bonair. The enemy, who had been lying concealed in the ravines and broken ground, suddenly rushed out, sword in hand, wildly attacked one of our Seik regiments, and for the moment even penetrated its ranks. The Seiks, however, were rallied by their officers, and supported by the 7th Fusiliers, and the enemy in a few minutes were driven back with great loss. In the meantime three field guns, under Captain Griffin, R.A., which had been brought down on elephants, got into action and shelled the crowded heights, the tribes withdrawing out of range. Our losses during the two days were: one officer killed,[1] four wounded, and there were 172 casualties amongst the men. As all tents and baggage had been left on the mountain, we bivouacked for the night outside Umbeylah, which was set on fire. The weather unfortunately was wet and cold, so that lying in the open wrapped up in a blanket was not luxurious; and, to add to my discomfort, all at once I felt what seemed to be a snake crawling about my legs. Having with difficulty obtained a lighted match, I suddenly threw aside the blanket, when a huge black rat darted out, but, as I found the next morning, had eaten large holes in my only pair of trousers, so that I presented altogether a somewhat damp and dilapidated appearance. These, however, were but minor incidents in a very interesting campaign.

The effect of our vigorous movements on the 15th and 16th was immediate and decisive. The men of Bajour and Dher, who had come so far and

[1] The names of the officers were, Lieutenant Alexander killed; Major Wheeler, Captain Chamberlain, Lieutenants Nott and Marsh wounded.

were so eager for war, now fled to their native fastnesses. The Akoond and his followers were no more to be seen; and the chiefs of Bonair, relieved from the presence of overbearing allies, came into camp the next day to discuss terms of peace. Under ordinary circumstances a force of sufficient strength would no doubt have been sent forward to drive away the original offenders, and to destroy their chief village—Mulka. But the Punjab Government were anxious to limit the scope of the expedition. and to withdraw from the mountains. Consequently a somewhat hazardous compromise ensued; Colonel Reynell Taylor, the commissioner, proceeding with one native regiment, about 400 strong, accompanied by an escort of the Bonairs, to burn the distant village. Roberts and myself, being anxious to visit a part of the country hitherto unexplored, joined the party. The first day's march, on December 20, was along the Chumla Valley to Kooria. We saw little of our new friends the Bonairs, but the inhabitants were civil and met our requirements as to food; the next morning we commenced our long and toilsome march up the mountain to Mulka; which proved to be a large, new, well-built village of wood, where we remained for the night. The inhabitants had all fled. The following morning the whole place was set on fire; the hill tribes of the Mahabun, armed and in large numbers, however, watching us at a distance. The native officers of our regiment represented that the tribes were greatly exasperated, and might at any moment fire off their matchlocks and make a rush at us. However, we kept well together, and as soon as the village had been destroyed, steadily marched back to the valley, and rejoined the main force under General Garvock. On Christmas day the British troops left the mountains and once more stood on the plains of Eusofzye, the Bonairs destroying the entrenchments and breaking up the roads as we marched away.

Thus ended the frontier war of 1863. Intended at the outset as a mere excursion against fanatical robbers, who had long infested the border, it speedily grew into a considerable war, the Mohammedan tribes, under the impression that their independence was in danger, combining against us. The campaign was interesting in its military aspect, in giving experience of the extreme difficulty and expense of carrying out offensive operations in a country composed of mountain ranges, devoid of communications, and inhabited by races of men whom we may consider half civilised, but who, at all events, possess the virtues of courage, independence, and love of their country, and physically are as active and handsome a people as exists anywhere. From a political point of view the north-west frontier of India is also full of interest. After a century of conquest, with dominions now extending

1,600 miles from Calcutta to Peshawur, we have at length arrived at a region which seems marked out by nature as the boundary of our Empire. The conditions of the north-west frontier no doubt involve difficult considerations, but it seems to me clear that, whilst guarding against incursions, our policy towards our somewhat turbulent neighbours should be one of forbearance and conciliation, combined in some cases with subsidies.

As Sir Charles Wood, the Secretary of State for India, wrote in 1864: 'Our true course ought to be, not to interfere in their internal concerns, but to cultivate friendly relations with them, and to endeavour to convince them, by our forbearance and kindly conduct, that their wisest plan is to be on good terms with us, in order that they may derive those advantages from intercourse with us which are sure to follow from the interchange of commodities and mutual benefits.' It is a policy necessarily requiring patience and somewhat slow in its effect, but will in due time bring its reward, and indeed it has already done so of late years. Our trans-Indus districts, which were formerly harried by the neighbouring tribes, are now comparatively safe and prosperous; and many Afghans who have served in our ranks have returned to their native villages with pensions, and with a kindly feeling and remembrance of those under whom they have served. Before leaving this subject, it may be well to point out that there is another and a far larger question beyond that of the immediate frontier which must be kept steadily in view by the British Government, and that is our relations with the ruler of Afghanistan in connection with the advance of Russia in Central Asia. I propose, however, to defer the consideration of those important questions until a later period, when the Afghan war of 1878–9 brought matters to a crisis.

CHAPTER XX

VISIT TO PESHAWUR—SIR HUGH ROSE RETURNS TO ENGLAND—SIR WILLIAM MANSFIELD APPOINTED COMMANDER-IN-CHIEF

THE good sense and judgment of Sir William Denison, with the cordial co-operation and support of Sir Hugh Rose, had extricated the Government of India from a somewhat dangerous military and political crisis on the north-west border; and although the fierce passions of the tribes had been considerably roused, the excitement gradually cooled down when our troops returned to the plains. One hill chief, however, had the temerity to come into the open, and make a dash at one of our patrolling columns, but was speedily driven back. I forget his exact name, but by the English soldiers he was commonly called Sawdust Khan. In the unsettled condition of the frontier, the Commander-in-Chief found it necessary to remain for some weeks at the large and important station of Peshawur, which stands half encircled by the Afghan mountains and only a few miles distant from the entrance to the celebrated Kyber Pass.

Peshawur, the central military position at this part of our territory, has a large old-fashioned mud fort, containing considerable reserves of armaments, munitions, and stores. It is probably strong enough to resist the desultory attacks of Afghan tribes; but in my opinion it would be more convenient, and more prudent from a military point of view, were the chief reserves of the district withdrawn to Attock, on the other side of the Indus.

The Afghan hill-men at the time of our visit were in a very lively condition, and constantly robbing the station. The very first night that the large camp of the Commander-in-Chief was pitched on the plain outside, although guards and patrols were plentiful, they succeeded in carrying off some bullocks and two camels, and the theft of horses was not of rare occurrence. The frontier chiefs, however, were friendly to a limited extent, and on one occasion accompanied a party of us for a few miles within the rocky defiles of the Kyber, which at that time had not been visited by any Englishman for years. They made it a condition, however, that we should trust ourselves entirely to their protection, and not take any military escort; and they loyally carried out the compact. Our relations with them at the time, were, in fact, a curious mixture of friendship by day, combined with occasional brigandage on the part of their followers by night.

Towards the end of February the camp of Sir Hugh Rose and the staff marched slowly southwards through the Punjab, crossing in succession by bridges of boats, the Indus, Jhelum, and Chenab rivers to Lahore. What with the elephants, camels, horses, bullocks, sheep, and goats which, combined with hundreds of followers, form essential features of military out-of-door life in India, the camp resembled an Oriental fair and menagerie more than anything else; and, owing to the vast impedimenta considered essential, the marches did not exceed twelve miles a day.

We took the opportunity one day of visiting the sandy plain of Chilianwallah, on which in 1849 the great battle had been fought between the British army and the Seiks. The 24th Regiment specially suffered great losses on that occasion, and an officer who had been present, informed me that on the evening of the battle the bodies of thirteen officers of that regiment were laid side by side in the mess-tent, including the colonel (Pennycuick) and his son, the adjutant. The obelisk erected on the plain in memory of the conflict bears the following inscription: 'Around this tomb was fought the sanguinary battle of Chilianwallah, 13th January, 1849, between the British forces under Lord Gough, and the Seiks under Rajah Sher-Sing. On both sides did innumerable warriors pass from this life dying in mortal combat. Honoured be the graves of these heroic soldiers! In memory of those who fell in the ranks of the Anglo-Indian Army, this monument has been raised by their surviving comrades, at whose side they perished, comrades who glory in their glory, and lament their fate.'

Having served for six years and a half continuously in India, and having obtained leave of absence, I left the camp on its arrival at Lahore, hurried to Calcutta, and embarked for England in April. As, however, many changes were still in progress, in respect both to the *personnel* and *matériel* of artillery, and in the Ordnance Department in India, it was deemed expedient that I should cut short my visit home; and in October I accordingly returned to resume my duties and landed in Bombay. As regards the Ordnance Department, the fact was that, owing to the triplicate system of military administration, which had prevailed in the days of the old East India Company, the arrangements in each presidency varied; and the armaments, munitions, and stores were not identical in pattern, whilst many were old and obsolete. The depots were scattered about without much reference to strategical considerations, and were too numerous. The system was not only costly but inefficient; and, in view of the great advances of artillery science, a general re-organisation had become necessary. During my visit to

England, I had been in communication with Sir Charles Wood, the then Secretary of State for India, on these matters.

On arrival at Bombay I had an interesting conversation with the Governor, Sir Bartle Frere, on military subjects; more especially as to whether the native troops should be thoroughly trusted and armed with the best modern weapons, or be relegated, as it were, to an inferior position, and be looked on as more or less subordinate auxiliaries. I gave my opinion that a policy of mistrust was not only a mistake, but would in reality defeat itself; that the native regiments should be armed and equipped like the English soldiers in every respect; the numbers to be maintained, and their nationalities, resting of course with the Government. It was a satisfaction to find that Sir Bartle Frere entirely concurred in these views.

Leaving Bombay, and being anxious to rejoin Sir Hugh Rose quickly, I travelled through Central India, first of all for about three hundred miles on a partly finished railway, with occasional breaks; and then for five hundred miles outside a mail-cart, passing hastily through Indore, Gwalior, Agra, and Delhi to Meerut. Although I found time to make a few hasty sketches, it has always been a matter of regret that military exigencies rendered me unable to pay more than mere flying visits to so many native cities of great historical and architectural interest. Delhi and its neighbourhood especially is rich in picturesque mosques, tombs, palaces, and forts of the former Mogul dynasties.

On arrival at Meerut I found that Sir Hugh Rose had seriously injured himself, having broken several ribs by a fall out hunting, so that for the time our movements were at a standstill. However, early in 1865, as soon as he had recovered, the head quarters staff continued their tour, and arrived at Lucknow, where a somewhat amusing incident occurred. During the Mutiny, an officer had gained the Victoria Cross for gallant conduct in the residency, but owing to some delay had not actually received the decoration; and the Commander-in-Chief was therefore glad of the opportunity of presenting it to him on the very spot where he had gained it. A general parade was ordered, the troops to be formed up round the ruins of the residency; and all the civilians and ladies of Lucknow were invited to be present. On the morning, when the hour of parade was at hand, the staff assembled in readiness in a bungalow, and it was understood that the Commander-in-Chief was preparing an appropriate speech for the occasion. Search was then made for the box containing the Victoria Cross, but it was nowhere to be found, and after an anxious hurried inquiry we discovered that by some mistake it had been left behind at Simla in the Himalayas. This was awkward, especially as Sir Hugh would naturally be annoyed at so unfortunate an error. The suggestion was made that some officer of the garrison should be asked to lend his for the occasion; but that also failed, no officer nearer than Cawnpore (fifty miles off) having gained one. There was no time to be lost, and at length Colonel Donald Stewart,[1] the Deputy Adjutant General, volunteered to inform the Commander-in-Chief: an offer which was at once accepted. Stewart on entering the room found Sir Hugh engaged in considering his speech, and then cautiously and gently announced that a slight mistake had occurred, and that the Victoria Cross had been left behind. The Commander-in-Chief, as anticipated, was angry, and complained that he had been treated with neglect. However, after he had cooled down, Donald Stewart said that in his opinion the difficulty could readily be got over; and, taking the cross of the Companionship of the Bath from his breast, suggested that it should be presented to the officer on parade, in lieu temporarily of the other; pointing out that the troops and the assembled company would not be near enough to distinguish the difference. Sir Hugh at once took in the situation, accepted the compromise, and acted accordingly. The decoration was

[1] Now Field-Marshal Sir Donald Stewart, G.C.B.

presented, the Commader-in-Chief made an appropriate speech, and the demonstration altogether was a success. My remark to the officer afterwards was that as the Queen had given him the Victoria Cross, and the Commander-in-Chief the Bath, I thought he was entitled to wear both for the future. There was a ball in the evening in honour of the occasion, and in default of a real cross he had to wear a painted leather imitation one.

In March 1866 the term of office of Sir Hugh Rose came to a close. His services in India had been of an eventful and distinguished character, not only in the field, in his celebrated march through Central India during the Mutiny, but also in military administration at a period of important changes. The position of a Commander-in-Chief in India, always a difficult one, was peculiarly so during his term of office. The extinction of a great institution such as that of the old East India Company could not be accomplished without considerable difficulty and delay; prejudices had to be overcome, and vested interests to be considered. All these circumstances must be borne in mind in judging the career of Sir Hugh Rose from 1857 to 1865. The appointment of Sir William Mansfield as his successor, an officer of long experience in the country, and of great ability as an administrator, tended to complete the work, and to produce unity of system, so essential an element of military efficiency. As he acted in concert with the Viceroy Sir John Lawrence, old prejudices and difficulties gradually disappeared, to the great advantage of the army and to the security of the Empire.

CHAPTER XXI

THE WAR IN BOOTAN

During 1865 another border war occurred in India; not as usual on the north-west frontier, but with Bootan, an almost unknown country away in the far East, and north of the great river Brahmapootra. The causes were of the usual character—incessant depredations in our districts of Assam and Cooch-Behar. The territory of Bootan, with a length of about 250 miles, lies amidst the southern slopes of the highest ranges of the Himalayas, the eternal snows forming its frontier towards Thibet. It is, in fact, a country of stupendous mountains, intersected by narrow, precipitous valleys and rapid streams. The rainfall is excessive;[1] and all along its southern border, in the low grounds at the foot of the mountains, are dense forests and marshy jungles, almost impenetrable and choked with vegetation. The whole of the lower district is very unhealthy, and is the home of wild elephants, rhinoceros, and tigers—natural zoological gardens, in short, free of

[1] The rainfall in that part of India is said to exceed 600 inches a year.

charge. The people of Bootan have little or no organised military force, and such fighting men as exist are only armed with knives, bows and arrows, and a few matchlocks; so that in a military sense they are not at all formidable. The inaccessible nature of the country is its best, and indeed almost its only, defence. The people are Chinese in type, and nominally Buddhists in religion; but, though brave and hardy, are almost entirely uncivilised, and the ruling authorities are weak and treacherous. The government of Bootan appears to be of a duplicate character; one rajah being a kind of spiritual head of the State without power, whilst another has all the power but apparently no head. The result, as might be expected, is frequent anarchy, whilst the subordinate rulers along the frontier district tyrannise over the people and plunder their neighbours at discretion. For a century past, indeed, the people, instigated by their chiefs, had incessantly committed depredations in our territories in the plains: carrying off men and women as slaves, and also elephants, buffaloes, and property of all kinds. Remonstrances had been made time out of mind, and missions sent to try and bring them to reason; but all our efforts were met by incivility, almost amounting to insult, and by evasion. The rulers of the country, no doubt, relied in a great measure on its inaccessibility; and, ignorant more or less of our power, were defiant and treacherous accordingly.

In 1864 the Government of India decided on sending a mission, under the Honourable Ashley Eden, to Poonaka, the capital. His instructions were to demand the release of all captives, and to endeavour to arrange for peaceful commercial intercourse in the future. Leaving Darjeeling in January, he crossed the river Teesta, the western boundary of Bootan; but throughout his long and difficult journey to the interior, although he succeeded in reaching Poonaka, and although the poor villagers appeared well-disposed, he was met with evasion and constant delay from those in authority; and, when he arrived at length at the capital, the conduct of the Government was so threatening and grossly insulting that he only got away with difficulty, having under compulsion signed an obnoxious treaty, which, on his return to India in April, was immediately disavowed and repudiated.

It was quite evident that, unless we were content to submit to violence and insult, the time had fully arrived for a recourse to arms. An expedition was arranged accordingly, and our troops entered Bootan from the plains in three separate, widely detached columns, of no great strength.[1] The one in the East marched a few miles up a gorge to Dewanghiri, and took it; but subsequently, on being attacked, abandoned the position, and fell back with the loss of

[1] See map of Bootan.

two guns. The temporary defeat was, however, speedily avenged by a force under the command of the late General Tombs, of which the 55th Regiment under Colonel Hume [1] formed part, and the place was retaken and held. The centre column also advanced into the hills and established itself at Buxa; whilst the third assaulted and captured Dalimkote, an old fort on a mountain ridge in the western ranges, and about 5,000 feet above the sea.

Dalimkote, a few miles from the plains, was only formidable owing to its almost inaccessible position; and our troops engaged in its capture had to climb the steep sides of the mountain, by tortuous and narrow paths, and through thick jungles. In fact, the whole neighbourhood was a mass of dense forest and luxurious undergrowth. The officers and men of a battery of artillery had managed with difficulty to carry a small mortar up the hill-side with a view to a short bombardment, preceding assault. Hardly had it been brought into action near the entrance gate than by some unfortunate accident a barrel of gunpowder exploded, killing Captain Griffin, R.A.,[2] both his lieutenants, and six gunners, besides wounding several others. The small garrison, however, did not wait for an assault, but bolted, and the fort fell into our hands.

[1] Now General Sir Henry Hume, K.C.B.

[2] Captain Griffin had been in command of a battery, and had done excellent service during the previous frontier war of Umbeylah. The names of the two lieutenants were E. Walker and E. A. Anderson.

Our columns had not penetrated for any great distance into the country, still the occupation of three important passes not only prevented the Booteas from plundering, but also put a stop to their commerce, which, though comparatively trifling in amount, proved a great blow to these isolated mountaineers; so that, after many attempts at evasion, towards the end of 1865 they were prepared to come to terms. Being desirous of visiting a part of the country so little known, and of so much interest at the time, I left Calcutta in January, made a rapid journey of about 400 miles due north to Darjeeling, and from that hill station started on an expedition for a fortnight along the Bootan frontier, returning by a voyage down the river Brahmapootra. The first part of the journey from Calcutta to the Ganges was by rail; and having crossed the river to Caragola, I was then carried by coolies in a palanquin, a sort of elongated bandbox, for 120 miles to the foot of the mountains, not meeting a single Englishman during the journey. The country was perfectly flat, and at night a native walked in front with a lighted torch, in order, so it was stated, to scare away the tigers. The coolies as they carried me along sometimes broke out into a low monotonous chant, occasionally varied by a dismal moaning chorus. I tried to ascertain the burden of their song, and found that it was myself, and that the coolie refrain was

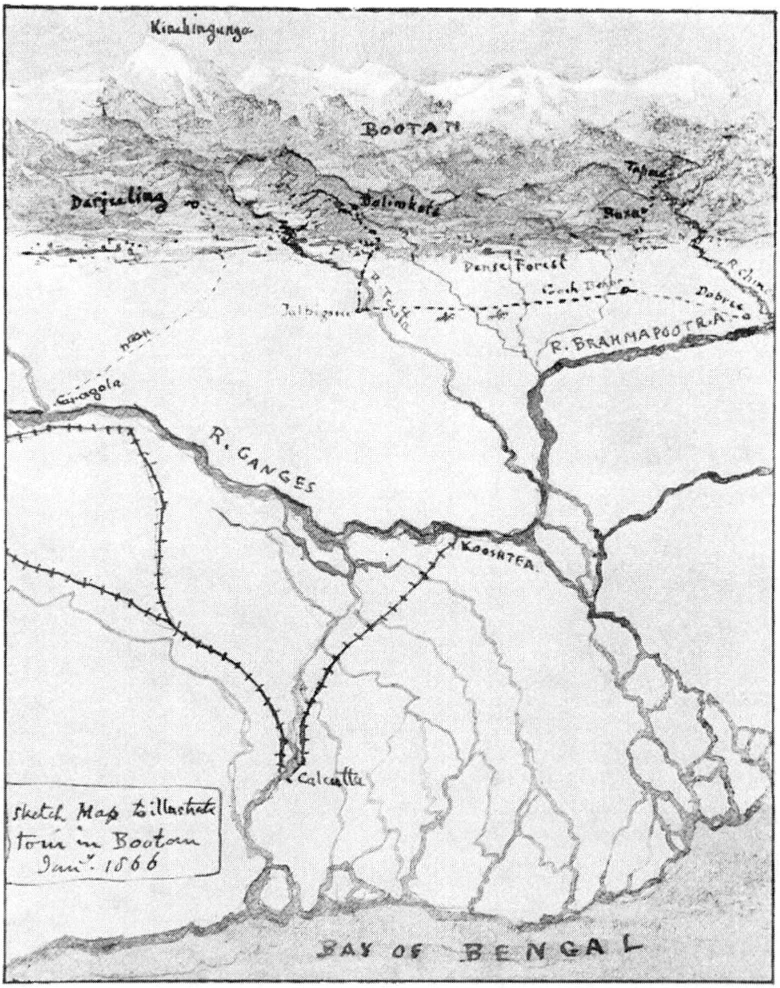

SKETCH MAP TO ILLUSTRATE TOUR IN BOOTAN, JANUARY 1866

somewhat as follows: 'This is a heavy man. Oh! what a fat man,' and so on. Colonel Bourchier, R.A.,[1] joined me in the 'Terai,' a narrow belt of marshy forest lying at the foot of the slopes; and then, on a couple of mules, we ascended the Himalayas to Darjeeling. Not being encumbered with any baggage to speak of, our arrangements for the expedition were simple. Leaving Darjeeling, we rode due East for about twenty miles, and by a gradual descent reached the banks of the Teesta, a rapid river about 100 yards wide, remaining for the night in the hut of a young officer who, with a picket of native troops, was in charge of this corner of the frontier. The scenery was charming, and we met occasional parties of Booteas carrying fruit to the Darjeeling market.

The passage across the Teesta was by means of a cane bridge; and, considering that the inhabitants are ignorant and uncivilised, was a wonderful specimen of ingenuity and skill. These bridges, of which there are several in different parts of the country, are on the suspension principle, and made entirely of bamboo canes fastened together. There is not a nail or a single piece of rope used in the whole construction. They swing about in an uneasy way in passing over them; and as the canes soon become rotten, the whole structure gradually perishes and falls into the river, and has to be renewed. Indeed, as I understood,

[1] Now General Sir George Bourchier, K.C.B.

they require re-building annually. Our mules were pushed into the rapid torrent and pulled across by a long line, also made of flexible bamboos and devoid of string. Altogether it was a curious experience; and we felt much sympathy for the young officer who had to pass months on guard in this secluded valley, without a fellow-countryman to speak to. After crossing the Teesta, we entered Bootan territory, began a long ascent, and at the top of a mountain found another officer with a picket in a solitary stockaded fort. The scenery all round was magnificent. Dense forests filled the deep valleys, and far away to the north stood the snowy crest of Kinchinjunga, 28,000 feet high, standing out clear in the horizon.

Proceeding along over the mountains, we passed an old monastery at Tasigimpoo, and in the evening reached a deserted Bootea stockade, where we remained for the night. The country seemed to be thinly inhabited, but the few people we met were good-natured and friendly. I had been warned not to sleep in the jungle, as we should be devoured by leeches; so, what with possible tigers on the one hand, and hungry leeches on the other, caution was necessary. However, I escaped, except that on one occasion a superfluous leech—not a tiger—attacked my leg during the night. Otherwise all went well, and the following evening, passing through glades of oak, we came in sight of the picturesque old walled fort of Dalimkote, overlooking the plains of Bengal, and surrounded with feathery woods of bamboo.

Although the war was supposed to be virtually at an end, I had been informed by Sir John Lawrence before leaving Calcutta that their chief warrior Tongso Penlow was still at large and defiant, and sure enough on arrival at Dalimkote it was found impossible to advance further into the country. Consequently, in order to reach the next column at Buxa we were compelled to return to the plains, and after a ride of fifty miles reached Julpigoree on the Teesta. During the night horses were placed along the road eastwards to Cooch Behar; and, sending on our baggage with a native servant on an elephant, we started early the following morning, galloped for sixty miles over the plains, and, crossing several rivers on rafts, reached Cooch Behar in the afternoon. There was no time to spare, so after a few hours' rest we turned our faces again northwards, and after another long ride reached the centre column at Buxa. The hostility of Tongso Penlow had thus compelled us to make a detour of about 150 miles; but leaving Buxa, pushing on over the mountains, and then down to the deep secluded valley of the Chin-chu, we at length reached our most advanced post at the small village of Tapsee, and were rewarded by a view of the magnificent scenery of a country hitherto unknown and unexplored. Our pioneers had for some months past been engaged in constructing a road towards the interior, cutting through forests, blowing up rocks, and constructing temporary bridges over precipitous gorges and mountain torrents. We were, in short, advancing steadily through a remarkable and very difficult country towards Poonaka; and the perception of this fact no doubt compelled the Bootan Government at length to sue for peace, and caused even the warlike Tongso to cease his opposition. Hurrying back by forced marches, I took leave of Colonel Bourchier at Cooch Behar; and then finally, after a long solitary gallop, reached Dobree, on the Brahmapootra, just in time to get on board a steamer on its return voyage. Although several hundred miles from its mouth, the river at Dobree resembled a great inland sea. Its navigation, owing to numerous sandbanks, is somewhat dangerous, so that we could only move during daylight, passing numerous picturesque native boats and occasional alligators, lying like logs of grey wood along its banks. After a few days we arrived at Kooshtea, near the junction of the Ganges and Brahmapootra, and then reached Calcutta by railway. The expedition was hurriedly carried out; still it was most interesting in its variety, and in giving a glimpse, at all events, of a country so peculiar and hitherto so little known.

WAR IN BOOTAN, 1866. OUTPOST IN VALLEY OF THE CHINCHU

CHAPTER XXII

FAREWELL TO INDIA—RETURN TO REGIMENTAL DUTY AT WOOLWICH—APPOINTED DIRECTOR OF ARTILLERY—WAR OFFICE ORGANISATION

HAVING completed an almost continuous service of nine years in India, the time had at length arrived for my return to England. After many wanderings in distant lands, it is always a happiness to return home; still, no one, I think, can derive other than benefit from a residence for a time in the great empire which England has established in the East. To a soldier the experience gained is invaluable, not only in regard to the incidents of camp life and of marching, but also from the exceptional character of the campaigns in which our troops are so often engaged. Desirous as the Government may be for peace, still even now other military expeditions may be looming in the future; and under any circumstances the preparations for possible wars require constant care and watchfulness. Indeed, in the wide range of their duties in India, the officers and men of the British forces gain a varied experience such as does not fall to the lot of any other European army.

The subjects of interest in our Eastern dominions are, however, by no means confined to arrangements for military expeditions. The various races of people whose customs, laws, and religions are so diverse in themselves, and so different from our own, the remarkable history of the country in the years gone by, and its successive invasions—all these are matters of a specially interesting character; and never more so than at the present time, when the results of our conquest, and the effects of modern civilisation, are beginning to exert so powerful an influence amongst the millions over whom we hold sway. Old customs and ancient superstitions are being rapidly and almost violently disturbed. In short, the establishment of our rule in the country is not only an unprecedented event, but involves a gradual and an almost entire change in the views and habits of the people. We have given them internal peace, sound laws, and safety of life and property, such as they have never enjoyed before; but we cannot stand still. Enlightenment, and the diffusion of what is termed education, are gravely affecting the character of the people; and it is not sufficient to guarantee them a mere peaceful existence; we must look forward to the results as they develop, and as we commenced by a bold policy, to subjugate a vast continent, so we must equally boldly be prepared to trust the people, and gradually to allow all ranks and classes to take part in the political, civil, and military events as they arise. By consistently and courageously following out such a policy, we shall present a noble spectacle to the world of a great, prosperous, and, what is more, an enduring empire established by England in the East. We have, indeed, but one course to pursue.

Military service at home in time of peace is naturally of a less interesting character than travels and occasional expeditions in distant lands; and the training of young soldiers at Woolwich, which fell to my lot for some time after my return to England, did not present incidents of a striking character. At one period, I remember, there was a considerable dearth of recruits, especially of drivers for the horse artillery, partially due to the frequent changes in war office regulations as to the height and dimensions of the men enlisted. We were allowed to take short men, provided they were of exceptional width of chest and shoulders. Meeting an old recruiting serjeant one day, I inquired if he had been successful, but he was by no means sanguine; and, on my pressing him for the reason of his comparative failure, he replied: 'Beg your pardon, sir, but the Almighty doesn't make the men the shape you order 'em.'

I received occasional curious letters from soldiers, one or two of which are worth quotation. The first was from a gunner who was anxious to be married, as in the days of long service it was necessary to obtain previous permission from the commanding officer. It is as follows: 'Sir, I beg you will pardon the liberty I take, in requesting the favour of your permission on a subject which depends on my future happiness. During my stay in Winchester, I have formed an attachment with a highly respectable young person, to whom I wish to develop my sentiments, by a matrimonial engagement, for which purpose may I beg, sir, the favour of your liberty?' The man, so far as my recollection goes, was duly married, and happy ever afterwards.

The second letter accidentally fell into my hands, and is of a romantic character, from a soldier to a girl to whom he was devoted. 'My darling Jane, it is with great Plesur that I sit down to right a fue lines to you, with the intenchun of cheering your drooping sperits, for the tempest that ranges before you, the storm is hie, the tempest's winds blows through the parish, the throushes is warbling their songs of melode, but by far the sweetest song thare singing, his hover the water to Charley' . . . and so on.

Whilst stationed at Woolwich an incident occurred connected with a young artillery officer, of Irish family, who had been absent for some years on foreign service; and who, on his return to Woolwich, was taken to the large handsome messroom to see some recent improvements. Amongst other things, a new patent stove was pointed out to him; and it was explained that, whilst it gave the same amount of heat as the old fireplace, there was a considerable economy of coal—in fact, there was a saving of half the fuel. The officer at once remarked: 'If one stove saves half the fuel, why don't you buy two of them, and save the whole of it?' This view had never occurred to the Mess Committee.

It was not until the early part of 1870 that I again took an active part in military administration, being unexpectedly offered the appointment of Director of Artillery at the War Office, by the Minister for War, Mr. Cardwell, whom until then I had never seen. It happened to be a period when considerable reforms in the army were under consideration; and I was fortunate in being associated for three or four years with a statesman of resolution and great ability, who, in the face of much opposition, parliamentary and other, laid the foundation of several important and beneficial changes, not only in the War Office itself, but also in the terms of soldiers' service and in general improvement of their condition. In order to understand the general bearing and scope of some of the chief reforms inaugurated by the late Lord Cardwell during his term of office as Minister, it will be desirable to give short accounts of the arrangements formerly existing in each case; and as some of his measures, from their nature, only arrived at maturity years after he had ceased to be Secretary of State, I propose to trace their gradual development, and the results achieved, down to the present day.

One of the first subjects which engaged the attention of Mr. Cardwell was the difficult one of War Office administration. The authority over the army was formerly more or less of a dual character; the *personnel* of the infantry and cavalry being under a Commander-in-Chief, whilst a Master General had charge of the ordnance corps, as well as the provision of armaments for the naval and military services. These arrangements would not in themselves at first sight appear to have much to recommend them, the responsibility being rather diffused. Still it must be remembered that they bore successfully the stress of the great wars at the end of the last and in the earlier years of the present century. As the Master General was always a distinguished officer, and was often a member of the Cabinet, and further was assisted by a board, some of whom were men of military experience and in Parliament, the system apparently suited itself more or less to our constitutional form of government. The great Duke of Wellington, who was for some time Master General, stated that the Ordnance Department was careful, economical, and efficient. He spoke of it as one of the most ancient departments of the monarchy, and that it was a pattern for others.[1] When, in 1849, a proposal had been made to abolish the board, he strongly opposed it, and said: 'I warn the Government of the danger of this alteration in a military view.' Sir Henry Hardinge, and other experienced General Officers who had held the same office, were of similar opinions.

When at length, after a peace of nearly forty years, we again in 1854 took part in a great European war, the difficulties which at once ensued, the enormous cost involved, and the sufferings of our troops during the winter in the Crimea, led the Government of the day suddenly to inaugurate a new *régime*; and early in 1855 the administration of the army in all its departments was vested in a Minister for War. In short, we made the somewhat hazardous experiment of swopping horses when crossing a stream. As a matter of general principle, it is probable that some such arrangement was desirable, an army being a department of the State which requires concentration of authority. But it is to be observed that the Minister for War is usually a civilian, and changes with each Government, so that neither concentration of knowledge nor unity of purpose neces-

[1] Clode's *Military Forces of the Crown*, ii. 765.

sarily followed on the change; and, further, when the new system came into force the Master General and board, instead of being simply absorbed, were abolished, their duties being divided in a slap-dash fashion amongst various departments. Mr. Clode[1] says that after the first Cabinet of Lord Palmerston as Premier, early in 1855, the Secretary-at-War 'brought home half a sheet of paper, containing a memorandum that the Ordnance Department was to be abolished.'

It is hardly a matter of wonder that this sudden concentration of the military departments in a new War Office, under a parliamentary chief, and in the midst of a great war, should have led to some confusion, which continued for several years. Soon after Mr. Cardwell became Minister, he appointed a committee under Lord Northbrook (then Under-Secretary) to investigate the matter; and the results of their inquiries led to a reconstruction, in 1870, of the various departments on an intelligible and sound basis. The War Office was then divided into three main branches: (1) *personnel*, under the Commander-in-Chief; (2) *matériel*, that is, armaments for navy and army, fortifications, barracks, commissariat and clothing, under a Surveyor General of Ordnance, who it was specially stated should be an experienced officer—in fact, it was a virtual revival of the office

[1] Clode's *Military Forces of the Crown*, ii. 251.

of Master General; (3) finance, to be represented by an Under-Secretary in Parliament.

The arrangement was simple, and soon in working order; but, unfortunately, after Mr. Cardwell had ceased to be War Minister one of its main principles was ignored, and the office of Surveyor General, which obviously required military experience, came to be regarded chiefly as a civil and political appointment, and was usually conferred on a member of Parliament, coming and going, of course, with the Government of the day. The result was a gradual weakening of the whole organisation. As a proof of the numerous changes which may occur, I may point out that between 1883 and 1887 there were no less than five Ministers for War, and four Surveyors General, all civilians, in office in rapid succession.

It so happens that in 1887 there were two Royal Commissions, the one under the late Sir James Stephen, and the other under Sir Matthew Ridley; both of whom advised the revival of the Master General. Sir James Stephen's Commission said: 'The office of Master General of the Ordnance should be revived, so far as the management of the stores and manufacturing departments is concerned. He should be a soldier of the highest eminence. . . . Sir Matthew Ridley said: 'That the intentions of Lord Northbrook's Committee of 1870 have not been carried out, and the idea of securing the highest professional acquirements for the position has been entirely abandoned. . . . We are of opinion that the Surveyor General of the Ordnance should in future be what he was intended to be, viz. a military officer of high standing and experience, and that he should not be a member of the House of Commons.'

Their views, however, were not acted on; and in 1888 the office of Surveyor General was abolished, and its numerous duties sub-divided, some being transferred to the already over-burdened shoulders of the military staff, and the rest handed over to the Financial Secretary; and this condition of affairs exists to this day. In short, the War Office is now divided into two branches: the one military, with great responsibilities; the other civil and financial, with great power.[1] In my judgment, should war occur, such a system would inevitably break down at once. Further evidence, however, exists, which will, I think, be conclusive on this point. In 1890 still another Royal Commission, that of Lord Hartington, examined and reported on this question, so vital to military efficiency; and it is to be observed that of its members three had already held the office of Minister for War—namely, Lord Hartington, the late Mr. W. H. Smith, and Mr. Campbell Bannerman. In their report they practically condemn the system

[1] See evidence of H.R.H. the Commander-in-Chief (*Second Report of Committee of the House of Commons on Army Estimates*, 1888, pp. 27, 35, 36, and 52.

then and now existing. In the first place, they point out that the various heads of the spending departments have no direct access to the Secretary of State and are subordinate one to the other. They consider that the present organisation of the War Office is defective in principle, and they go on to recommend that the heads of departments should be directly associated with the Minister for War[1]—in short, a board of officers, such as now exists at the Admiralty.

In considering this great national question I would point out that this country holds quite an exceptional position as regards its military arrangements and preparations for war. Other nations maintain far larger armies, but their troops as a rule have no foreign duties, or distant possessions to protect. Our condition is much the reverse. We are a great naval, military, Indian, and colonial empire; with fleets, troops, fortresses, and reserves of munitions to maintain in every quarter of the world; and it is essential, not only that the two fighting services should act in unity, but that their armaments should be identical in pattern, and that the reserves at home and abroad be available for both. Then, again, on entering on a foreign expedition, we have at once to undertake a most difficult operation in the rapid embarkation

[1] See *Commission on the Administration of the Naval and Military Departments*, February 1890, pp. 57, 67, 70, 78, and 114.

of men, horses, guns, munitions, engineer, medical and commissariat stores; so that from every point of view a strong administration is required, and one in which the unrivalled experience of our officers should be fully utilised and trusted.

No doubt the requirements of constitutional government must be considered and provided for. Indeed, it is essential that the naval and military services should be adequately represented in Parliament, and this principle was fully recognised in the years gone by. For instance, in 1829, when the Duke of Wellington was Prime Minister, and when our military expenditure was far less than now, the army was officially represented in the two Houses of Parliament as follows:—

Secretary of State, War, and Colonies	General Sir George Murray, G.C.B.
Commander-in-Chief	General Lord Hill, G.C.B.
Master General of Ordnance	General Lord Beresford, G.C.B.
Secretary at War	General Sir Henry Hardinge, K.C.B.
Clerk of Ordnance	Rt. Hon. Spencer Percival
Lieut.-General of Ordnance	Lieut.-Gen. Lord Edward Somerset.
Surveyor General of Ordnance	Major-Gen. Sir Henry Fane, K.C.B.
Principal Storekeeper	Colonel Trench
Clerk of Deliveries	General Phipps
Secretary to Master General	Colonel Lord Downes
Treasurer of Ordnance	William Holmes
Paymaster-General	Rt. Hon. J. Calcraft
Judge Advocate General	Rt. Hon. Sir John Beckett

We must always bear in mind that the army is no mere inanimate piece of machinery. On the contrary, it is one of the most vital and powerful elements of the State; and its efficiency can only be maintained by placing the administration of its various departments in the hands of competent and experienced general officers, and investing them with adequate power. If I have dwelt at some length on this abstruse subject, it is because, having served both as Director of Artillery and Surveyor General of Ordnance, I have gained some insight into its difficulties, and feel earnestly the necessity of re-organising the department.

Although the War Office, as will be seen, is a department of hard work and great responsibility, still even within its gloomy portals there are now and then incidents and stories of an amusing character. Many years ago, when the late Sir Cornewall Lewis was Minister for War, on one occasion he visited the infantry depot at Warley in Essex, and was shown a handsome room.[1] After admiring its proportions he inquired as to its use, when, suddenly observing a wooden vaulting horse at the far end of the building, he said: 'Oh! I see—the riding school.'

The late Lord Longford, who had seen much active service both in the Crimea and India, was Under-Secretary for War in 1867. He was an excellent administrator, and occasionally very humorous in

[1] The gymnasium.

his minutes. At the period in question it so happened that there were two officers of high rank and position in the War Office who disagreed in their views on almost every subject, and were constantly in collision—on paper. The correspondence became so voluminous, and the difficulty so perplexing, that at length the whole matter was placed before Lord Longford. I am unable to give his exact words, but his minute to Sir John Pakington, then Minister for War, was to the following effect. 'Secretary of State,—This is a very interesting correspondence. From a careful perusal I have arrived at the conclusion that both these gentlemen are in the *right*. The case is now for your disposal.'

On another occasion, another Under-Secretary wrote a minute as follows: 'Secretary of State,—This is a very important subject. You will observe that the paper is folded the wrong way.' When Sir Henry Storks was Surveyor General of the Ordnance, he was waited upon by an excellent old messenger, who, however, in his conversation was apt to omit his h's. One day he came into the room, and said: 'Sir 'Enery, Mr. Owl wishes to see you.' 'Who?' asked Sir Henry. 'I never heard of him.' 'Beg your pardon—it is Mr. Owl, the Director of Contracts.' 'Oh, Mr. Howell; show him in!'[1]

[1] I once knew a gentleman of far higher rank than a War Office messenger who laboured under the same defect. We were at one time interested in an association which, though useful, constantly met with opposition. Coming across him one day after a meeting which

Some years ago the Minister for War, so it is said, being desirous of acquainting himself with the work of the different branches, visited the various rooms and inquired as to the details. Meeting a gentleman in the passage, he asked at what hour he usually came to his duty. 'Oh!' said the gentleman in reply, 'I usually stroll in about eleven or twelve o'clock.' 'Stroll in,' said the minister, in surprise; 'then I presume you do not leave until a late hour?' 'Well,' replied the gentleman, 'I generally slip off about three o'clock.' 'Slip off at three?' said the minister, much scandalised. 'Pray, sir, may I ask what department you belong to?' 'Certainly,' said the young man; 'I come every Saturday to wind up the clocks!'

I also remember a curious incident which happened to Lord Cardwell, but which is social rather than military. After he had ceased to be minister, it so happened that the wife of one of his former colleagues in the Government gave birth to a child, and Lord Cardwell called to make inquiries. When the butler opened the door, he announced that her Ladyship was going on well. 'A girl?' said Cardwell, inquiringly. 'No, my Lord.' 'Oh, a boy?' remarked Cardwell. 'No, my Lord.' 'Why, surely—' but before he could say more, the butler interposed, 'Beg pardon, my Lord, but it's a little hare' (heir).

he had attended, I inquired how matters were going on, and he replied, 'I was determined there should be no 'itch, so I brought them up to the scratch.'

CHAPTER XXIII

SHORT SERVICE AND RESERVE

Among the numerous measures carried out by the late Lord Cardwell during the period of his administration of the War Department, none has exercised a wider or more beneficial influence than the introduction of short service and reserve for the non-commissioned officers and men of the army. Indeed, when we consider the results achieved, it seems rather surprising that such a change had not been made long ago, not only in the interests of the men, but also in the reserve of strength which it gives to the country in the event of war.

In considering the subject in its various bearings, both military and financial, it will be desirable to refer shortly to the methods by which we had endeavoured to maintain our forces in former days. During the great wars in which this country was engaged at the end of the last and in the earlier years of the present century, although the arrangements for recruiting occasionally varied, the main principle adopted was one of long service with high bounties on enlistment, and small pensions on retirement. Yet, so difficult was it found to keep the ranks complete, that debtors and even criminals were pardoned on condition of serving abroad.[1] The cost was enormous. For instance, in 1808 the levy and bounty money alone exceeded 40*l.* for each man, before he had been trained or had done a day's service. This was not only wasteful, but led to drunkenness and desertion[2]; and, notwithstanding its cost, the plan failed in providing sufficient recruits, and the army at critical moments was lamentably behind the numbers required. For instance, early in the Peninsular war it was about 43,000[3] short of the desired establishment, and during the Crimean war the deficiency was over 46,000.[4]

The real fact was that the system of recruiting up to 1870 was, and always had been, unpopular. The service was a very hard one. Regiments were kept abroad for upwards of twenty years, often in tropical, unhealthy climates; and of the thousands who enlisted yearly but few ever returned, and even those were often prematurely aged and broken down. It is no wonder that the poor people of the country looked upon enlistment of their sons with dread, and as almost equivalent to a sentence of banishment and

[1] Clode's *Military Forces of the Crown*, vol. ii., pp. 25–60.

[2] *Commissions on Recruiting*, 1861, p. xiii., and 1867, p. x.

[3] *Militia Report of* 1877, app. xvii., p. 546.

[4] *Commission on Recruiting*, 1867, p. 221.

of death. So great was the difficulty, that between 1861 and 1869—although the men were then better paid, fed, and clothed than in former years—the average number of recruits obtained was only 12,546 per annum.[1] In 1867 General Peel, the Minister for War, said that 'the question now is whether the British army should be allowed to collapse.' In that year another Royal Commission was appointed to consider the subject, and in their report said: 'The military history of this country, even up to the date of the last great war in which we were engaged, shows that it has been our practice during periods of peace to reduce our military establishments to the lowest possible point . . . No preparations for a state of war were thought of; and the consequence has been that, when war occurred, everything had to be done in a hurry at the most lavish expense. . . . Men were enrolled and sent half-trained into the field, material manufactured, transport provided, and accommodation for the sick and wounded devised and organised.' They went on to say that 'wars will be sudden in their commencement and short in their duration, and woe to that country which is unprepared to defend itself.'

The above remarks will probably be sufficient to demonstrate the difficulty which the country had experienced over and over again, not only in

[1] *Army Return for* 1880.

maintaining its forces in the field during a campaign, but even in providing sufficient numbers for our garrisons at home and abroad in time of peace. But whatever may have been the merits or shortcomings of the arrangements up to 1870, one point, at all events, was perfectly clear—that the army had no reserve. One or two feeble efforts in that direction had been made, but had failed. When a great war came upon us, the only resource was to try and stimulate recruiting by lowering the physical standard and by raising the bounties, so that often the campaign was over before the desired numbers had been obtained.[1]

The time, indeed, had fully come for a change of system. In March 1869, Mr. Cardwell, speaking in the House of Commons, indicated his intention of abolishing the plan of long enlistments, and the following year introduced the bill affirming the principle of short service and reserve. What he said was 'that in time of peace the army would feed the reserve, and in time of war the reserve would feed the army.' Having confidence in the scheme, he boldly abolished the old costly system of bounty on enlistment. The principle, when first established, was tentative and optional, and naturally required time before a correct opinion could be formed of its

[1] See *Commission on Recruiting*, 1861, p. iii.

progress; indeed, it is only within the last few years that the reserve has developed to its normal figure. The change was much criticised at the time, and it was confidently asserted that men would not care to engage for a short period; and that even were they to do so, the reserves would not be forthcoming if called out. No sooner, however, had the system been adopted than its success year by year became apparent. Not only did the numbers enlisting largely increase, but the proportion of those selecting long service rapidly declined. Then again, although the formation of a reserve was necessarily gradual, we have had two proofs of its reliable nature; the men composing it having been called out, first in 1878 under apprehension of war, and again partially in 1882 during the Egyptian campaign; and in both cases the percentage of absentees was very small. I have already mentioned that during the last years of the long service system the average annual number of recruits was only 12,546, whereas in 1892 no less than 41,659 men joined the army, and the reserve had in January 1894 reached the large figure of 80,349. Before leaving the subject of reserves, it will be as well to mention that Lord Cardwell, in 1870, also gave effect to the Militia Act of 1867, by which a certain number of men of that force, on receiving a small annual bounty, engage to join the regular army in case of war. This reserve now amounts to 30,103, in addition to the numbers just quoted.

These facts are undeniable proofs, not only of the popularity of the present arrangement, but also that the army can at once be largely augmented in case of necessity by men thoroughly trained and in the prime of life. There are, however, other satisfactory elements in the present system. The old feeling that the man who enlisted was virtually lost to his family is becoming a tradition of the past. In former times, as I have said, but few returned, and even they were often prematurely aged by long residence in unhealthy climates; whereas now-a-days the men who come back to civil life are, on an average, little over twenty-six years old, and their numbers amount to more than 17,000 per annum, whilst their few years passed in the army have been beneficial in giving them habits of discipline and obedience.

From a financial point of view—which, it is needless to say, is an important feature—the results are equally satisfactory. In the first place, the enormous sums formerly spent in bounties and levy money are now in a great measure saved. Then, again, the pension list is decreasing. Had the old plan continued, with the army at its present strength, the annual cost of pensions would have been nearly

3,000,000*l.* per annum. It will now gradually decrease to less than one-third of that amount. By an actuarial[1] calculation it is estimated that, taking all charges into consideration, the economy of the present system over the old one will be a saving in the normal of 21·71 per cent. for Great Britain and of 47·2 for India. The above statements are made, not as mere matters of opinion, but as facts founded on official records and parliamentary reports; and afford proofs that whilst military service is more popular, and our strength and elasticity for war considerably greater than formerly, at the same time the annual cost is much less. It may, perhaps, be said that the army estimates are increasing; and my reply is that as the Empire is expanding, it requires not only more men, but more numerous and costly armaments for defence, than in the past.

Even the results just quoted do not conclude the story. Several other incidental advantages arise from the abandonment of long service, which may be shortly alluded to. Many persons, for instance, appear to be under the impression that a large proportion of the men now serving are less efficient in point of age than formerly, but the evidence points the other way.

The following are the ages of the non-commis-

[1] *Actuarial War Office Report*, January 1889.

sioned officers and men serving in January 1871 and 1894 respectively.[1]

Proportion per 1,000 *men*

Year	Under 20	Between 20 & 30	Over 30	Total
1871	190	490	320	1,000
1894	170	742	88	1,000

The above figures are somewhat remarkable, as showing that the number of men of the most serviceable ages (that is, between 20 and 30) has largely increased since the introduction of short service; and I believe that experienced officers will concur with me that the army of 1894 is, in respect of age, superior to that of former days.

Then, again, in the consideration of the foreign duties which devolve on our forces, it is often urged that long service, at all events, is best adapted to meet Indian requirements, on the two grounds that young soldiers cannot stand tropical climates and that frequent reliefs are costly. Neither of these views will bear the test of examination. The report of the sanitary condition of the army in India said that 'upon the whole, early entry into India appears to be an advantage, not only at first, but in after life.'[2] At a subsequent period, Sir Ranald Martin stated that 'all statistical observations go to disprove anything like acclimatisation in the East

[1] *Annual Army Returns*, 1880 and 1894.

[2] *Sanitary Condition of the Army in India*, 1868, p. xxxi.

Indies.' On the contrary, he declares that 'disease and death increase with length of service and age.' Dr. Brydon also said: 'The death-rate of 1871 shows that the death-rate for the men above thirty has been consistently double that of men below that age.'

Lord Airey's Commission of 1880 [1] quoted figures proving that the proportion of deaths, and of invalids sent home, increases in a rapid ratio with age. For instance, the number of deaths and invalids per 1,000 men on the average of ten years is—

	Deaths	Invalids
Under 25 years old	16·06	25·84
Over 85 and under 40	88·71	76·11

The above figures indicate that men should be sent to India young, and not be kept there beyond a few years. If men, whose service in India is prolonged, die twice as fast after thirty as they do when under that age, it is evident that, as they must be replaced by drafts from home, even from a financial point of view such a system is not to be commended. So far from a short period not being adapted for India, it is the only one which ought to be allowed, on grounds alike of humanity, efficiency, and economy.

There still remain a few other points, regarding the men serving in the present day, which are

[1] *Lord Airey's Committee of* 1880, p. 19.

worthy of notice. The effects of the Education Act of 1870 have been very marked on the Army. For instance, the proportion of men in the ranks of what is termed 'superior education' was in 1861 74 per thousand, whereas in 1889 it had risen to 854.[1] Again, as regards crime, in 1868[2] the proportion of courts-martial per thousand was 144, whereas in 1892 it was only 54.

Desertions also are steadily decreasing. In 1858[3] upwards of 20,000 men disappeared. In 1874 the net loss from desertion per thousand was 20. In 1893 it was 12.[4] Finally, there remains one more subject regarding the men in the army on which I would say a few words, and that is the marriage question. So long as a system of long service prevailed, a married establishment of only 7 per cent. was recognised by the Government. The virtual result was, that the great majority of men serving year after year were not allowed to marry; and this state of affairs was neither natural nor desirable, tending also to render military service unpopular. Under the present system, as the great majority of the men only remain for a few years in the ranks, they are for the most part single, and on return to civil life can marry at will.

[1] *Army Annual Returns*, 1881 and 1893.
[2] *Army Annual Returns*, 1880 and 1894.
[3] *Recruiting Commission of* 1861, p. iii.
[4] *Annual Army Return of* 1894.

The foregoing remarks will, I hope, be of some interest in indicating the beneficial effect of the changes introduced as regards service in the army by the late Lord Cardwell, when Minister for War in 1870. The men who now enter the ranks are probably of much the same class as formerly, but they serve under improved conditions; and whilst I believe that they retain all the enterprise and courage of those who preceded them, they are undoubtedly far better educated, and therefore to some extent require more discrimination in their treatment than formerly prevailed.

CHAPTER XXIV

LOCALISATION AND COUNTY REGIMENTS.—INTERVIEW WITH THE EMPEROR NAPOLEON III.

ANOTHER important measure introduced during the administration of the late Lord Cardwell was that of localisation. In the old days, when the infantry regiments were scattered all over the world, and for the most part consisted of single battalions, it had been the custom, on their proceeding abroad, to leave behind a small depot, which was constantly moved about in the United Kingdom and obtained recruits as best it could, without regard to local ties or associations; so that, although many of the older regiments bore county titles, which had been given them so long ago as 1782 by King George the Third, in reality men of the various counties and nationalities served together indiscriminately. Field Marshal Conway, who was Commander-in-Chief at the time in question, specially stated that the object of the King was 'to create a mutual attachment between the county and the regiment, which may at all times be useful towards recruiting.'

The scheme, however, for all practical purposes had no force or reality until 1871. Lord Cardwell first of all established fixed depots in the counties, each representing two battalions; and thus not only engendered local ties, but also brought the regular army into permanent association with the militia and volunteers. In his speech in the House of Commons in February 1871 he emphasised the desirability of combining our military institutions. He said: 'There is the standing army, with its historical association and glorious memories, and having a larger amount of foreign service than any other army in the world; there is the militia, whose theory is conscription, but whose practice is voluntary enlistment; and then there are the volunteers, who have most of the attributes of military life, and all the independence of the most perfect civil freedom. To combine these different institutions in one complete whole is, as I believe, the desire of the House of Commons and of the English nation.' He quoted Mr. Pitt, who in 1803 spoke as follows: 'I am of opinion that to a regular army alone, however superior, however excellent, we ought not solely to trust; but that in a moment so eventful we ought to super-add to the regular army some permanent system of national defence. . . . The army must be the rallying point; the army must furnish example, must furnish instruction, must give us the principles on which that national system of defence must be formed; and by which the voluntary forces of this country, though in a military view inferior to a regular army, would, fighting on their own soil, for everything dear to individuals and important to a State, be invincible.'

These quotations will, I think, give a general idea of the views which were uppermost in the mind of the Minister for War when he gave vitality to the principle of localisation. The change, like many others, was criticised and somewhat retarded, and was not brought into full maturity until several years afterwards. In 1877 a committee on the militia, of which Colonel Stanley[1] was chairman, however, gave the subject a fresh impetus. In their report they spoke strongly of the advantage of unity between the line and the militia, and said: 'We have no hesitation in replying that they should be constituent parts of one body. . . . We consider that this is best to be effected by their being treated as one regiment, such regiment bearing a territorial designation; the line battalions being the first and second, the militia the third and fourth, of such territorial regiment, the depot being common to all.' There was still hesitation and delay, but on Mr. Childers becoming Minister for War in 1880 the recommendations of Colonel Stanley's committee were adopted, and are now in full force; and the beneficial results are

[1] Now Earl of Derby.

becoming more apparent year by year. For instance, General Sir Edward Bulwer, in his report on recruiting in 1887,[1] stated 'that the number of men in infantry regiments, who were born in the district to which the regiment belongs, increases every year.' He also mentions, that upwards of 14,000 militiamen transferred their service to the regular army in the preceding twelve months. The most recent Committee on Army Service, that of Lord Wantage of 1892, speaks plainly on the subject. It says 'the evidence as to the value of the territorial connection is overwhelming;' and added, that the double battalion system is the most economical and best machinery for furnishing foreign drafts and reliefs.[2]

I might go on to allude to other measures connected with the army and its administration which were introduced by Lord Cardwell—to the vigour and influence which he imparted to the Intelligence Department, to the doubling the Field Artillery at home, to the rank of field officer given to captains of batteries, and so on—but it is perhaps hardly necessary. Lord Cardwell did not live to witness the results of some of his measures; but there was hardly a branch of the army which did not feel the benefit of his wise and far-seeing administration.[3]

[1] *Report of Inspector-General of Recruiting*, 1887.

[2] *Report of Lord Wantage's Committee*, pp. 11 and 18.

[3] An important reform carried out by Lord Cardwell was that of the abolition of purchase; but I do not propose to enter into the

In May 1872 I had an interesting interview with the late Emperor Napoleon III. at Chislehurst, only a few months before his death. During his career, he had always shown great interest in artillery questions, and had published works on the subject.[1] In May he expressed a wish to see me, being desirous of discussing a plan for checking the recoil of guns, by means of water compressed within the bore. The nature of his proposal is contained in the following letter.

Camden Place, Chislehurst: Mai 1872.

'Mon cher Général,—Il y aurait une expérience d'artillerie, assez intéressant à faire, et qui, si elle réussissait, pourrait diminuer le recul des grosses bouches à feu. Il s'agirait comme dans le dessin ci-

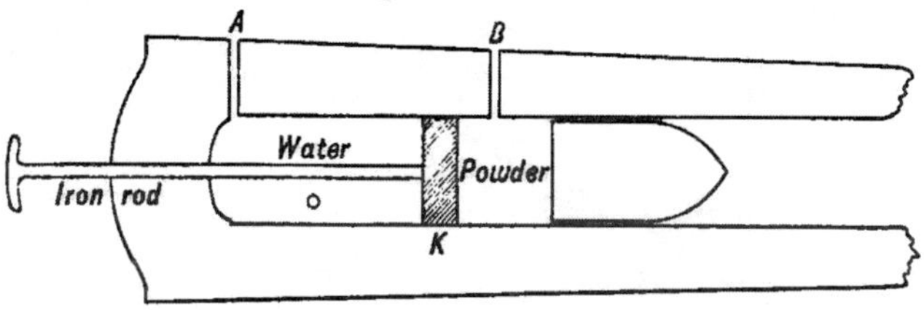

Copy of Sketch by Napoleon III.

joint de prendre un ancien canon, de forer au point A un trou d'un certain diamètre, de forer à un point B une lumière pour mettre le feu. La partie O près

question, as it had been virtually decided before I entered the War Office.

[1] One of his works is entitled *A New System of Field Artillery*, by Louis Napoleon Bonaparte, 1854.

de la culasse serait remplie d'eau. On mettrait auparavant à K une rondelle à gutta-perka pour séparer la poudre de l'eau, et en chargeant le canon comme à l'ordinaire.

'En mettant le feu, à la charge, l'eau jaillirait en dehors par l'orifice A, et la force employée pour rejeter l'eau en dehors du canon diminuerait d'autant le recul. Je ne prétends pas que ce système soit très pratique, mais il serait néanmoins assez intéressant de l'essayer. Je vous confie cette idée pour que vous en fassiez l'usage que vous croirez convenable. Je vous renouvelle, Général, l'assurance de mes sentiments d'amitié.

'NAPOLÉON.

'La question serait de savoir quelle est la quantité d'eau qu'il faudrait introduire dans le canon, et quel diamètre il faudrait donner à l'orifice.'

During the interview, which lasted about half-an-hour, we were quite alone; and he made some pen-and-ink sketches, which he gave me, to illustrate his views. The proposal was ingenious, although it would probably be difficult to apply it in the field.

The Emperor also referred shortly to one or two incidents of the great war of 1870, especially as to the employment of mitrailleurs; and I ventured to point out that, although of use against savage races, they had not, in my opinion, much future in a campaign against a modern army; as, although efficacious for short distances, they were of limited range and power, having neither shattering nor incendiary force, as compared to artillery, whilst they would add considerably to the impedimenta of troops in the field. I was particularly struck by the quiet unimpassioned way in which he alluded to the past; and he certainly appeared to bear his great reverses with fortitude and calm resignation. When the interview ended, I left with him at his request, a small pamphlet on rifled ordnance; and on returning it he sent me the following note:

Camden Place, Chislehurst: le 8 Mai, 1872.

'Je vous renvoie, Général, avec mes remercîments, la brochure que vous avez bien voulu me prêter, et je vous prie de recevoir l'assurance de mes sentiments distingués.

NAPOLÉON.'

Monsieur le Général Adye, Woolwich.

Subsequently, Her Majesty the Empress Eugénie was kind enough to present me with the Emperor's work, 'Organisation Militaire,' dated 'Wilhelmshoehe, 1871,' with her name inscribed upon it.

It so happened that a few months before seeing the Emperor Napoleon I had had an opportunity of discussing the subject of mitrailleurs with General von Blumenthal, who had been chief of the staff to the Crown Prince of Germany during the war; and his views agreed with those I have just expressed. He said that the German soldiers at the outset were considerably impressed with the numerous batteries of mitrailleurs with which the French began the campaign of 1870; but they soon found out that their range was limited, and that by concentrating the distant fire of field guns upon them the mitrailleurs could not hold their ground, but were driven off the field. Prince Frederick Charles said 'that for near ranges he would rather have ten good riflemen; for far ranges a field gun.'

CHAPTER XXV

VISIT TO THE CRIMEA WITH CHARLES GORDON. REPORT ON THE CEMETERIES

In the autumn of 1872 I was sent by the Government to the Crimea, to report on the condition of the British cemeteries and monuments, and also as to their restoration and care for the future. Colonel Charles Gordon (of Khartoum), an old friend of mine, was associated with me in the work. He was at that time a member of the International Commission for improving the navigation at the mouth of the Danube. Travelling rapidly through Europe, I met him at Galatz at the end of August; and we embarked on board H.M.S. 'Antelope,' which had been sent from Constantinople to convey us across the Black Sea. Gordon's views about the work of the Danube Commission were, as usual, rather peculiar. He explained to me that, as the river had been adequately dredged and buoyed, and as the lighthouse at its mouth was completed, there was really nothing more to do; and that the Commission was practically useless. As I understood, he had written to the Foreign Office to that effect, adding also that his salary was too large. In the ordinary concerns of life he was actuated by one principle which is rare—namely, a contempt for the accumulation of money. In fact, he gave it away almost as fast as he received it. His experience in Eastern countries, also, had given him a distrust of pashas and men in high places; and all his sympathies were for the poor and friendless. Soon after our visit to the Crimea he was appointed Governor-General of the Soudan, and it is said that at an interview with Ismail Pasha before starting for Khartoum he objected to the large amount of his salary, as being more than necessary; and when he left, the Khedive remarked: 'What an extraordinary Englishman! He doesn't want money!'

On leaving Galatz, we went first of all to Odessa, to call on General Kotzebue, the Governor-General of Southern Russia, who, however, was unfortunately absent; but we had an opportunity of meeting, and of receiving assistance from him later on. Indeed, during the whole of our visit to the Crimea, every attention was paid to us by the authorities; and two Russian officers were specially detailed to accompany and assist us in our investigations. We arrived at Sebastopol on August 29, and found the city in ruins, and almost exactly in the same condition as when the allied armies had left it seventeen years before. The churches, barracks, theatres, and storehouses were all roofless; and the Malakoff, Redan, and other defences mere crumbling earthworks. All was so quiet and still, and such a contrast to the stirring times of the years gone by, in the hardships and vicissitudes of which Gordon and myself had shared. We seemed to know every inch of the ground, and for many days wandered about, taking notes of the various cemeteries, great and small, scattered over the country.

Although comparatively few officers and men remain of all those who took part in the great Crimean war of forty years ago, its reminiscences will still, no doubt, be of interest to many in the present day; and I will therefore quote some extracts from the report made by Gordon and myself on our return home:[1] 'From the day of our arrival until September 9, we were engaged many hours each day in making a careful inspection of every cemetery and memorial of the British Army in the vicinity of Sebastopol.' 'It will be remembered that after the battle of the Alma the Allies marched on Sebastopol, and in consequence of their long detention before that city the great body of the British Army did not move again during the war, but remained encamped on the plateau on the south side; consequently, with the exception of a few monuments at the Alma and at Kertch, the whole of the cemeteries,

[1] *Report on the Crimean Cemeteries*, December 1872.

one hundred and thirty in number, are to be found on the ground which extends from Sebastopol to Balaclava, and from Kamiesch to the Tchernaya.' 'The cemeteries vary much both in their position and size. Some are in the rocky ravines leading down to the trenches, whilst others are on the hills and downs which surround Balaclava. Some lie in the sheltered valleys about Kadikoi and Karani; but by far the greater number extend along the bare plateau in front of the city, upon which the army so long remained encamped; and pre-eminent among them is that on Cathcart's Hill, distinguished alike by its commanding central position and by the numerous monuments it contains, many of them to officers of high rank and distinction.'[1]

'The cemeteries also differ considerably in the number of graves and monuments which they relatively contain. Some are large, with hundreds of graves, and many inscribed tablets and crosses; others in isolated spots with only a few. A considerable number contain no monuments whatever. The majority are those to officers; but there are also many to soldiers, and a few to women, nurses, or the wives of soldiers.' 'A small proportion of the monuments have been erected since the termination of the war.

[1] We found no less than 122 graves of English officers on Cathcart's Hill, including those of Generals Sir George Cathcart, Fox-Strangways, Goldie, and Sir John Campbell.

Some are of marble, but as a rule they are of the soft stone found upon the spot. They were for the most part hurriedly erected toward the end of the campaign, often by unskilful hands, without sufficient foundations, and with slightly cut inscriptions. Originally there were also a considerable number of wooden crosses. Under these circumstances, it is not surprising that, exposed to the vicissitudes of climate, especially to the rigour of Crimean winters, a large number of them have perished, and almost all of those remaining show signs of weather and decay.' 'The walls which enclose the cemeteries were in the first instance roughly built, without mortar or foundations, and of the loose uncut stones in the neighbourhood. Time and weather have led to their rapid decay, and the shepherds have occasionally hastened the destruction by making entrances for their flocks.' 'We endeavoured to visit every cemetery and memorial of which we could find a record; the total number in the neighbourhood of Sebastopol and Balaclava amounting to 130.[1] The farm-house which was so long the head-quarters of the British Army is well cared for, and in good preservation; and in the room in which Lord Raglan died a marble slab has been inserted in the wall, with

[1] To those persons who had relations or friends buried during the Crimean war, it may be interesting to know that, in the report of 1872 details are given of all the names found on the various tombstones.

the following inscription: "In this room died Field-Marshal Lord Raglan, G.C.B., Commander-in-Chief of the British Army in the Crimea, June 28, 1855."'

'The circumstances of the French Army were very similar to our own, and they had numerous cemeteries widely dispersed from Kamiesch to Baidar. Feeling the inconvenience and difficulty as regards their care and preservation which have so long perplexed ourselves, they determined to disinter the remains of their officers and men, and to remove them to one central spot near the former French head-quarters. This arrangement was carried out in 1863, each cemetery being denuded of its dead, and then abandoned. About 28,000 bodies are said to have been removed; those of the officers having been as far as possible identified.' . . .

'Although a course similar to that followed by the French has been from time to time advocated, with regard to the remains of our officers and men, it does not appear to Colonel Gordon and myself that any general disinterment or removal is necessary or even desirable. Independently of the difficulty, it might almost be called impossibility, after the lapse of so many years, of collecting the remains or of in any way identifying them, we believe that it would be repugnant to the feelings of the Army and of the British public generally that any such plan should be attempted. Our officers and men were buried by their comrades on the ground where they fell; the whole scene is sacred and historical; and the remains of the dead should not be disturbed. As regards the cemeteries generally, our view is that those which contain no monuments should be covered with mounds of earth and turf, and that the ruined walls should be removed.' . . . 'We are of opinion that the larger cemeteries, which contain numerous mementoes and tombstones, should be preserved, a substantial wall being built round them, and that all monuments, tablets, and crosses should be repaired and the inscriptions renewed. The three memorial obelisks at Inkerman, Balaclava, and the Redan, should be protected by a good wall, with a substantial railing. . . .'

These extracts will probably suffice as a general view of the condition of the British cemeteries in the Crimea at the time of our visit, and of the proposals for their restoration, which were subsequently adopted and carried out by the Government. The cost was estimated at 5,000*l*.

Leaving Sebastopol in the 'Antelope,' we called at Yalta, and had an interview with General Kotzebue, who was much interested in our work, and anxious that the British memorials should be respected, at the same time pointing out the difficulty of adequately guarding so large a number. The late Empress of Russia was at the time residing at the Palace of Livadia at Yalta, and sent us a kind message, regretting her inability owing to illness to receive us, and wishing us *bon voyage.* Having paid a short visit to Kertch and Yenikale, at the entrance of the Sea of Azoff, we then returned to Constantinople, and were immediately, for some inscrutable reason, placed in quarantine for a week, although we were all perfectly well.

As soon as we were free, the British Ambassador, Sir Henry Elliot, kindly received us for a few days at his palace at Therapia, on the Bosphorus; and at his request, I paid a visit, accompanied by an interpreter, to the Grand Vizier, Midhat Pasha, who was anxious to discuss the Turkish armaments and defences. I had previously inspected the arsenal and manufacturing departments; and frankly told him that they were in considerable confusion, and that a great deal of money had apparently been wasted in the purchase of second-rate half-obsolete material, partly on the Continent and partly in America; and that, in view of the rapid advances in the science of artillery, and in small arms, I advised prudence and economy. He listened attentively, and his reply was 'Pekki,' which I found meant approbation (literally, 'Very good'); and went on to say, that the lavish expenditure had been incurred by his predecessors, but that he would be careful. He then alluded to the defence of Constantinople against naval attack; and I pointed out that, considering the comparative narrowness of the Bosphorus, it offered great facilities for the employment of ground torpedoes. Midhat Pasha was apparently ignorant on the subject, so I explained as lucidly as possible that a torpedo was a case of gunpowder, which, placed at the bottom of the channel, could be exploded by electricity as the enemy's vessel passed over it; and that such defence was simple, efficient, and cheap. This gave him much satisfaction, and he replied, 'Pekki, Pekki,' with great fervour. I heard afterwards that he had been pleased with the interview, and especially with my economical views. He had, however, no opportunity of acting on them, having been dismissed from office almost immediately afterwards.

Having taken leave of Gordon, who returned to his improvements on the Danube, I then proceeded to Smyrna, where a few British tombs and memorials of the war existed; and on my arrival called on the British Consul, who lived in a charming house overlooking the bay. On expressing my admiration of his residence, the Consul's wife explained that there was a difficulty in keeping it in order, on account of incessant earthquakes; although lately they had been more free from them. Hardly had I returned to the hotel than I heard a rumbling noise. Then the whole house commenced rocking violently to and fro, and it became evident that the overdue earthquake had arrived. Fortunately not much damage was done.

During my stay at Smyrna I paid a visit to Ephesus, meeting Mr. Wood, who had been sent out by the authorities of the British Museum, and was excavating the recently discovered ruins of the temple of Diana. My duties, however, required me to return home; and travelling through France, I took an opportunity, when at Paris, of sketching ruins of a very different character—those of the Tuileries, on which were inscribed in large letters, 'Liberté—Egalité—Fraternité.'

On arriving in England I was invited by Mr. Lowe, the Chancellor of the Exchequer, to call in Downing Street to discuss the purport of my report. The conversation began by his inquiring, somewhat abruptly, whether I considered it one of the duties of the British Government to keep in repair the cemeteries and monuments of the Army in all parts of the world. My reply was that I had never considered so wide and interesting a question, but had limited myself simply to those in the Crimea. He at once said, that the report was sensible enough, involved no great expenditure, and should be carried out; and so we amicably left the main problem unsolved.

Subsequently I sent a few copies of the report

RUINS OF THE TUILERIES, NOVEMBER 1872

Liberté—Egalité—Fraternité

and some photographs to those who had assisted us at Sebastopol; and one of the Russian officers sent me a reply, which, although not altogether perfect in its English, is very friendly in its tone: 'My General,—I have the honour to accept your lovely letter, with the photographie of mitrailleuse, and I your transport my deep thanksgiving. I observe of your letter, that you forget not Sebastopol and cemetery, who to ask by repair. Your report of British Cemetery I have forward of General Kotzebue, and if you possess one copy, take my,' &c.

CHAPTER XXVI

RIFLED ORDNANCE AND NAVAL AND MILITARY RESERVES—APPOINTED GOVERNOR, ROYAL MILITARY ACADEMY—THE BRITISH ARMY IN 1875

ONE of the most important and interesting subjects connected with the Navy and Army of late years, and with the changes in which I was at one time much associated, is that of the gradual advance of modern armaments, not only in size, but in range, power, and accuracy. Until forty years ago the science of artillery had practically remained stagnant ever since the time of the Tudors. Indeed, it may be said that the guns used during the Crimean War, although less cumbersome, were in all essential particulars much of the same type as those of the days of Queen Elizabeth. The introduction, however, of rifled small-arms, and of armour-plating for vessels of war, indicated the necessity of improved ordnance; and what may almost be termed a revolution commenced, which has had many vicissitudes, and even now has hardly reached its final solution.

It was in 1854 that Lord Armstrong first took up the subject, of which he has ever since been acknowledged as one of the chief authorities. He has also rendered good service in the establishment of a manufacturing arsenal at Elswick, which, in the event of a great war, would become of national advantage. The first rifled breech-loading guns of his pattern were adopted in 1859, and gave results in range and accuracy far beyond anything that had hitherto been achieved. They were followed by the introduction of others of a larger calibre; and so enthusiastic were the navy and artillery, that many of our vessels of war and fortresses were speedily supplied with them. Between 1859 and 1862, two millions and a half sterling were expended on new armaments.

Notwithstanding their great success and superiority, however, they developed considerable defects in regard to breech mechanism; and numerous accidents occurred both by sea and land, due in a measure to want of skill in their handling. It became evident from experience in the war in China in 1860, and in Japan in 1862–3, that they were somewhat delicate weapons.[1]

In 1863 the Armstrong and Whitworth competition took place, in which both firms were represented on the committee; and after lengthened trials

[1] *Treatise on Construction of Ordnance*, 1877.

they reported[1] in 1865 that the breech-loading system was inferior for purposes of war to that of muzzle-loading, and was more expensive. Other experiments followed, leading to a similar conclusion, and as a consequence the latter was adopted, and continued in force for many years; the guns rising rapidly in size and in weight from five up to one hundred tons. In 1867 a committee of thirteen artillery officers, under the late Field-Marshal Sir Richard Dacres, inquired into the subject as regards field guns, and reported unanimously in favour of muzzle-loaders. In 1868 the Admiralty were asked whether they wished the subject re-opened as regards naval guns, but they declined.

Having served in India from 1857 to 1866, I had, of course, no practical knowledge of the earlier stages of this difficult and much-debated subject; but on becoming Director of Artillery in 1870, I found that the two services were in practical unanimity as to the advantages of the rifled muzzle-loading system—that it was simpler, better adapted for war, and cheaper than the other. In 1871 the Admiralty were again consulted on the question, but with the same result as before. In that year, a German 9-pounder breech-loading field gun was obtained for comparison with our own; and after a long series of trials the committee re-

[1] *Textbook on Rifled Ordnance*, 1872.

ported that the English gun was superior, not only in simplicity, but in range and power, and in rapidity of fire.[1] It was also known that during the great war of 1870 upwards of two hundred German guns had become unserviceable. All experience, therefore, appeared at the time to point in one direction; but a change gradually arose, the causes of which were partly scientific, partly mechanical.

Whilst the attention of experts was engaged in the effort to produce the best gun, it ultimately proved that the real solution rested not so much with the weapon as with the motive power which gives life and force to the projectile. The question of gunpowder had until about 1870 remained much in the same stagnant, neglected condition as that of ordnance. Long and careful researches were, however, carried out at that time, chiefly by Sir Andrew Noble and Sir Frederick Abel, which led to the introduction of a comparatively mild and slow-burning explosive, and finally determined the system of gun-construction. In the first place, owing to its gradual combustion, the excessive strain on the breech mechanism was much diminished; and further, as an improved system of closing had been adopted, the difficulties, and the accidents at critical moments, which had been so perplexing, were in a great measure at an end. That was one important result;

[1] *Treatise on Construction of Ordnance*, 1877.

but there was a second. As the explosion was no longer instantaneous, but comparatively gradual, it followed that larger charges could be employed, and in order to utilise them greater length of bore became necessary, as, within limits, the longer the gun the greater the initial velocity and consequent range and power.

These altered conditions were manifestly both in favour of breech-loading, not so much as a matter of principle, but of convenience. Sir Andrew Noble, in writing to me on the subject in 1875, said: 'As regards the effects to be produced from a gun, precisely the same results can be attained, whether it be made in the form of a muzzle or a breech-loader. There is no magic, as many seem to imagine, in one form or the other. . . . As regards convenience in using, there may be, and undoubtedly are, differences.' Between 1875 and 1880 experiments were somewhat slowly carried out, with a view to re-introducing breech-loading. Having been appointed Surveyor-General of the Ordnance in the latter year, I advised that the experiments should be pushed on vigorously, and on a larger scale. The adoption of steel, to the exclusion of wrought iron, in the construction of guns, was another important change about to take place; and, with a view to a full consideration of these great questions, Mr. Childers in 1881 re-established a permanent Ordnance Committee, which for some reason had been abolished in 1867. The main principles thus established, the naval and military armaments have since proceeded uninterruptedly. Many improvements, especially as regards quick firing, have recently been introduced; and we have every reason to believe that they are fully equal in all respects to those of any other nation.

That this subject has been a difficult and an anxious one is evident. Lord Armstrong, in his address to the Civil Engineers in 1882, said: 'All breech-loading mechanism is of a nature to require very accurate fittings, and require care both in use and for preservation.' Again, in a work published as late as 1893 by Commander Lloyd, R.N., and Mr. A. Hadcock, late R.A., of the Elswick establishment, they say 'that it has taken all the ingenuity, backed by all the mechanical resources of the present day, to obtain a satisfactory breech-loading arrangement.'[1] The whole question is extremely technical; but I have endeavoured to give an outline of its broad characteristics; and it is evident that the consideration of so vital a question requires a permanent committee of naval and artillery officers, and of scientific civil engineers; we may then feel confidence that the requirements of the two services will be adequately dealt with.

[1] *Artillery, its Progress and Present Position*, 1893. By Commander Lloyd, R.N., and A. C. Hadcock, late R.A.

Even the placid and scientific temperament of an Ordnance Committee may, however, occasionally be subject to a severe strain. Many years ago, a proposal was submitted by some inventor that a small gun, strapped broadside across a horse's back, and fired from that position, would be useful, especially in mountain campaigns. The experiment was made in the Arsenal at Woolwich, the horse's head being tied to a post, with the muzzle of the gun pointed to an old earthen butt; the Committee standing on the other side of the horse to watch the result. The gun was loaded, and, in order to give time, a slow-burning fuse was used to fire it. The Committee, however, in tying the animal's head, had omitted to take the precaution of also making fast its tail. The first result was that, when the horse heard the fizzing of the fuse on its back, it became uneasy and walked round the post, so that the gun, instead of pointing at the butt, was thus directed straight at the heads of the Committee. Not a moment was to be lost; down went the chairman and members, lying flat and low on their stomachs. The gun went off; the shot passed over the town of Woolwich, and fell in the Dockyard; the horse being found lying on its back several yards away. The Committee were fortunately unhurt, and gradually recovered their equilibrium, but reported unanimously against any further trial.

Armaments and Reserves.—Amongst the many subjects which constantly occupy the attention of the War Department is the provision of adequate reserves of armaments, small arms, gunpowder, accoutrements, camp equipage, harness, clothing, and the numerous Engineer, medical, and commissariat stores which have to be maintained in readiness for war, not only in the United Kingdom, but at our stations in various parts of the world. The great majority of these reserves are required for both the fighting services; and until recently have been provided and cared for by the War Office, acting in co-operation with the Admiralty. The subject is not only complex, but very little is known by the public as to its administration and cost. Formerly, the provision of these costly armaments and stores rested with the Ordnance Department; and, as the successive Master Generals were men of the highest distinction and experience in war, the country had a guarantee that the national requirements would be duly considered and maintained. As the Duke of Wellington wrote in 1843, 'the Ordnance Department and the office of Master General is constituted for the service of the Navy as well as that of the Army.'

It is not necessary, nor indeed would it be proper, to give details of the amount of these various reserves, which, of course, have been modified and increased from time to time according to circumstances. It may be sufficient to say that in 1858[1] their value was reckoned as being upwards of eleven millions sterling; and since that date has undoubtedly risen, partly from the increased cost of modern armaments and appliances, and partly from the additional requirements of our enlarged empire.

It is sometimes asserted that, owing to financial pressure, or to false ideas of economy, the maintenance of these essential requisites for defence is apt to be starved and neglected. My experience does not confirm this view. Having served at the War Office for years, under three Ministers of War, statesmen of divergent political views, I have found them all of one mind as to the necessary provision year by year of sufficient funds for the purpose. Naturally and properly they looked into the details. The estimates are presented to Parliament annually, and no reluctance is shown to vote the requisite supplies. Indeed, there are many influences in the House of Commons which rather tend the other way—that is, to extravagance.

An unfortunate change, however, was made a few years ago—namely, in the separation of the naval and military reserves at home and abroad; and duplicate establishments, storehouses, and staff, now exist, which are leading to increased cost, some loss

[1] Clode's *Military Forces of the Crown*, ii. 214.

of efficiency, and eventually to diversity of patterns. As a great naval, military, and colonial Power, with fleets, fortresses, and depôts all over the world, it seems apparent that, both in regard to efficiency and economy, unity of system is essential. Not only the great Duke of Wellington, but successive Master Generals of Ordnance, concurred in this view, and agreed that the Ordnance was an efficient department of the State,[1] and should hold the reserves of both services. According to my judgment, we should revert at once to the former arrangements, and indeed, should war unfortunately arise, we should in all probability be compelled to do so.

Having been appointed Governor of the Royal Military Academy at Woolwich in July 1875, I left the War Office, and did so with much regret. Although, as I have tried to explain, its system of administration is not altogether adapted to meet the requirements of parliamentary government, and although in some respects the Navy and Army are not in such close association as seems desirable, still these defects are capable of remedy, and, at all events, are in no way attributable to the chiefs of the various departments, military and civil, of the War Office, who are men of the highest character and experience,

[1] See Appendix to Fifth Report of Committee of House of Commons on Army and Navy Estimates, 1887, in which correspondence is quoted between the Treasury, War Office, and Admiralty, confirming the above views.

and who carry out very difficult duties with loyalty and success, even under a somewhat imperfect system.

During my five years of office as Director of Artillery, the following sovereigns and foreign princes visited the manufacturing departments of the Arsenal: the late Emperor Alexander II. of Russia—the late Emperor Napoleon III.—the late Emperor of Brazil—the late Grand Duke Constantine of Russia—the late Comte de Paris—and the Shah of Persia.

Some years after the inspection of the Arsenal by the Shah he paid a second visit to England, in 1889, and I had then an interesting interview with him at Lord Armstrong's in Northumberland. Having heard that I had served in India, the Shah came up during the evening and alluded to our position on the North-West Frontier. It must be understood that the conversation was entirely through a Persian interpreter, the Shah knowing only a few English words. He discussed the subject in a very sensible manner, and said we should avoid entering into war with the Afghans, and should endeavour to keep on terms of friendship with the Ameer at Cabul; to which I cordially assented.

Looking about the room, and seeing a general officer at some distance, he inquired: 'Who is that great man in a red coat?' I replied that it was Sir Edward Blackett, High Sheriff of the county. Perhaps that did not convey much to his mind, so I said to the interpreter: 'Tell the Shah that five and thirty years ago, Sir Edward was in the Crimean war, and one day a shot came and took off his leg.' The Shah threw up his hands and was much impressed, but presently the interpreter said that his Majesty couldn't understand it, as he had two legs now. 'That is quite correct,' I observed; 'but tell the Shah that one of them is made of wood.' His Majesty said at once: 'I must go and talk to that great man.' He went up to Sir Edward, and remarked: 'You lost your leg in the Crimea?' to which Blackett assented. 'Ah,' says the Shah, 'I remember. It was in the same battle that Lord Raglan lost his arm!'

The late Emperor of Brazil also paid a second visit to England, after he was dethroned, and on one occasion was shown a wheel by Lord Armstrong, which by some scientific arrangement made rapid revolutions, and he remarked: 'How very interesting. Its revolutions appear to me to be quicker even than those in South America.'

The record of the Royal Military Academy during my period of command was like that of a nation without a history. As the Governor has been invested of late years with adequate power, and is assisted by a competent staff, civil and military, he has only himself to blame if its administration is not successful. The two hundred gentlemen cadets, youths just rising to manhood, no doubt require tact and discretion in those having authority over them; but if they are treated with confidence and kindness, we may feel assured that no real difficulties will arise. Indeed, during my period of office, speaking generally, the conduct of the cadets was admirable throughout; and it is a gratification to me to know that many of those who were then at the institution are now becoming distinguished as officers of Artillery and Engineers. As regards education, the cadets, in my opinion, have too many subjects imposed upon them during their two years' residence at Woolwich. In addition to following up their previous studies in mathematics, French, and German, they have to learn artillery, fortification, military surveying, landscape drawing, chemistry, military history, riding, gymnastics, and drills of all kinds. There is, however, another point, not due to any defect in the regulations, which injuriously affects candidates for the military colleges—namely, the apathy of many of the great public schools, in not teaching the boys who may desire to follow a military career the subjects which are held to be essential to the profession. The result is that a large proportion of those who go up for the competitive examinations are compelled to leave the colleges at a critical period, and to be hastily educated by special teachers. Unjust criticisms are often made on what are commonly called the 'crammers,' whilst the real fault lies elsewhere; and if those in authority at the public schools would take more pains to have the boys educated for the profession in which they are ultimately to serve, the army and other branches of the public service would reap the benefit.

During the year 1875, the late Mr. John Holms, then member of Parliament for Hackney, constituted himself a vigorous critic of the army reforms which had been instituted by Lord Cardwell, and also put forward a distinct plan of his own of military organisation. His view was that we should maintain three separate armies—one for home, a second for the Colonies, and a third for India—all recruited and organised on different systems. It is not necessary now to discuss these proposals; but as his criticisms at the time attracted some attention, I was asked by Lord Cardwell in 1876 to publish a short reply; and as soon as it was ready he gave me a letter of introduction to the late Mr. John Murray, the well-known publisher of Albemarle Street, with a view to his bringing it out. When Mr. Murray had read Lord Cardwell's note, he turned to me and said: 'So you wish to publish a pamphlet—why, an archangel wouldn't read a pamphlet!' My reply was that we were not thinking so much at the present moment of archangels, as of members of Parliament and others, who were of quite a different class. The argument was so conclusive that he published the article in the course of a few days, and it may, perhaps, to some extent have accomplished the intended object.[1] At all events, I received many letters of approval of its contents, and amongst others, the following from my old friend the late Lord Airey, who had been Governor of Gibraltar:—

'Lowndes Square, March 1876.

'My dear Adye,—You were so kind as to send me and ask me to read your reply to Mr. Holms. When I was at Gibraltar, Drummond Hay, our Minister at the Court of Morocco, sent me over the Grand Vizier and the Commander-in-Chief of the Moorish Army. 'They were solemn, silent, but not unobservant parties. Amongst other things, I showed them some long-range seaward artillery practice. When they saw the little flag shot down two or three times, they turned to me, and simply said, "The Spaniards may go to bed!" I think Mr. Holms may go to bed.

'Yours truly, my dear Adye,

'RICHARD AIREY.'

I also received the following letter from Mr. Gladstone:—

'September 1876.

'Dear Sir John Adye,—Amidst a great pressure and many interruptions, I have been able to gather

[1] *The British Army in* 1875 *: a Reply to Mr. John Holms, M.P.*

very interesting information from your valuable pamphlet. For the last three years my attention to current public questions has been much relaxed, while the work of dilapidation incident to an unrefreshed memory has gone on. I do not now recollect as I ought, the precise terms of the present contract of the soldier with regard to the three years, which I have been accustomed to regard as the proper term of short service. To reaching that term for the British Army, I attach (ignorantly) a great value, with this idea among others, that it will very greatly popularise the service, besides its favourable bearing on the question of marriage.

'It will be a great pleasure as well as advantage to me, if I should have an opportunity of resuming the conversation which we began under Lord Sydney's hospitable roof.

'Believe me, faithfully yours,

'W. E. Gladstone.'

CHAPTER XXVII

CENTRAL ASIA AND THE AFGHAN WAR OF 1878–79

THE gradual advance of Russia, and its conquest of the ancient principalities of Central Asia during the present century, have from time to time formed subjects of great interest to the people of this country, chiefly on account of the possible effect of the Russian approach to the borders of our Indian empire; and, having studied the question for many years, I propose to give a short summary of its rise, progress, and present position, more especially from a military point of view. At the beginning of the century, the southern boundary of Russia extended from the north of the Caspian by Orenburg and Orsk, and then across to the old Mongolian city of Semipalatinsk, and was guarded by a cordon of forts and Cossack outposts. This line was no less than 2,000 miles in length, and abutted on the great Kirghis steppe, and to a certain extent controlled the tribes pasturing in its vicinity, but by no means established the hold of Russia on that pathless, and for the most part lifeless waste. Nevertheless, even in those early days, we experienced occasional alarms from imaginary invasions of our Eastern possessions. In 1801 we were threatened with a joint attack of the French, Persian, and Afghan armies; but finally we made a treaty with the Shah, in which it was stipulated that 'should an army of the French nation, actuated by design and deceit,' attempt to establish themselves in Persia, a conjoint force of English and Persians should be appointed to put an end to them.

In 1808, another great expedition against the East India Company's possessions was planned—on paper—between Napoleon and the Emperor Alexander of Russia; but this danger was also averted by a second treaty at Teheran in 1809, in which the Shah covenanted 'not to permit any European force whatever to pass through Persia.' Again, for a third time, in 1837, we were supposed to be threatened by a combined attack of Persians, Russians, and Afghans, of which Kaye gives the following account: 'It was believed,' he says, 'that the danger was great and imminent. There was a Persian army, under the command of the King of kings himself, investing Herat, and threatening to march upon Candahar and Cabul. There were Russian diplomatists and Russian engineers in his camp, directing the councils of the Shah and the operations of the siege. The Barukzye sirdars of Afghanistan were intriguing with the Persian Court;

and far out in the distance, beyond the mountains of the Hindoo Koosh, there was the shadow of a great northern army, tremendous in its indistinctness, sweeping across the wilds and deserts of Central Asia towards the frontier of Hindostan.'[1] All these shadows, however, passed harmlessly away; and the so-called great northern army, as we now know, but as we did not know then, was the Russian column of Perofski, consisting of a few thousand men, which had left Orenburg with a view to chastise the Khan of Khiva, and which perished from famine and pestilence in the snowy wastes of the Barsuk desert, north of the Aral.

It was not until 1847, contemporaneously with our final conquest of the Punjab, that the Russian advances in Central Asia assumed an important aspect. She had held nominal sway since 1730 over the Kirghis tribes in the western division of the great steppe; but, except in the vicinity of Orenburg, had little real control. In 1847–8, however, Russia erected three fortresses in the heart of the steppe—thus forming a connecting link with the Sir Daria—and established Fort Aralsk, near the embouchure of the river. The Russians having thus crossed the great desert, came permanently into contact with the three khanates of Central Asia, and their progress and conquests since that date have been comparatively

[1] Kaye's *History of the War in Afghanistan in* 1838.

easy and rapid. The principalities had no military strength which could long withstand the advance of a great Power, and the Russians are now predominant in that part of the world, and are masters on the Aral and Caspian Seas. Drawing a line from east to west, their outposts are dotted along the crests of the Tian-Shan mountains, looking down on Kashgar; in the centre their frontier touches the outlying provinces of Afghanistan which lie to the north of the Hindoo Koosh; whilst on the west their possessions run along the border of Persia.

What we have to consider, therefore, is the fact that a great Power, within the last forty or fifty years, has virtually advanced its old frontier for many hundred miles southwards, rapidly overrunning the country like a tidal wave over sands; absorbing decaying principalities, establishing forts at strategic points, taking possession of inland seas, routes, and river communications, until its frontier posts not only approach our own, but are on the confines of countries with which we are closely associated, and some of which are more or less under our direct influence and control. Her long line of frontier is devious, and not always perfectly defined; it wanders along the crests of mountains, is marked sometimes by the course of rivers, and occasionally almost lost in pathless deserts. So far as the principalities themselves are concerned, it is admitted that their conquest by

Russia is an unmixed blessing to the inhabitants. In their bare outline these changes are certainly matters of interest to us; but they do not necessarily constitute a great danger. There is undoubtedly a difference between the present and the past. The military forces of a great Power are now in comparative proximity to our Indian empire, and hold ground formerly in possession of governments which, although usually unfriendly, had no real means of injuring us. We need not now discuss the causes of Russian activity; whether they have been the result of the apocryphal will of Peter the Great, or of the military restlessness and ambition of her generals on the spot, or the inevitable consequence of collision with half-civilised decaying States. What we have to consider is the effect on our position in India.

Perhaps the most striking feature is the vast extent of country absorbed by Russia. From Orenburg in the north to Samarcand in the south is more than 1,000 miles in a straight line, and from the Caspian to Kuldja, west to east, about 1,500 miles. Increased military power is not, however, a necessary result of extended dominion. The annexation of a country well peopled, fertile, rich, and civilised, and whose inhabitants are in accord with their new rulers, may give a great accession of strength, but when none of these conditions are fulfilled, conquest may lead to military weakness. The population of Central Asia is not only extremely sparse, but, owing to extensive deserts and to the vicissitudes of climate, many of the tribes are nomadic in their habits. The whole population is estimated not to exceed four millions and a half. When we consider that our empire of India, which approximately is of about the same geographical area as Russian Central Asia, contains a population of over 250 millions, we have at once a striking example presented to us of the difference of the two regions.

The power of conducting military operations on a great scale depends not only on the resources of the country to be traversed as regards supplies of food, pasture, fuel, and water, but also on facilities of communication and transport. In discussing, therefore, the possible future danger to our Eastern possessions from a further advance of Russia, the sterility and general characteristics of the country in which she has established herself, and also the great distance of her troops from the main resources of the empire, become important elements for consideration. War is a science which depends for its success not only on the courage of well armed, disciplined hosts, and of skilled generals as leaders, but also on the means of rapid concentration and of bringing up reserves of munitions and *matériel*. Modern armies are specially tied by such considerations. Now Central Asia is exceptionally deficient in all these essential requirements, and these conditions are abiding. It therefore forms a very weak base of operations against a great empire like India, whose general characteristics are of an exactly contrary character; and although the construction in recent years of a railway from the Caspian to Samarcand will to a certain extent give facility for transport, still it will not in itself alter the general features of the pathless deserts of which the greater part of the country consists.

Between the recently conquered provinces of Russia and our empire of India lies the mountainous country of Afghanistan, inhabited by warlike tribes of brave, fanatical Mohammedans who certainly have no love for Russia. In a geographical and indeed in every sense, it is laid out, as it were, as the natural frontier of an empire. All along its northern provinces stands the snow-capped range of the Hindoo Koosh, stretching away from east to west: a line of mountains between 15,000 and 20,000 feet high, with few practicable passes, and even these are closed in winter. It thus presents for the greater part of its length a natural barrier against aggression, which a few military works at the passes would render impregnable. Even as far west as Herat, the ranges to the north of it are several thousand feet high. But this is not all. The great ridges which run away in a south-westerly direction from the Hindoo Koosh, and which, enclosing long narrow valleys of limited fertility, form the greater part of Afghanistan—all these present a series of additional natural defences. Afghanistan resembles Switzerland, but its mountains are higher, its defiles more difficult, its resources very scanty, and it has no roads properly so called; so that an enemy advancing from the north can only come in any force by one route—that is, by skirting the successive ridges where they sink into the southern deserts. It is indeed remarkable that India is surrounded for hundreds of miles to the north-west by a vast zone of barren country, including Afghanistan, Persia, and the principalities; territories unequalled perhaps in the world for their misery and desolation; but which, regarded from a purely military point of view, offer a great impediment to projects of invasion. The Afghans are poor, but brave, hardy, fanatical, and no doubt somewhat turbulent. They hate all intruders. In former days the hordes of Asia, composed chiefly of cavalry, could disregard bases of support and supply, and, being unencumbered with siege trains or other modern appliances, could sally out from these desert wastes, and, braving all risks, overflow the comparatively rich fertile plains of India. But all such incursions are now happily impossible. Circumstances have entirely altered. Modern science has so expanded the means of defence that armies of invasion must necessarily bring with them a corresponding power; and this entails vast encumbrances, numerous depôts, good roads, and safe communications.

It now becomes time to consider the military position of our empire in India, and here we are met at once by conditions the very opposite of those I have described as prevailing in Central Asia. Whilst Russia has been engaged for many years past in the almost futile effort of establishing her power amongst the remains of decaying principalities, and of introducing civilisation in regions where almost every element of prosperity is deficient, we have also consolidated our empire in the East. Order now reigns in India in place of anarchy, the government of the law has replaced that of the sword, and provinces formerly almost depopulated by depredations and misrule have become fertile and prosperous. Life is safe, and religion and property respected. The value of land has increased; great commercial cities have arisen and trade flourishes.[1] Good civil government, in causing contentment to the people and in developing the resources of the country, gives vast additional strength to our military power. In addition to the British troops, we maintain highly efficient armies recruited from the many martial races under our rule, and are able to increase them

[1] *What England has done for India*, Dr. W. Hunter, 1879.

almost at will. At the same time, the improved means of communication by railways, roads, and rivers enable us to concentrate our forces, supplies, and munitions with comparative ease. It may seem almost unnecessary to dwell upon facts so well known; but judging from much of what we often hear and read, the enormous latent strength we possess in India appears not to be fully appreciated.

We hold a central position of great concentration and power, whilst that of Russia is necessarily much the opposite; so even were the two empires in contact, the danger would not be on our side. We are the great and predominant naval and military power in the East, and Russia is comparatively the weak one; and there is nothing in the present aspect and condition of affairs likely to cause any important alteration in these respects. Russia may not have the wish to attack us in India, but she has not the power, which is a far more important consideration. But the two empires are not in contact, or near it. The most advanced Cossack outpost on the Murghab is several hundred miles from the Indus; so that, far as the Russians have already advanced, and far removed as their outposts are from the bases of supply, they have still a whole continent of very difficult country to traverse before they would even be in sight of our frontier river and of the plains of India.

The views on this important question which I had formed and published years ago, were fully confirmed in 1887 by Sir West Ridgeway, who was our representative at the Joint Commission, which, between 1885 and 1887, finally marked out the northern frontier of Afghanistan; and who, from his position and the accurate knowledge he obtained of the country, was able to give an authoritative opinion. He wrote: 'If any Russian general were so reckless as to attempt the invasion of India, and, relying on the single line of lightly constructed rails which connect the Caspian with the Oxus—and which are liable in summer to be blocked by the moving sands of the desert, and in winter by the falling snows of heaven—if, relying on this frail and precarious base, he were to move an army through the barren plains bordering the Oxus, and, leaving in his rear the various hostile and excited races of Central Asia, he were to cross the difficult passes of the Hindoo Koosh and entangle his army in the barren mountain homes of the fanatical and treacherous Afghan, then indeed our fortunate generals may well congratulate themselves that the Lord has delivered the enemy into their hand. The same objection applies to an invasion of India by the Herat road. Imagine the plight of the Russian army when it arrived before our entrenched camp at Candahar, connected, as it would be, by railway with our immense resources in India. The Russian army would find itself in a country stripped of supplies and carriage, with a powerful enemy in its front, and fanatical tribes waging a guerilla war on its flanks and rear.'[1] Sir West Ridgeway also bore testimony to the beneficial rule of Russia in Central Asia, and that her officers on the frontier were conciliatory, moderate gentlemen.

If the foregoing statements and the opinions which I have offered upon them are sound, then it is evident that our general line of policy towards the people of Afghanistan is simple and clear. They hold important outworks, as it were, just outside our frontier; and, whilst not interfering with their independence, we should do all in our power not only to maintain the authority of their ruler, the Ameer of Cabul, but also to keep on friendly terms with the tribes, many of whom, especially those along our frontier, are more or less independent. Our policy should be one of conciliation and of subsidies; and although in dealing with half-civilised, turbulent chiefs and tribes the beneficial results are achieved slowly, still, year by year, a patient and forbearing policy will bear good fruit, and indeed is now doing so in a marked degree. It is important to note that in our dealings with the Ameer, and in granting

[1] 'The New Afghan Frontier,' by Col. Sir West Ridgeway, K.C.S.I., C.B.; *Nineteenth Century*, October 1887.

him subsidies and arms, we only claimed in return that his foreign policy should be under our guidance. Our principle for years past had been that Afghanistan should be strong, friendly, and independent.

The gradual approach of the Russian frontier towards India led to a diplomatic correspondence in 1872–3[1] between Lord Granville, then Secretary of State for Foreign Affairs, and Prince Gortchakoff, with a view to a clearer definition of the Afghan frontier north of the Hindoo Koosh. It was not that the forces of either Power were then on the ground, nor had the country been accurately surveyed; but the object was to avoid complications in the future, and it is to be observed that the Russian Government ultimately acquiesced in all Lord Granville's proposals as to the provinces and districts which were to be considered as Afghan territory. Though Russia claimed independence of action so far as the principalities[2] were concerned, it also fully accepted the principle that Afghanistan was within the sphere of our influence.

During the period from 1864 to 1876, when Lords Lawrence, Mayo, and Northbrook were successively Viceroys of India, the general policy which I have indicated was carefully pursued, but in the

[1] *Parliamentary Paper*: Central Asia, C 2164, 1878; also C 699, 1878.

[2] Central Asia, No. 1, 1878.

latter year a serious change occurred which eventually led to a great war in Afghanistan in 1878–9. There were apparently two main causes for the alteration in the views of the British Government. One was a restless feeling that we were somewhat in the dark as to the conduct of affairs in Cabul, and that the then Ameer Shere Ali was becoming unfriendly; the other that the long range of the Suliman mountains trans-Indus formed a somewhat insecure border line, and that we should take possession of some of the passes with a view of establishing what was called a scientific frontier. In pursuance of the first a violent effort was made to force English representatives on the Ameer at Cabul, Candahar, and Herat, a policy known to be specially feared by the Afghans, and which we had hitherto engaged more than once not to adopt.[1] In January 1877 an Afghan envoy, Noor Mahomed Khan, held prolonged meetings with the late Sir Lewis Pelly on the subject at Peshawur, and begged that the proposal might be dropped. He said: 'Why all this pressing to send British officers, when you declare that you have no wish to interfere in the internal affairs of Afghanistan? It has roused the suspicion of the Ameer. . . . He is now convinced that to allow British officers to reside in his country will be to relinquish his own authority.' . . . Again he said:

[1] *Parliamentary Paper:* Afghanistan, 1878.

'Your Government is a powerful and a great one; ours is a small and weak one. We have long been on terms of friendship, and the Ameer clings to the skirt of the British Government, and till his hand be cut off he will not relax his hold of it.' Sir Lewis Pelly, however, stated that the presence of English officers in Afghanistan was a *sine quâ non*; and as Lord Lytton, the Viceroy, had already, in speaking of the position of Shere Ali between Russia and England, described it as that 'of an earthen pipkin between two iron pots,' it was evident that no friendly arrangement was likely to ensue. During 1877 our native agent at Cabul was withdrawn, our subsidy ceased, and Shere Ali remained in a position of isolation, and was left to form friendship elsewhere. In fact, we washed our hands of him and were evidently drifting into war.

As regards the other cause of dispute—the rectification of the trans-Indus frontier—the opinion of our Government at the time was that we should march into Afghanistan, and establish what was termed a strategical triangle between Cabul, Ghuznee and Jellalabad, and thus guard, as it were, the avenues to India.[1] Being greatly interested in the proposed military operations at the period in question, I wrote a letter to the Times,[2] pointing out the serious

[1] *Parliamentary Paper:* Afghanistan, No. 2, 1881, C 2811.
[2] *Times*, October 18, 1878.

results which were likely to ensue on our advance into Afghanistan, and of which the following are extracts. 'In my opinion such an idea is a dangerous delusion. Afghanistan is a country of mountains, and the Suliman range, which forms our boundary, is merely the first of a series of great ridges running down south-westerly from the Hindoo Koosh. If we enter the country and merely hold the nearest passes, we shall at once find ourselves in a maze of mountains, with dozens of other passes and strong positions in our front. Not only that, but we shall become involved with other tribes; and as soon as our flag is seen flying within the Afghan mountains, our influence will begin to extend, political and military complications will arise, and we shall inevitably be carried forward.' Alluding to the policy which had for some years past been followed, I went on to point out that 'the frontier throughout its length is far quieter now than in the years gone by. Occasional acts of outrage and robbery are treated as matters of police. Many of the men of the Afghan tribes beyond the border now enter our service, and do their duty well. . . . Therefore, I maintain that a conciliatory policy has been in a great measure successful, and was leading straight to the object we had in view, although time, patience, and forbearance are required before the results become palpable and confirmed.' Lord Lawrence, the greatest authority then living on the subject, wrote several letters to the 'Times' in 1878 strongly deprecating our change of policy, and I had the satisfaction of receiving from him a note expressing his entire agreement with the military views which I had put forward.

Whilst the two causes I have described gradually led to the estrangement of the Ameer of Cabul, an additional fear arose in his mind owing to our dealings with the ruler of the neighbouring country of Beluchistan.[1] Here also we had for many years past, and amidst some difficulties, pursued a course of conciliation and subsidies with the ruler, the Khan of Khelat; one of our objects being to insure the safe passage of caravans with goods through the Bolam. In 1877, however, a new treaty having been made, a small British force entered the country, and, marching through the Pass, occupied and fortified Quetta, on the borders of Afghanistan, ostensibly as a protection to our representative. It was, perhaps, only natural under the circumstances, that Shere Ali should look with some distrust at the presence of our troops on his immediate southern border, and on the direct road to Candahar. Matters drifted on during 1878, but Shere Ali having finally rejected our ultimatum, war was declared in November, and British troops entered Afghanistan in three columns—one by the Khyber as far as Jellalabad, the second occupied

[1] *Parliamentary Paper:* Beluchistan, February 1878.

the Koorum valley, whilst the third, marching through the Bolam, reached Candahar in January 1879. These operations were accomplished with comparative ease, and for the moment our success seemed complete. Shere Ali fled from Cabul, and died soon afterwards, and his son and successor, Yakoob Khan, having sued for peace, a treaty was signed in May, the chief items of which were that we should permanently retain the Koorum and Pisheen valleys, and also send an English officer with a suitable escort as our representative at Cabul, Major Cavagnari being selected for the purpose.[1] So far all seemed well; but in reality the war, instead of being at an end, was only at its commencement. In September, Cavagnari and his escort were surrounded and murdered, and the whole country was disorganised and seething with excitement. The treaty of peace was torn up,[2] and the Khyber and Koorum columns marched at once upon Cabul, and after severe fighting established our authority at the capital.

So completely had these serious and untoward events changed the aspect of affairs that Lord Lytton, the Viceroy, in January 1880 stated that we must recognise disintegration as the basis of our policy. The province of Cabul was to be given over to one

[1] Afghanistan, No. 7, 1879, C 2401.
[2] Afghanistan, No. 1, 1881, C 2776, and No. 2, 2811.

Afghan chief, Candahar to another, and as to Herat, the most flourishing and important district of all, it was proposed to hand it over to Persia. It is not necessary to describe the military measures which followed, which were brilliantly carried out, but towards the close of the campaign we had about 60,000 men either actually in Afghanistan or on the frontier, and even then we only commanded the ground on which we stood; whilst the cost of the war amounted to nearly twenty millions sterling. In the end, and after much discussion, however, the British Government reverted to the original policy of a strong, friendly, and independent Afghanistan; and Abdul Rahman Khan, who had been a refugee for years in Russian territory, was acknowledged by us as the ruler of the country. Our forces were withdrawn early in 1881, and the strategical triangle was, by common consent, consigned to the waste paper basket.[1]

In my opinion the war of 1878–9 was bad in policy and unjust in principle from beginning to end. It is a matter of history now, but we not only were fighting against those we ought to have conciliated, but nearly ended in disintegrating the country and taking a large portion of it ourselves. Subsequent to the withdrawal of our army the country became more settled, although the position of Abdul Rahman was for some time precarious. By our support,

[1] *Afghanistan*, 1881, No. 1, pp. 60-87.

financial and other, however, he slowly established his authority, and has continued on terms of friendship with our Government.

Reverting to Central Asia, the capture of Merv by the Russians and their gradual approximation to the northern provinces of Afghanistan, combined with the somewhat overbearing conduct of their military subordinates on the spot, led in 1885 to a conflict at Penjdeh between the Russian and Afghan outposts, which at one time threatened to lead to a great war. I have already explained that although by the Granville-Gortchakoff agreement of 1873 the northern Afghan provinces were settled, their actual boundaries, in the absence of full information, remained somewhat indefinite. Indeed, in countries chiefly inhabited by nomadic tribes, wandering about in search of pasture, such questions are often more or less uncertain. As a proof of the doubtful nature of the facts at that time, I may point out that in the official English maps published a few years before the Penjdeh incident, that hitherto almost unknown village was marked as outside the Afghan frontier. It would answer no good purpose to re-open a subject which involved no great principle, and the issues of which were exaggerated at the time by violent and imprudent language, both in England and Russia. It was eminently one for diplomatic arrangement and not for war, and found its solution in the joint Boundary Commission which was originated by Lord Granville,[1] and brought to a friendly conclusion in 1887. The Marquis of Salisbury, who was Prime Minister at the time, alluding to the arrangement, said: 'I believe a more well-balanced and equable settlement could hardly have been arrived at. There has been no great sacrifice on either side; but I value the settlement for this reason, not because I attach much importance to the square miles of desert with which we have been dealing—and which probably after ten generations of mankind will not yield the slightest value to any human being—but because it indicates on both sides that spirit which in the two Governments is consistent with continued peace.' That, in my judgment is the spirit in which two great Powers should always be prepared to act in international disagreements.

One more subject remains, as regards Central Asia, which deserves a few remarks—that of the Pamirs, on the north eastern confines of Afghanistan. The country, until recently very little known, is an elevated desolate plateau ringed round with snowy ridges, and is the point of junction of the three great mountain ranges—the Himalayas, the Hindoo Koosh, and the Tian-Shan. The fact that some of the lakes on this elevated region are over 12,000 feet above the sea is a proof of its exceptional character. The

[1] *Central Asia:* No. 2, 1885, C 4387; and No. 1, 1887, C 5114.

climate is very severe, and its inhabitants appear to be chiefly nomadic tribes from Afghanistan, Russia, and China respectively, who bring their flocks there for pasture during the three or four summer months. The actual delimitation of the frontiers, it is understood, is now being amicably arranged between the Powers concerned. As a base for military operations for an advance on India, the very nature of the country offers insurmountable obstacles and hardly needs discussion. I have dealt in some detail with the subject of Central Asia, as one of great and general interest, and have endeavoured to explain the military aspect of the case, because it is the one perhaps not so generally understood. There are people who say that war, sooner or later, is inevitable. As the late Lord Derby once very sensibly remarked: 'Of the two I prefer it later.' It appears to me that there is no cause for war, or indeed probability of it, between Russia and England in that part of the world; but should such unfortunately arise, the danger would not lie on our side.

CHAPTER XXVIII

APPOINTED SURVEYOR GENERAL OF THE ORDNANCE—PRINCIPLES OF ARMY PROMOTION—EGYPTIAN WAR OF 1882

On the formation of Mr. Gladstone's Government in 1880 I was offered by him, and accepted, the appointment of Surveyor General of the Ordnance.

Mr. Childers, on becoming Minister for War in 1880, at once took vigorous measures to bring to maturity the changes which had been instituted by Lord Cardwell, but of which some, from one cause or another, had been rather retarded. One of his first acts was to complete the localisation of the infantry regiments in counties, which had been so strongly recommended by Colonel Stanley's[1] Commission of 1877; and which is now exercising so beneficial an influence in welding the regular and militia forces, and in the gradual formation of local ties and associations. Another measure, introduced in 1881, was an increase in the pay and pension of non-commissioned officers, and the appointment of those in the higher grades as warrant officers. Essential as it is

[1] Now Earl of Derby.

to maintain the system of short service for private soldiers, as affording the only method of creating a reserve and of giving strength and elasticity to the army in war, it is at the same time desirable that a proportion of the non-commissioned officers should be induced to prolong their duties in the ranks. The same difficulty, it may be observed, is felt, and the same remedy adopted, in the chief European armies, where considerable advantages as to pay, pensions, and ultimate civil employment are given to non-commissioned officers who extend their service.

Principles of Promotion and Retirement of Officers

Amongst the many problems which have to be considered and solved by the War Office, none perhaps is more complex than that of providing a system of promotion for officers in order that a sufficient proportion of the most capable may attain to the higher positions at a time of life when their previous experience can be fully utilised. The great and real difficulty may be explained in a few words. In the army, as probably in every profession more or less, the number of employments available for the higher ranks is comparatively limited, whilst the junior branches are crowded with young men, all full of life and energy, gradually gaining experience, and all animated with the one laudable hope of rising to the top. In the military profession perhaps more than in others, the organisation of ranks is strictly defined as to numbers, and is supposed to require a considerable excess of officers in the lower grades, who, in time of peace at all events, have not adequate occupation, and some of whom as the years pass away, losing their zeal and activity, become unfitted for responsible posts, when their long deferred opportunity arrives.

There are two methods of partially solving the difficulty: one, which is now mainly in force in the British army, is a graduated scale of compulsory retirements with pensions at certain fixed ages. No doubt it tends to clear the list, and thus to make room for the juniors. But it has great drawbacks; first of all in its excessive cost, and secondly, that it does not in reality discriminate between the efficient and the inefficient. Age alone being the criterion, it often happens that promising officers who have no wish to retire, are compelled to do so—and this is not only a hardship on individuals, but injurious to the State, in depriving it of men who carry away with them into private life valuable experience gained in various parts of the world. It is, in short, a system which, if rigidly enforced, is costly in both senses, without adequate benefit to the army. In 1876 a commission under Lord Penzance investigated and reported on the subject, and it is chiefly on their recommendations that the above arrangements were adopted.

There are, however, other ways of meeting the difficulty which would at all events tend to remove some of these objections. In the first place it must be remembered that the duties of the British army are far more varied and severe than is the case with the Continental powers. More than half our troops are always at foreign stations. Many officers, therefore, as they arrive at middle life, and whose health has suffered from tropical climates, find themselves compelled to retire; and a scheme of voluntary, in lieu of compulsory, pensions would meet their cases without injuring capable officers, and without inflicting individual hardships. But there is another and a more efficacious mode of meeting the difficulty; namely, by a careful reorganisation of ranks. Lord Penzance's Commission was quite alive to this alternative, and said that a reorganisation of ranks would meet the question in another way, would be less costly, and would prevent the loss of valuable officers, but that it was beyond their instructions. As I have already mentioned, the present organisation rests on the hypothesis that a fixed proportion of officers is requisite in each rank, with a vast preponderance of juniors. But is this really essential? Now it so happens that of late years considerable modifications have been made in every army in Europe except our own, tending to reduce the disparity. On the Continent the infantry regiments, for instance, are now organised in double companies under mounted officers, and the cavalry in squadrons. It is held that under the modern system of fighting such arrangements are more efficient; and they virtually lead to an increase in the upper, and a diminution in the lower, ranks, which in point of promotion is exactly the remedy wanted.

Mr. Childers in 1881 introduced changes with this two-fold object in view, and the following table exemplifies the result in an infantry regiment of two battalions.

Ranks	Establishment before 1881		Establishment after 1881	
Lieut.-Colonels .	2	6	4	12
Majors . . .	4		8	
Captains . .	20	52	14	44
Lieutenants . .	32		30	
Total . . .	58		56	

By the old plan the number of field officers to juniors was, as will be seen, 6 to 52–or 1 to $8\frac{2}{3}$. By the new one it became 12 to 44 or 1 to $3\frac{2}{3}$. It will be evident at once that the prospects of the juniors as regards promotion were greatly improved, and it had the additional merit of being more economical as regards pensions, and further, as it is held by many that the new organisation is more efficient for war, it would appear to have everything in its favour. Unfortunately, owing to diversities of opinion, although the ranks were thus re-arranged, the battalions have never been divided into double companies; so that the most important part of the scheme has not been completed and remains untried. Indeed, the tendency during the last few years has been of a retrograde nature. In my opinion, the proportion of the ranks should be rigidly enforced so as to reduce the juniors to a minimum in time of peace, as being better in the interests of the officers, more in accordance with the requirements of modern warfare, and more economical to the State. The following figures giving the proportion of senior officers to juniors in the army in 1884 and 1894 respectively, will illustrate my argument, and will afford proof that the changes made three or four years ago have injuriously affected the prospects of young officers in respect to promotion.

—	1884	1894
Number of General and Field Officers	2,586	2,128
Number of Captains and Lieutenants	5,601	6,728
—	8,187	8,851

It will be observed that the proportion of seniors to juniors in 1884 was nearly 1 to 2, whereas in 1894 it is about 1 to 3. Again, the annual cost of pensions in 1884 was about £737,000, but in 1894 it has risen to about £1,000,000. So that not only are the prospects of promotions less, but at the same time the cost to the country in pensions is greater. There remains one more point connected with the subject which must be mentioned—namely, that of selection. The principle is a valuable one, and should be carefully carried out in the higher ranks. It will affect individuals and be beneficial to the army; but it will not in itself have much bearing on promotion generally.

Speaking of retirement, it is related that some years ago the late Lord Airey went to the German manœuvres, and on being introduced to the old Emperor William, his Majesty said: 'I hear, Lord Airey, you are going to retire. What is your reason?' Lord Airey replied that, being seventy years old, by the regulations he had no option in the matter. 'Retire at seventy!' said the Emperor; 'why, all my best generals are over that age!' 'Oh yes, your Majesty,' said Airey, 'I quite agree with you, but in England they get tired of us at seventy, and get rid of us.'

Expedition to Egypt

At the beginning of 1882 the War Office in Pall Mall had for a time to put aside what may be called its domestic reforms, and, in concert with the Admiralty, to prepare for an expedition to Egypt, in which our naval and military forces were destined before the close of the year to take a leading and a successful part. The causes of the revolution in Egypt (which commenced in 1881) appear to have been a complicated mixture of intrigues, military discontent, and a sham national uprising; and it is difficult now to understand how a man like Arabi Pasha, who had neither political experience nor military skill, could, even for a time, have become the virtual master of the situation. But if the local causes are somewhat obscure, the diplomatic action, or rather inaction, of the various Powers of Europe is almost equally strange. England alone from the first seems to have perceived the true issue, and by denouncing Arabi as a mere mutinous adventurer, and by insisting on the necessity of crushing the rebellion and restoring the authority of the Khedive, she protected not only her own interests in the country, but also those of Turkey, and, indeed, of Europe generally. The Government of France at the outset appeared to be quite in accord with our own. In January a joint assurance was given to the Khedive of adequate support, and in May the French and English fleets accordingly arrived at Alexandria for the maintenance of order. It is further to be observed that the other European powers, recognising the superior interests of France and England, acquiesced in their proposed intervention. So far unanimity apparently prevailed. And yet, when an insurrection headed by Arabi occurred in Alexandria the following month, France for some reason withdrew her ships and left England alone. And again, when it became evident in July that a military force could alone restore order, notwithstanding the oft repeated desire of the British Government that the two nations should act in concert, the French Chamber, which on the 19th of July had voted the necessary supplies for their part of the expedition, on the 29th reversed their policy, and by a majority of 375 declined to take any part in the campaign.

Judging by the debates in the French Chamber at the time, it would appear that their Ministers were disinclined to embark on a distant expedition on two grounds: (1) that they had anxieties nearer home and wished to keep themselves free; (2) that the people of France were really sick of campaigns, and would not therefore give their support to a policy of distant adventure—not perhaps an unnatural view on their part. So uncertain, indeed, was the policy of the French Government up to the last moment that towards the end of July, when I was appointed Chief of the Staff to the expedition, I received instructions to proceed to Paris, to discuss with the French military authorities as to the place of landing, and to ascertain their views on the joint operations. The vote of the Chamber on the 29th, however, of course rendered my visit unnecessary.

The policy of Turkey as to Egypt was still more uncertain. It would naturally have been supposed that when one of its tributary States had broken out into insurrection, and when the power of the local ruler had been subverted, the Sultan's Government would have been anxious to quell the revolution, as we invited them to do, and would have welcomed the assistance of allies like ourselves who had a similar object in view. Instead of that the Turkish Government not only hesitated, but after the outbreak at Alexandria in June actually conferred the Grand Cordon of the Medjidi on Arabi Pasha, the rebel leader. The Sultan, however, must be a man of great impartiality and discrimination, for when I arrived at Cairo in September, after the short desert campaign, he also conferred on me the Grand Cordon of the Medjidi. Whether he was under the impression that I was a friend or an enemy of Arabi I never cared to inquire.

Before proceeding to give details of the preparations for the expedition to Egypt, it will be as well to allude shortly to certain misconceptions which appear to prevail as to the supposed want of concert between the navy and army in war. Even as recently as 1890 these misconceptions were prominently alluded to, and indeed endorsed in the report of Lord Hartington's Commission.[1] Whilst pointing out that the two services are 'to a large extent dependent on each other,' the report goes on to say that 'little or no attempt has ever been made to establish settled and regular relations between them.' This, if correct, would be serious. My experience in the Crimea, in Egypt, and at the War Office does not lead me at all to the conclusion stated by the commission. The two professions are so distinct in themselves that they require separate administration, but that does not necessarily entail any want of co-operation in war. On the contrary, they thoroughly understand their relative positions; and whether as regards preparations for national defence, or in operations for the expansion of the empire in various parts of the world, our success has been remarkable, and the results are due to the united efforts of the navy and army. The present arrangements are, in my opinion, efficient, and should be left alone.

The Egyptian expedition of 1882 affords the most recent proof of what I have urged. No sooner was it determined on, than the Minister for War and the First Lord of the Admiralty, with their chief advisers, held constant meetings, and discussed and decided difficulties and details day by day, and

[1] *Report of Royal Commission on the Relations of the Naval and Military Departments to Each Other*, 1890.

nothing could be more complete than the cordial co-operation of the two departments—a co-operation which was not limited to the authorities at home, but was equally conspicuous at the seat of war. Throughout the operations the naval and military authorities on the spot fully appreciated their relative positions; and it was due to their combined efforts, backed by the discipline and courage of the officers and men of both services, that the campaign was carried to a speedy and successful conclusion.

Although the Egyptian expedition of 1882 bears no comparison either as to its duration, difficulties, or hard fighting with that of the Crimea, still in respect to the number of troops embarked at the outset the two closely approximate. The force sent to Egypt from England, and from the Mediterranean garrisons, amounted to about 26,000 men, with 54 field guns and 5,000 cavalry and artillery horses. To these were shortly added about 8,000 men from India, consisting of the Seaforth Highlanders, a battery of artillery, and several regiments of native cavalry and infantry. The troops from home commenced embarking towards the end of July; and so complete and satisfactory were the arrangements of the Admiralty, due in great measure to the energy and experience of Admiral Sir William Mends, the Director of Transports, that after a voyage of 3,000 miles they arrived at Alexandria without a *contretemps* of any kind.

The general outline of the campaign and of the movements to be undertaken had been discussed before the departure of the expedition, and it was virtually decided to take temporary possession of the Suez Canal; Ismailia becoming the base of operations with a view to an advance upon Cairo. There were obvious political and strategical reasons for the decision. In the first place the occupation of the canal would secure its safety, and prevent its being blocked or injured by the enemy—a most important European interest in itself; and it is curious that the late Monsieur de Lesseps, who was in communication with Arabi and who was at Ismailia at the time of our arrival, was violently opposed to our action in this respect. In the next place Cairo was then the centre of disaffection, and as it was known that the Egyptian army, reinforced by Bedouins, was in considerable strength and entrenching at Tel-el-Kebir, on the verge of the desert, it was probable that a rapid advance from Ismailia and a severe defeat of the enemy would cause a general collapse, and thus save Cairo from fire and pillage. These various considerations determined the general plan of the operations, and the result amply justified the anticipations formed. To have advanced from Alexandria, or from the neighbouring Bay of Aboukir, would have entailed a long and difficult march south, through the Delta of the Nile, a country without roads and intersected by irrigating canals. Further, the distance to Cairo was about 120 miles, as compared with 75 from Ismailia. In short, no striking or rapid result could be anticipated by an advance from Alexandria, and in the meantime Cairo would have been left at the mercy of a mutinous army, and of other elements of disaffection and disorder.

It was very important that the decision as to entering the canal, and using it as a base, should be kept secret; and therefore, on the arrival of our troops at Alexandria, during August, it was ostentatiously announced that our great object was to land in strength at Aboukir Bay, and from that position and from Alexandria to attack Arabi Pasha, who with a large force was entrenched at Kaffr-Dewar, a few miles distant; and fortunately the device succeeded.

All being ready, the British fleet and transports left Alexandria on the afternoon of August 19, a considerable force having to be left behind temporarily for the protection of the city. In order still further to mislead Arabi Pasha, the fleet and the great majority of the transports proceeded in the first instance to Aboukir Bay, and anchored for the night; a few shots being fired at the works on shore. One brigade, however, went on to Port Said, which was reached on the 20th, when the two ends of the canal were temporarily closed. On August 21, Sir Garnet Wolseley [1] and staff arrived at Ismailia with the brigade of General Graham, which was landed, pushed on at once, and seized the railway station at Neficè, two miles outside. From the moment, indeed, of our arrival it became an urgent necessity to land troops of all arms as fast as possible, in order to take possession of what was called (somewhat figuratively) the Sweet-Water canal and also the single line of railway which ran parallel to each other in the direct line of our destined march across the desert.

Ismailia, from its limited resources and with only a small wooden pier, was not well adapted for the disembarkation of an army. However, in the course of three days nearly 9,000 men, with a portion of the Household Cavalry and two Horse Artillery guns, had been landed. As the water in the Sweet-Water canal began to fall rapidly, it was evident that the enemy were at work not far off and were obstructing its flow. Accordingly, at daylight on the 24th a small force advanced into the desert, and found the enemy in considerable strength at Magfar, about six miles from Ismailia. They had constructed a dam across the canal, which after some sharp fighting was captured, the Egyptians falling back two or three miles to some sandhills at Mahuta, where they were in considerable numbers and entrenched.

[1] Now Field Marshal Viscount Wolseley, G.C.B.

As a serious engagement was likely to take place at Mahuta, reinforcements of all arms were pushed on during the day and following night as soon as landed; the Brigade of Guards under H.R.H. the Duke of Connaught having to make a hurried and harassing march across the desert in the extreme heat, on the afternoon of the 24th. At daylight on the 25th the British troops were formed up across the desert at Magfar in order of battle, and advanced to the attack on Tel-el-Mahuta. But the Egyptians at once lost heart, and were observed to be retiring in haste, partly by rail; and, being followed by the cavalry and horse artillery, they not only evacuated their strong position at Mahuta, but were driven out of Mahsamah, eight miles further on, where seven Krupp guns, large numbers of rifles, and a quantity of ammunition, food, stores, camp equipment, and seventy-five railway waggons fell into our possession. Considering that the troops had only just landed, that the heat was extreme, and that the cavalry and artillery horses were in bad condition from their long voyage, these operations of the 24th and 25th were not only highly successful, but were very creditable to the various arms engaged.

Sir Garnet Wolseley did not fail to take full advantage of the demoralisation and feeble tactics of the enemy, and on the following day General

Graham's brigade made a farther advance of two or three miles to Kassassin Lock on the canal, and within a few miles of the Egyptian main position at Tel-el-Kebir. Thus, within five days of our arrival at Ismailia, notwithstanding the restricted facilities for landing, and in spite of the difficulties of marching during the hottest season of the year across the desert, we had been able to drive away the enemy and to take possession of twenty miles of the fresh-water canal, and of the railway and telegraph line.

As an interval of some days now elapsed before further movements of importance took place, it may be interesting to give a short summary of the strategy of the Egyptian leaders, which appears to have been faulty throughout. In the first place they divided their main forces into two parts far removed from each other, one being placed in front of Alexandria, and the other behind a long weak line of entrenchments across the desert at Tel-el-Kebir. They may no doubt have been somewhat uncertain at the outset as to our general plan; but at all events, when the arrival at Ismailia had made our intentions clear, their troops outside Alexandria should have gone forthwith to the scene of active operations. Instead of doing so, they remained stationary throughout the short campaign, with the result that they had eventually to disband without firing a shot. In the desert they were equally blind to the real position. If on our arrival they had at once blocked the fresh-water canal, diverted its stream before it had reached the desert, and had entirely destroyed the railway and telegraphic lines, they would at all events have greatly added to the difficulties and hardships of our march. By neglecting these obvious precautions, they enabled us within a week to advance and hold these important resources, and to establish ourselves at Kassassin Lock, where, as soon as our army was concentrated, we crushed their power by capturing their main position and brought the war to an end.

In addition to the guns, ammunition, and railway plant secured at Mahsamah on the 25th, we were fortunate also in taking prisoner Mahmoud Fehmi Pasha, one of the chief leaders of the insurrection. I had a short interview with him on his being brought to Ismailia. He was naturally rather excited, and, speaking in French, said that as he had been fighting against us we could dispose of him as we chose. 'Fusillez-moi, si vous voulez,' he remarked; but he begged not to be handed over to the Khedive's Government, as they would torture him. He added, that he knew the English were just people; and I replied that he might feel sure that the British Government would treat him as a prisoner of war, and give him a fair trial.

In sketching the history of a campaign, it is

always desirable, if possible, to ascertain the views of the combatants on both sides; and as regards the earlier incidents in the desert, it so happens that we were fortunate enough to find at the railway stations copies in Arabic of various telegrams which had been sent from Cairo, and also from Arabi Pasha to the Egyptian leaders on the spot; and I will quote English translations of a few of them, as examples of the different conclusions which two opponents may come to on the same events.

1. 'From Under Minister of War, Cairo, to Mahmoud Pasha Fehmi, informing him that his telegram had been read in council, and complimenting him on his victory over the English at Mahsamah.'

2. 'From the Military Commander, Cairo, to H. E. Rashid Pasha Husni. We, and the entire Egyptian nation, congratulate your Excellency on your defeat of the enemy. May God be pleased to bless your crusade.'

3. 'Telegram of three pages from Arabi Pasha, complimenting Rashid Pasha Husni, the Commander of the Eastern Division, on his frequent defeats of the English, who are the enemies of religion and of humanity. Hopes the honour of the Egyptian nation may be written with the blood of the English.'

Speaking of telegrams, towards the end of September, when the British army had arrived at

Cairo a rather bewildering message was received by us from Kaffir-Zoyat. 'Atrocity has taken place in all the stations from the inhabitants and immigrants. The station master is helpless, and now is the time for the arrival of local train. The station master requires help soon. A copy has been sent to Sultan Pasha.'

Notwithstanding the congratulations which the Egyptian generals in the desert had received on their imaginary victories, they became gradually alive to the necessity of making an effort to recover their lost positions, and on August 28, Arabi Pasha having arrived, they seriously attacked Kassassin with about 10,000 men and 12 guns. The battle lasted all day, with occasional intervals, but General Graham (who had rather less than 2,000 men under his command), supported by the cavalry and horse artillery from Mahsamah under Sir Drury Lowe, at length drove off the enemy, and their retreat was hastened by a brilliant cavalry charge after dark in the desert. Our losses on the occasion in killed and wounded were 97.

Subsequent to this attack on Kassassin there was a lull in active operations for about a fortnight. Although the rapidity of our earlier movements had gained us possession of the fresh-water canal and railway, still, as both had been blocked with large dams and embankments, they were for the moment of limited service for transport, and in reality we had, as it were, out-run our commissariat. Consequently for a few days the troops suffered some hardships, although their general health was not apparently affected, the sick list being less than six per cent. There were no resources, of course, in the desert, and it was calculated that we had to send forward about sixty tons a day of food and forage. By incessant exertions, however, the obstructions were removed, and early in September many barges were placed on the fresh-water canal; and, the single line of rail and the telegraph having been repaired, the chief difficulties were thus overcome, and we were able to send up about 250 tons of supplies daily. From that moment we became masters of the situation, and gradually accumulated a large reserve of food, forage, munitions, medical and other stores.

The Highland Brigade of four battalions, with Sir Edward Hamley and Sir Archibald Alison, had arrived at Ismailia on September 1, and by the 12th the British forces were concentrated at Kassassin in readiness for decisive action. Previously, however, on September 9, a considerable portion of the Egyptian army from Tel-el-Kebir again attacked the position at Kassassin at daylight; but we were too strong for them, their opportunity was gone, and under the orders of General Willis our troops advanced boldly across the desert, and drove the enemy back, capturing three of their guns.

Our losses on the occasion were: killed, 3; wounded, 77; total, 80.

Arabi's estimate was very different. In his telegram, September 12, to the Ministry of War, Cairo, he says: 'Moreover, from true observation it has been proved to us that the number of the enemy killed and remaining on the field of battle is about 2,500, and their carts were insufficient for carrying off the wounded.'

During the early part of September, reconnoissances were made with a view of ascertaining the general position of the enemy's defences, and, as far as possible, their armament and progress. Our reconnoitring parties consisted of one or two officers with a small mounted escort, who approached the Egpytian entrenchments at daylight and made careful observations from different parts of the desert; the enemy taking little or no notice of their appearance. Indeed, it was rather remarkable that, although the Egyptian leaders must have been aware of the near approach of the British army, they apparently sent out no cavalry at night, and even their infantry pickets were, as a rule, lying about close to their works and only roused themselves at dawn. The right of the enemy's earthworks rested on the fresh-water canal, and then stretched away northerly for nearly four miles across the desert, their left being *en l'air*. Their very extent was a great weakness. So far as could be ascertained before the battle, the entrenchments towards the canal, which were subsequently stormed by the Highlanders, were the most complete and formidable, being armed with many Krupp field-guns, and supported by retrenchments inside. About 1,000 yards in advance of that part of the defences the Egyptians had constructed and armed a detached outwork, which, curiously enough, escaped the observation of our reconnoitring parties. Most fortunately when we advanced on the 13th, and when a portion of our troops must have passed close to it just before daylight, they were not discovered; otherwise out great object of reaching the main line of works unperceived might have been prematurely divulged at a critical moment. The Egyptian forces were estimated as being about 38,000 men, with 60 guns, of which we captured 59.

The plan of attack of the lines of Tel-el-Kebir was one requiring the greatest care and consideration. The enemy had been for several weeks on the spot, and had not only entrenched their position and armed it with many guns, but the whole of the ground in their front was a flat, sandy desert, without cover of any kind. An attack by us in open daylight under such circumstances must inevitably have entailed a prolonged conflict and enormous losses. By a wide flank movement we might, no doubt, have turned their left with comparative ease, and have captured the position without great loss, experience at Tel-el-Mahuta and elsewhere having proved that the enemy were not prepared for, and in fact would not stand against such a

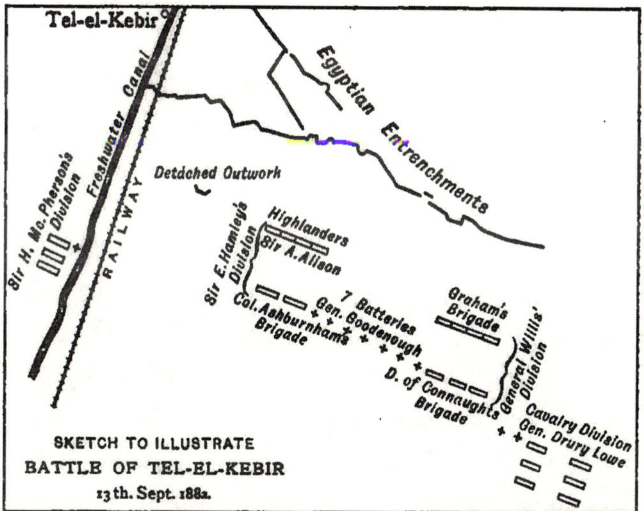

SKETCH TO ILLUSTRATE
BATTLE OF TEL-EL-KEBIR
13th. Sept. 1882.

Walker & Boutall sc.

manœuvre; but, as Sir Garnet Wolseley clearly stated in his dispatch after the battle, 'It would not have accomplished the object I had in view—namely, to grapple with the enemy at such close quarters that he should not be able to shake himself free from our clutches except by a general flight of all his army. I wished to make the battle a final one. . . . My desire was to fight him decisively when he was in the open desert, before he could take up fresh positions, more difficult of access, in the cultivated country in his rear.' All these considerations led to the decision to make a night march across the desert, to be followed by an assault along the whole line of entrenchments at dawn. No doubt there was risk, but the object to be attained was supreme, and Wolseley relied, and with good reason, on the steadiness and courage of his troops.

Early on the morning of September 12 (twenty-four hours before the battle) Sir Garnet Wolseley, accompanied by all the general officers, rode out towards Tel-el-Kebir, so as to arrive at daylight in sight of the works, and as near as prudence would allow; and he then explained to them his plan of attack, and gave to each a rough sketch of the intended formation, which is shown by the diagram on preceding page.

The day preceding the battle passed quietly, and no movements of any kind gave signs of the coming event. As soon as it was dark the whole of the tents were struck, rolled up, and, with the baggage, stacked alongside the railway and left behind. The strength of the army was about 12,000 infantry, 2,700 cavalry, and 2,400 artillery, with 60 guns.

During the early part of the night the troops moved out about 2,000 yards into the desert, and, having taken up their respective positions, bivou-

EVE OF TEL-EL-KEBIR. ENCAMPMENT OF BRITISH ARMY AT KASSASSIN LOCK

Colonel Tuson remained in reserve with head quarters. The troops, who were now approaching the Egyptian position, moved steadily forward over the firm, dry sand, and so complete was the silence that it was difficult to realise the fact that two armies were close to each other and just about to meet in dire conflict. At about 4.45 A.M. the first faint glimmerings of the dawn were observed, and in the course of a few minutes some straggling musket shots were heard, fired evidently by the feeble pickets of the enemy just outside their works. Then all along the line in front of the Highlanders a perfect blaze of musketry fire commenced, and continued for the next half-hour without intermission. The Egyptian artillery were also in action, but, being fired at a high elevation, their shells for the most part burst wildly all over the desert. General Graham's brigade on the right had slightly deviated from its course in the darkness. This, however, was soon rectified, and as the day dawned the leading brigades, in the most gallant and determined manner, stormed the whole line of the enemy's works; and followed up by the Guards under the Duke of Connaught, and by Colonel Ashburnham's brigade in rear of the Highlanders, they swarmed over the parapets and held their ground inside. In the meantime the seven batteries of artillery under General Goodenough, in the centre of the line, had also continued their advance; and although from the nature of the assault they were unable to give active support to the infantry at the first onset, they watched their opportunity, and as soon as our men were on the crest of the parapets, several batteries succeeded in getting through the works, and, by following up the Egyptians, contributed to their defeat and flight. One battery, just before entering the entrenchments, was brought into action against the detached outwork which I have previously mentioned, and, taking it in reverse, led to its immediate abandonment by the enemy.

At length came the opportunity for the cavalry and horse artillery under General Drury Lowe. They had purposely been held back until the infantry had established their footing on the works, but then, sweeping round the northern extremity, they charged the retreating Egyptians, who were now in headlong flight all over the country, and also captured several trains and locomotives on the railway. It is necessary now to turn to the movements of Sir Herbert McPherson, who, with the Seaforth Highlanders and part of the Indian contingent, marched from Kassassin during the night on the south side of the canal, supported on their right by a naval battery of Gatlings, which moved along the railway. Their advance was never checked, and after some smart skirmishing in the cultivated ground near the village, and taking twelve guns, they arrived at the bridge at Tel-el-

Kebir on one side, just as our other victorious troops had reached it on the opposite bank.

The short account I have given of the various movements in the field during the eventful night march, and the battle at the dawn, will, I think, afford proofs not only of the gallantry and perfect discipline of the troops of all arms engaged, but also of the skill and care with which the general officers in command had carried out their arduous and anxious duties. The severe fight within the entrenchments did not last much more than half an hour, and the Egyptians, finding their works and guns all captured, broke and fled in thousands, throwing away their arms, Arabi having been one of the first to make his escape. The entrenchments inside were crowded with dead and wounded; and in addition to 59 guns, an immense quantity of arms, ammunition, and stores, together with the whole of their large camp, fell into our possession. The Egyptian losses amounted to 1,500 killed and about 3,000 prisoners, large numbers of them being wounded. The losses of the British army in killed, wounded, and missing were 459.

The victory was complete, but no time was lost in taking advantage of the flight and utter disorganisation of the enemy. Sir Herbert McPherson's force, strengthened by a battery of artillery, marched at once along the line of railway to Zagazig, and, arriving during the afternoon, captured several trains and locomotives, the Egyptian soldiers bolting without firing a shot. The movements of the cavalry division are graphically described in Sir Garnet Wolseley's despatch: 'Major General Lowe was ordered to push on with all possible speed to Cairo. . . . These orders were ably carried out, General Lowe reaching the great barracks of Abbassich just outside Cairo, at 4.45 P.M. on the 14th instant. The cavalry marched 65 miles in these two days. The garrison of about 10,000 men, summoned by Lieutenant Colonel H. Stewart to surrender, laid down their arms, and our troops took possession of the citadel. A message was sent to Arabi Pasha calling upon him to surrender forthwith, which he did unconditionally. He was accompanied by Toulba Pasha, who was also one of the leading rebels in arms against the Khedive.'

The divisions of General McPherson and Drury Lowe having thus been despatched to Zagazig and Cairo, the head quarter staff and remainder of the army rested for the day on the field of Tel-el-Kebir, awaiting the final *dénouement*. In fact, the result of the battle of the 13th and the flight of the Egyptian forces became known by telegraph throughout the country in the course of a few hours, and the war came to a sudden termination. The medical arrangements at Tel-el-Kebir were admirably carried out. As soon as the position had been taken, large marquees were erected close to the fresh-water canal, and our wounded officers and men, having been attended to, were then conveyed in covered barges to Ismailia; thus avoiding a long rough journey in carts across the sandy desert. Late in the afternoon, I rode along the captured entrenchments, the ground being covered with dead and wounded Egyptians—the latter faint and helpless, and praying for water. Parties of our men had been sent out during the day with carts of provisions and barrels of water, and did all in their power to mitigate the sufferings of these poor creatures. Thousands of muskets and vast quantities of ammunition lying about were broken up, and then buried.

On the afternoon of the 14th the head quarter staff, accompanied by the Duke of Connaught and Prince Teck, with a part of the Brigade of Guards, left the field of battle by rail for Zagazig; but the line was a single one and in disorder, so that we were constantly delayed, and did not arrive till 9 o'clock P.M. Our baggage animals were wandering about somewhere in the desert, and none of us had even a change of clothes; and, with the exception of a tin of meat, a few biscuits, and bottle of claret—fortunately brought by the Duke of Connaught, who kindly shared his scanty supplies with us—we had no food. Our troops of all arms were marching along the line of railway, and once, when we were detained, a weary gunner passed the carriage, and on being asked where he was going replied, 'To Zig-zag.' Two other gunners had captured a dromedary, and were riding along in high spirits. The inhabitants of the villages as we passed through the cultivated country came out and salaamed, and seemed quite happy. They had stuck poles with white rags flying on the tops of their houses in token of surrender. Altogether it was an interesting and amusing scene. I slept that night on the railway platform at Zagazig, surrounded by myriads of flies. However, these were the last of our hardships, if such they can be called; and on the following morning we arrived by train at Cairo, and were cordially received; in fact, the whole population had turned out in the streets to give us welcome. Every English soldier walking about was followed by an admiring crowd. The Khedive, telegraphing from Alexandria, placed the Abdin Palace at the disposal of the staff and begged us to consider ourselves as his guests. From a small tent in the desert to a royal palace in two days—with a battle in the interval—was certainly an unusual but welcome change of scene. There was, however, one drawback. Although the Abdin Palace contained suites of handsome state apartments, gorgeous in satin and gold, there were no bed-rooms! Whether rulers in Egypt never sleep, or whatever the explanation, we had to make

A A

the best of it, and I took possession of one large state room; but my little camp-bed looked very shabby and insignificant amidst such splendid surroundings. There were upwards of 100 wax candles in glass chandeliers hanging from the ceiling.

As several thousand Egyptian soldiers were still in arms on our arrival at Cairo, many of them in a large barrack just opposite the palace, an order was sent over that they were to give up their muskets and were then free to return to their homes. Hardly had the order been received than it was acted on, and crowds of them, divested of their uniforms, were seen running as if for their lives, and in a few minutes the barrack was deserted. I inquired the reason of their extreme haste, and was informed that the news was so good they could hardly believe it to be true, and were afraid we might change our minds and detain them. The incident I have mentioned affords a good indication of the real feeling of the inhabitants, who were not anxious to fight anybody, but rather to be allowed to return and live in peace in their native villages. Egypt is probably not the only country in which these sentiments largely prevail, but do not always find expression.

In the prison within the citadel we found a large number of people in chains; criminals, political prisoners, even Arab women and children, and two

English subjects (Maltese) all jumbled together, ill-treated, and nearly starved. Separating the real criminals, after inquiry, the remainder were set free, and by way of a change the jailor was placed in one of the cells.

In some small rooms in a corner of the great barrack, in Abdin Square, Arabi and Toulba Pashas were confined as prisoners, with an English guard over them. As there were several passages and staircases about the place, with Arab servants and others constantly going to and fro, and as, to an English sentry, one native is very like another, there seemed a possibility of Arabi's attempting to escape. So, under pretext of calling to inquire as to his health (for he had been unwell), I paid him a visit, with an interpreter, in order to inspect the premises. Arabi came up and shook hands, and, on my asking if he were better, he replied that now I had come to see him he was quite well—which was encouraging. Then he went on to say that the English were famous for their love of freedom, of liberty, and of justice, and that, relying on our honour, he had surrendered unconditionally. He seemed inclined to enter into a discussion, so I replied that no doubt his case would receive careful consideration and justice from the British Government. He did not strike me as a man of much education or intelligence. Subsequently, Colonel Thynne, Grenadier Guards, was specially appointed to take charge of him.[1]

Although during the short period of active operations our troops had enjoyed excellent health, notwithstanding the heat and the occasional hardships they had undergone, soon after their arrival at Cairo considerable numbers were struck down by fever and dysentery; probably attributable to the bad water in the canal at Kassassin, and partly to the insanitary condition of Cairo itself. Acting on advice, large numbers of the sick were conveyed by rail to Alexandria, embarked for home, and speedily recovered at sea.

Without wishing to exaggerate the events of the campaign, I think it will be admitted that the difficult arrangements connected with the embarkation of our troops were carefully carried out; and that the ex-

[1] Visiting card of Arabi Pasha, found at Tel-el-Kebir.

pedition was conducted with great promptitude and success. These results testify to the efficiency of the naval and military administration at home, and also to the courage and discipline of the two services under somewhat trying circumstances. From a financial point of view, the rapidity of the operations enabled us on arrival at Cairo at once largely to reduce expenditure, by cancelling contracts for food, forage, transport animals, and stores at various ports in the Mediterranean. So sudden, indeed, was the transition from war to peace, and so completely had the insurrection collapsed, that in the course of a few weeks a large proportion of our forces were withdrawn from the country and returned to England. The campaign being at an end, I left Egypt early in October in order to resume my duties as Surveyor General in the War Office; but before embarking had a farewell audience with the Khedive, Ibrahim Tew-fik. I had had interviews with him on one or two occasions previously. He was quiet and friendly in manner, and apparently of a gentle disposition; was cordial in his recognition of the good services rendered to him by the British forces. I said I hoped that the conduct of our men since their arrival at Cairo had been satisfactory, and he at once expressed his admiration of their good discipline, and remarked that in every respect, whether in the streets or in the bazaars, their conduct had been most orderly. What vexed him was that some of his people in the bazaars cheated our men, and demanded extravagant prices for their goods. I assured him, however, that he need not worry himself on that point, as the English soldiers would readily discover the market value, and matters would soon find their level; and that they enjoyed their visit to Cairo.

Statements were current at the time that the Khedive was not really loyal to England. On this being brought to his notice, it is said, and I believe truly, that he observed: 'Not loyal to the English? When my country was in insurrection and my authority and life in danger, there was only one power in Europe which would move a finger to help me—and that was England. If I am not faithful to them it would be strange indeed!"

CHAPTER XXIX

GIBRALTAR—ITS VALUE FROM A NAVAL AND COMMERCIAL POINT OF VIEW—ZOBEHR PASHA A STATE PRISONER—SANITARY CONDITION OF GIBRALTAR.

SOON after my return from the expedition to Egypt I was appointed Governor of Gibraltar, and on January 2, 1883, took over the command from my distinguished predecessor, Field Marshal Lord Napier of Magdala.

Before alluding to the present position of Gibraltar, and to the duties in connection with it during my tenure of office, it may be as well to refer shortly to its eventful history in the past. One of the most ancient fortresses in Europe, it owes its exceptional interest and importance partly to its position at the entrance to the Mediterranean and partly from its vicinity to the kingdom of Morocco. From the early part of the eighth century, when first occupied and fortified by the Moors, it became, as it were, their chief base of operations in the gradual conquest of the greater part of Spain. Its history in those days is indeed one continual record for several centuries of sieges, and of battles fought in its vicinity; and although retaken in 1309, and held for a few years by the Spanish forces, it may be said to have been in possession of the Moors during almost the whole of the eight hundred years of their rule in that country. During that long period its value was chiefly of a military character; and it is only in more recent times, as circumstances in Europe gradually changed, that its unique position in regard to naval power in the Mediterranean has been fully recognised and developed.

Subsequently to the expulsion of the Moors in the sixteenth century it was held by the Spanish Government, but its defences were apparently neglected and its importance little appreciated; so that when attacked by the British fleet under Admiral Rooke in 1704 it was captured with comparative ease, its possession being confirmed to us by the Treaty of Utrecht in 1713. Since that date, although it has undergone several sieges—notably that by the allied

GIBRALTAR FROM QUEEN OF SPAIN'S CHAIR

armies and fleets of France and Spain, which lasted from 1779 to 1782, it has successfully resisted all attacks; and its past history would appear to prove that, if properly armed and resolutely held, it is practically safe from capture by land or sea.

Coming down to modern days, the first and perhaps the most important point relates to its value as a harbour; and in this respect it is, and always has been, somewhat defective from a naval point of view in time of war. Although its anchorage is so far good that well-found vessels can remain there in safety during the heaviest weather, still it cannot be considered a harbour in the ordinary technical sense. It has no narrow entrance or channel which by means of land armaments, lines of torpedoes, or other means can be absolutely denied to a hostile fleet. In fact, it is an open bay several miles wide. These general conditions are, of course, permanent; but it is to be observed that the increased range, power, and accuracy of modern ordnance have to some extent given the fortress a greater command over the sea approaches than it had in former days; so that, although hostile vessels cannot be absolutely interdicted from paying flying visits in war, they would be unable without great risk to remain for any length of time within range. The conditions of modern warfare, therefore, have not been of an unfavourable character in that respect. Another point has to be noticed. The shores of the bay consist for the most part of territory belonging to Spain; consequently, its waters are more or less under the command of that country, and the improvement in modern artillery, no doubt, has extended their power in this respect. It is, however, clear that only in the event of war with Spain would this aspect of the case assume importance; and, as a matter of fact, so little is the contingency regarded that no batteries containing modern armaments have been erected along their coast. On the whole, although the position of Gibraltar may not in all respects be an ideal one, its general conditions remain very much as they always have been; and to a great naval, colonial, and commercial nation such as Great Britain it is of the highest value, not only in war, but also in peace.

Its possession gives us a place of rendezvous and of observation for our fleets; so that in time of war, with ordinary vigilance, no hostile vessels can enter or leave the Mediterranean without our knowledge. That of itself is an important consideration. We are also enabled to maintain within the fortress reserves of naval munitions, food, coals, and stores, available for our vessels of war, either in the Mediterranean or coming from the Atlantic. Its value, however, is not limited to a period of war. Gibraltar has been for many a year to a certain extent a centre of trade, not only with the neighbouring towns of Spain, but also with the ports along the coast of Morocco. And since the opening of the Suez Canal its mercantile interests have greatly increased, the number of trading and passenger vessels of all nations calling in daily for provisions and coals and other requisites being much larger than of yore, as will be seen by the following table, giving the number and tonnage of vessels calling at Gibraltar during 1868 and 1893 respectively :—

Year	Number of vessels calling	Total tonnage
1868	4,471	1,519,046
1893	5,172	4,687,454

As a proof of its commercial activity I may point out that Linea, which five and twenty years ago was a mere Spanish village at the other end of the neutral ground, is now a town of twelve thousand people, large numbers of whom visit Gibraltar daily, bringing in supplies of food, forage, vegetables, and fruit, &c., and leaving again at night with English goods. In fact, it has become a suburb, as it were, of the city. The trading facilities of Gibraltar are beneficial to the country round, and are fully appreciated by the inhabitants of that part of Andalusia. Taking all these matters into consideration, it will, I think, be apparent that the value of the city and fortress to this country are greater now even than in former days.

It is no doubt quite natural that the Government and people of Spain should feel regret at the permanent occupation of Gibraltar by a foreign power; and it has been suggested that we should accept in exchange the town and fortress of Ceuta, which holds a somewhat analogous position on the other side of the Straits and which belongs to Spain, and thus remove any cause for unfriendly feeling on their part. The question, however, is not so simple as at first sight it would appear. Assuming for the moment that the strategical value of Ceuta as a naval station equals that of Gibraltar, on which I offer no decided opinion, it is by no means certain that the proposal if made by us would be accepted. The Spanish Government are very tenacious of their possessions on the coast of Morocco, as giving them great influence in that country. Their apparent desire is to hold a powerful, if not a predominating, influence on both sides of the straits; and, although they would no doubt gladly obtain possession of Gibraltar, it does not therefore follow that they would give up possession of one of their most valuable positions on the opposite coast in exchange. Other Mediterranean powers also are carefully watching events in Morocco, and it is very possible they might not acquiesce in our occupation of Ceuta. These are diplomatic rather than military questions, and I only allude to them as proofs that the subject is rather involved and goes beyond a mere exchange of territory. So far as Morocco is concerned, its present condition is deplorable. It is a country situated only a few miles from Europe, with an excellent climate and great agricultural and mineral resources; inhabited, moreover, by a fine, brave race of people, and yet, notwithstanding these advantages, owing partly to the jealousies of its neighbours, its resources remain undeveloped, whilst its government is weak and cruel to a degree.

In considering the two-fold aspect of Gibraltar as a fortress and a commercial city combined, it is sometimes argued that its dual interests are antagonistic, and that the presence of a large civil population would add to the difficulties of its defence. To a certain extent no doubt the position is anomalous, as in other fortified cities. Should hostilities occur, and should the fortress be seriously threatened, its trade would certainly suffer and a considerable proportion of the inhabitants would probably seek temporary refuge elsewhere. Still we must bear in mind that war is the exception; and as not a shot has been fired at Gibraltar for upwards of a century, it would appear senseless to paralyse its commercial advantages in time of peace in anticipation of what an enemy might attempt to accomplish in war. In short, the remedy would be far worse than the disease.

The shipping trade of Gibraltar in the present day is subject to one disadvantage, from the absence of any wharves for coaling the numerous steam vessels which call daily throughout the year. In order to remedy this deficiency, the coal reserves of the mercantile marine are stored in large old wooden hulks, about thirty-five in number, which are moored in *échelon* down the bay, inconveniently crowding the anchorage. The arrangement is not only costly in the purchase and maintenance of the hulks, but in time of war they would be liable to be sunk either by ramming or by torpedoes. The difficulty, however, could be met by an extension of the new mole pier, and by the construction of a wharf from the Ragged Staff bastion; which would not only enclose a considerable area of deep water and give facilities for coaling vessels, both of war and of commerce, but would also enable a large reserve of coals to be maintained on shore, under protection of the guns of the fortress. The enclosed area would also be an appropriate site for the proposed dock.

One of the first subjects brought to my consideration on arrival as Governor, was that of coaling merchant vessels at night. Ever since the days of the great siege it had been the custom to close and lock up all the gates of the city at sunset, and to prevent any communication with the outer world until the following morning; just as if an enemy at the gate outside were waiting to rush in and take possession. One consequence of this extreme vigilance was that all vessels arriving after dark had to remain at anchor for many hours before their wants could be supplied. A deputation of merchants represented to me that great advantage would arise if the detention could be avoided. Their request seemed reasonable enough, and as on inquiry it appeared that their wishes could be met by permitting a few coal-heavers to leave the city at night, orders were given accordingly; and the result not only obviated the inconvenience, but led to an increase in the vessels visiting the port, thus adding considerably to the harbour dues.

The old records of Gibraltar[1] during the eighteenth century contain some interesting and amusing regulations concerning matters both of civil administration and army discipline, and I will quote a few examples.

'Any donkeys loose in the town are to be the property of the person taking them away, and any straying on the ramparts are to be shot by the sentries.

'Fishermen are only to sell their fish after the servant of the Governor has bought what he requires.

'Whatever suttler doth not inform against men

[1] See *Gibraltar Directory*, in which many others are recorded.

that swear in their houses contrary to the orders given out shall be turned out of town.

'A hat having been taken from the Convent by some gentleman who left his own instead, Mr. —— takes this method that the gentleman may exchange hats *if he pleases.*

'No gaming to be allowed in wine houses, particularly including the games of the devil-and-the taylors and skuttles.

'All oysters which come from Portugal are to lie in the sea for at least a fortnight before they are brought into the garrison, as they are found very unwholesome without this precaution.

'If sentries are attacked by bullocks in the streets or on the Line Wall, they are to retire into an embrasure or get upon the parapet; but they are not to fire inconsiderately.

'A loose ball and a charge of powder in a cane is to be issued to each man on guard to save their cartridges. The loose ball to be carried in the cock of their hats.

'On account of the scarcity of flour soldiers are not to have their hair powdered till further orders.

'Officers and non-commissioned officers commanding guards are frequently to send out patrols through the day with their arms unloaded to kill every dog they see going about the streets.

'The Governor recommends it to the commanding officers of regiments to give directions that the cartridges may not be made too large for firing at exercise or reviews, some barrels of firelocks having split in firing.

'No person whatever is to be suffered to go on the Line Wall or ramparts in a night-gown, night-cap, or binyan on any pretence whatever, and all sentries are to turn off such as shall attempt to come near their posts in any of the said dresses without distinction of persons.

'All sentinels who do not call out "All's well" every half minute shall be punished with two hundred lashes.

'The queue is to be fixed to the hair of the head, but when an officer's hair is not long enough for this purpose he may be allowed to fix the queue otherwise till his hair is sufficiently long, but this is not to continue longer than two months on any account.

'No one to suffer any person to stand at their doors or go into the streets that has marks of the small-pox. No mackerel to be suffered to come into town.

'No woman to beat a soldier; the first that doth shall be whipped and turned out of town.'

'Any man who has the misfortune to be killed is to be buried by the guard where it happens, and his clothes to be sent to his regiment.

'Officers at guard-mounting will bring their

espantoons to a half recover and come to the right about together upon a flam and not upon the ruffle, which will be previous to it.' [The terms are meant for certain beats on the drum. The espantoon for officers was done away with in 1786.]

The conditions under which our soldiers serve in the present day as compared with those of the last century are certainly of a much improved character, and the results in all respects are very satisfactory. They are better paid, clothed, fed, and generally cared for than in the days gone by. During my residence at Gibraltar, I obtained permission from the War Office to convert some old store-houses within the city into reading and recreation rooms for the garrison, and it was carried out on a considerable scale. The chief room was capable of seating 1,200 persons; and every week a free smoking concert or entertainment was given, open to all soldiers, their wives, and friends; each regiment taking its turn to arrange a programme. Ladies and officers were sometimes kind enough to take part in the concerts, which were always crowded. The institution also contained a library, a billiard room, and was provided with games, such as bagatelle, chess, draughts, &c. Tea, coffee, and non-intoxicating drinks, at moderate prices were sold all day at a buffet; and after sunset until roll-call a bar was opened, at which the men could get glasses of beer, &c.

The expenses were not large, and the financial results were satisfactory. The non-commissioned officers and men of the garrison only paid one half-penny a month each, and were then free to use the institution every day during their leisure hours; and to attend the free concerts and other entertainments at will. Their subscriptions, added to contributions from officers and to the profits from sale of beer and refreshments, &c., were found to be sufficient for the purpose. The furniture and gas were supplied by Government. During the period of my command there was not a single case of disturbance or trouble of any kind; and in my opinion such institutions are excellent in every way, not only as places of innocent recreation, but, especially in a place like Gibraltar, as tending to draw the men away from the numerous wine-shops in the lower parts of the town. I may add that during the visits of the Channel fleet the seamen and marines were invited to make free use of the rooms, and did so in considerable numbers: the institution thus contributing to promote that friendly association between the men of the two services which is so desirable from every point of view.

A somewhat singular story is told of General Sir Robert Wilson on his arrival as Governor of Gibraltar in 1843. It may be premised that Sir Robert's services in the army had been of a very distinguished character. Born in 1777, he was appointed a cornet of dragoons in 1794, and saw active service in Flanders and in Holland, and then in Egypt in 1801. In 1802 he became a Lieutenant Colonel and went to Brazil, and was also at the capture of the Cape of Good Hope in 1806. In subsequent years he served in Poland, and also in Portugal and Spain during the Peninsular war. He was with the Russians in the campaign of 1812, and with the allied armies on the Continent up to 1814. From 1818 to 1830 he was Member of Parliament for Southwark. In September 1821, however, he was dismissed from the service by King George IV. on account of his participation in the London riots which occurred on the death of Queen Caroline. On the accession of William IV, in 1830, he was restored to his rank in the army, and in 1843, was appointed Governor of Gibraltar, in succession to Sir Alexander Woodford. It is related that on his arrival he inquired of Sir Alexander if he remembered the last occasion on which they had met? Woodford's reply was that so many years had elapsed that he was unable to recall the exact time or incident. Sir Robert Wilson then said: 'The last time we met was in 1821, when you were at the head of the Guards and I was with the mob, and you were driving us through the streets of London!' It is not often, perhaps, that two general officers meet on two occasions under such very different circumstances.

ZOBEHR PASHA

In March 1885 Zobehr Pasha, accompanied by two sons, an interpreter, and several servants, arrived at Gibraltar from Egypt as a state prisoner by order of the British Government, and he was detained there during the remainder of my period of office. I had many conversations with him on the subject of the Soudan, and found him to be a man of considerable ability; and, although cautious in the expression of his views on Egyptian affairs, I gathered from him that the people of the Soudan specially detested the rule of the Egyptian Pashas, and that the cause of their hostility to us arose solely from a belief that in sending an expedition up the Nile to Khartoum in 1884, our object was to reinstate the rule of Egypt in that country.

Without entering at any length into this much discussed question, it must be borne in mind that until conquered in 1821 by the late Mohammed Ali the Soudan was entirely independent of Egypt, and separated from it by a great desert. Colonel Charles Gordon wrote: 'From Wady Halfa southwards to Hannek, a distance of 180 miles, an utter desert extends, spreading also for miles eastwards and westwards, on both sides of the Nile. . . . It was this boundary that kept the warlike and independent tribes of the Soudan quite apart from the inhabitants of Egypt proper, and made the Soudanese and the Egyptians two distinct peoples that have not the least sympathy one with the other.' Of the result of Egyptian rule, the late Sir Samuel Baker, writing in 1864, drew a melancholy picture. He described the provinces as utterly ruined and only governed by military force, the revenue unequal to the expenditure, and the country paralysed by taxation; shut in by deserts, all communication with the outer world was most difficult, and the existing conditions rendered these countries so worthless to the State that their annexation could only be accounted for by the fruits of the slave trade. Zobehr Pasha's opinion as expressed to me was, that if the people of the Soudan were assured that no attempt would be made to restore the authority of Egypt, their hostility would cease, and they would be anxious to open their country to trade. Speaking generally, it appeared to me that his views were sound, and that if we were to proclaim a policy of peace at Souakim, combined possibly with some annual payment to the neighbouring chiefs, the road to Berber and Khartoum would soon re-open and commerce be renewed. At all events I cannot see that it is any part of our duty to assist the Egyptians to reconquer the Soudan.

Gibraltar, like many another ancient fortress, has undergone frequent changes in its defences from time to time, owing to the advances in military science, and to the constantly increasing power of modern artillery. These changes have been incessant during the present century, and it has been re-fortified and re-armed over and over again. It is said that many years ago the Inspector General of Fortifications of the day, desirous of bringing it up to date, recommended an extra expenditure of 100,000*l.*, and had an interview with the Chancellor of the Exchequer for the purpose of obtaining his consent. He explained to the Chancellor the steep and isolated nature of the rock, and, after giving him a graphic account of its numerous sieges, asked his opinion. The Chancellor of the Exchequer's reply was discouraging, and he said that, from the lucid and interesting description of the Inspector General, it appeared to him that Gibraltar would be perfectly impregnable if the military authorities would only leave it alone. The money, however, was ultimately granted, and I only mention it as an example of the different conclusions which financial and military authorities may arrive at from a consideration of the same facts. The one was evidently thinking of bastions and the other of budgets.

Gibraltar has a population of about twenty-four thousand persons, of which between four and five thousand are military, and as it is said to be one of the most thickly inhabited places in the world[1] its sanitary condition is a matter not only of importance,

[1] *Colonial Office Book*, 1894.

but under the circumstances one of some difficulty. In the early part of the century it was frequently visited by severe epidemics of fever, and more recently by serious attacks of cholera. Of late years, however, its sanitation has been under the careful supervision of a Sanitary Commission, which during my period of office consisted of twelve members, four official, and eight civilians selected from the grand jury list, and all unpaid. They had charge of the drainage, water, gas, and general improvements of the city; and, under the authority of the Governor, levied an annual rate on the inhabitants to meet the necessary expenditure. It is evident that their duties were arduous and responsible. The Sanitary Commission may be said to be the only form of representation given to the people, and it is one which should be carefully preserved. However necessary it may be that the governor of a city, such as Gibraltar, enclosed within a fortress should have full power and authority, still it must be an advantage to him and to the public service that in a matter of vital interest to the people, in which also their local knowledge can be utilised, they should be consulted and associated with the Government. I may go farther and record my opinion that at Gibraltar, as elsewhere, it is desirable that representatives of the people should be freely consulted, not only in regard to sanitation, but also in commercial and other matters; and during my residence there I derived much assistance from their knowledge and friendly co-operation.

The results of the care bestowed, for many years past, on the sanitary arrangements at Gibraltar have been very satisfactory. Not only is its condition far better than that of the neighbouring towns of Spain, but it is now one of the healthiest stations of the British army at home or abroad, as the following statistics will prove.

Annual death rate per thousand of the troops at various stations at home and abroad, on the average of ten years from 1882 to 1891—[1]

United Kingdom	5·78	Bermuda	10·11
Gibraltar	6·08	Ceylon	12·38
Malta	8·18	India	14·78
Egypt [2]	23·78		

A striking proof of the excellent sanitary condition of the city was afforded in 1885, when the greater part of Spain was visited by a severe attack of cholera, which gradually spread southwards; and early in August several cases suddenly occurred both in Gibraltar and in the neighbouring town of Linea. Bearing in mind the crowded population, the matter was very serious, and certain additional precautions were at once taken in order as far as possible to mitigate the severity of the attack. One difficulty

[1] *Army Medical Department Report*, 1892.

[2] Average of nine years.

which has always existed more or less is that of good drinking water. The chief supply is obtained from rain water, collected from the surface of the rock during the wet season, and stored in large reservoirs above the town. A considerable quantity is also pumped up from shallow wells on the north front, but although available for flushing, washing, &c., it is brackish and unfit for drinking. As a consequence of this scarcity, there always has been a considerable trade in water brought from Spain in barrels and sold in the streets; but as on analysis it was found to be very impure, its introduction on the appearance of cholera was stopped. Fortunately, my predecessor, Lord Napier of Magdala, with a view to the possible requirements of a state of siege, had commenced in 1882 the erection of works for distilling sea water in large quantities; and, as they were just completed, they were put into operation, and for some weeks about 8,000 gallons a day were distilled and sold to all comers at the rate of six gallons for a penny. A medical authority, speaking not long since, said that 'cholera is an exclusively water-carried disease, and all European countries may be rendered impervious to its attacks by close attention to the purity of water.' That, I may say, was the view of my medical advisers at Gibraltar at the time, and I attribute our escape from a severe attack very much to this supply of pure water to the inhabitants.

Another precaution taken was the establishment of a camp just outside the fortress for the inhabitants of the houses attacked. Indian experience has proved that it is very advantageous to regiments when visited by cholera to move them out of their barracks and place them under canvas on fresh ground. The cases at Gibraltar nearly all occurred among the poorer inhabitants living in very crowded dwellings; and the families attacked being at once sent to the camp and supplied with pure water, the disease was immediately checked. Their houses were temporarily closed, the drains disinfected, cisterns emptied, and rags and rubbish burnt; and in the course of a few days they returned home, and the cholera, so far as they were concerned, was at an end.

The epidemic at Gibraltar lasted for about two months, and great misery resulted amongst the poorer classes, owing to the city being placed in quarantine by the other ports of Europe. As a consequence very few vessels called, and large numbers of the inhabitants were out of employment. So great was the poverty that public soup kitchens were established, and for some time about 2,000 persons a day received free rations of soup and bread. In the meantime the disease was raging at Linea and other neighbouring towns, and, considerable alarm being felt, I was constantly urged to establish a cordon of troops across the neutral ground, and to prevent all communication from the outside. But although the precise causes of cholera may be somewhat obscure, it appeared to me that, as the chief supplies of food came from Spain, had a cordon been established, prices would have risen at once, and the misery already existing would have been considerably increased. All Indian experience proves that such arrangements are useless. In fact, a line of sentries cannot stop the march of a disease; and therefore, advised by experienced medical officers who had served in the East, I refused to close the communications with Spain.

The actual cases of cholera at Gibraltar and at Linea respectively in the autumn of 1885 were as follows:

—	Population, Approximate	Number of cases of cholera	Number of deaths
Gibraltar	24,000	32	24
Linea .	12,000	429	206 [1]

So that whilst in Gibraltar one person in 750 was attacked, in Linea it was one in 28. These facts speak for themselves, and prove that adequate sanitary measures and precautions will to a great extent serve to prevent the spread of epidemic disease.

Before leaving this subject, I would mention

[1] These figures were given me by the Spanish authorities.

that at the end of 1885 a numerous committee of distinguished members of the medical profession, including amongst others, Sir William Jenner, Sir William Gull, and Sir Joseph Fayrer, conducted an inquiry into the subject of Asiatic cholera, and at the end of their report they state as follows: 'The Committee feel that they ought not to separate without expressing their conviction that sanitary measures in their true sense, and sanitary measures alone, are the only trustworthy means to prevent outbreaks of the disease, and to restrain its spread and mitigate its severity when it is prevalent. Experience in Europe and in the East has shown that sanitary cordons and quarantine restrictions (under whatsoever form) are not only useless as means for arresting the progress of cholera, but positively injurious; and this not merely because of the many unavoidable hardships which their enforcement involves, but also because they tend to create alarm during periods of epidemics of the disease and to divert public attention at other times from the necessity which constantly exists for the prosecution of sanitary measures of assured value—measures which, moreover, tend to mitigate the incidence of all forms of disease.'

The story of my 'Recollections' now draws to a close. Whatever vicissitudes or occasional hardships I may have experienced during my long service in various parts of the world, I was in great measure free from them during the period of my government of Gibraltar. There were, of course, numerous duties, and sometimes anxieties, connected with its administration, but these were rendered comparatively easy by the warm support of all classes which was so heartily given during the four years of my residence amongst them. They are a loyal people, and were most grateful for any efforts of mine to promote their welfare. The conduct of the troops in garrison throughout was excellent, and a friendly spirit prevailed at all times between the civil and military population. I left Gibraltar with much regret, feeling deeply the kindness shown to my family and myself by the inhabitants who came to bid us farewell on our embarkation for England in November 1886.

I hope that the narrative which I have given of the campaigns in which I bore a small part, and the views which I have expressed on military and political matters, may be of some interest to the public generally. It will always be a gratification to me that throughout my career I have been so closely associated with the officers and men of the Royal Artillery, a corps in which members of my family have served in uninterrupted succession from 1762 down to the present day.

Spottiswoode & Co. Printers, New-street Square, London.